Line Grenier, Fannie Valois-Nadeau (eds.)
A Senior Moment

Aging Studies | Volume 12

Editorial

The series is edited by Heike Hartung, Ulla Kriebernegg and Roberta Maierhofer.

Line Grenier is a full professor at the Département de communication at Université de Montréal in Canada.
Fannie Valois-Nadeau is a postdoctoral researcher at CELAT (Centre Culture-Arts-Société), Université du Québec in Montréal, and a lecturer in sociology at Université du Québec en Outaouais in Montréal, Canada.

Line Grenier, Fannie Valois-Nadeau (eds.)
A Senior Moment
Cultural Mediations of Memory and Ageing

[transcript]

Bibliographic information published by the Deutsche Nationalbibliothek
The Deutsche Nationalbibliothek lists this publication in the Deutsche Nationalbibliografie; detailed bibliographic data are available in the Internet at http://dnb.d-nb.de

© 2020 transcript Verlag, Bielefeld

All rights reserved. No part of this book may be reprinted or reproduced or utilized in any form or by any electronic, mechanical, or other means, now known or hereafter invented, including photocopying and recording, or in any information storage or retrieval system, without permission in writing from the publisher.

Cover concept: Kordula Röckenhaus, Bielefeld; Antonia Hernàndez
Cover illustration: Antonia Hernàndez, 2020
Typeset by Francisco Braganca, Bielefeld

Print-ISBN 978-3-8376-3683-3
PDF-ISBN 978-3-8394-3683-7
https://doi.org/10.14361/9783839436837

Printed on permanent acid-free text paper.

Contents

Introduction
Thinking Memory *with* Ageing, and Ageing *with* Memory
Line Grenier and Fannie Valois-Nadeau 7

Chapter 1: Remembering, Ageing and Musicking
Stories from the Archive
Sara Cohen 33

Chapter 2: Soundtrack of My Life
Ageing, Autobiography and Remembered Music
Ros Jennings 77

Chapter 3: It's a Man's World for *The Iron Lady*
Truth, Prosthetic Memory and the Organized Forgetting of Feminism
Josephine Dolan 101

Chapter 4: Ageing with Waves
The Im/material Worlds of Two Quebec Ondists
David Madden 133

Chapter 5: "Dis-placement," Ageing and Remembering
Case Study of a Transnational Family
Helmi Järviluoma 165

Chapter 6: Resoundingly Entangled
Ageing and Memory in Étoile des aînés in Quebec
Line Grenier, Kim Sawchuk and Fannie Valois-Nadeau 195

Acknowledgements 221

Contributors 223

Introduction
Thinking Memory *with* Ageing, and Ageing *with* Memory

Line Grenier and Fannie Valois-Nadeau

This book focuses on cultural processes of memory and ageing, teasing out their complex and largely unpredictable relationships and interconnections. Its overall purpose is to explore how different practices, commodities, daily routines, sounds, images and technologies through which memory and ageing are constituted and configured in our societies affect our experiences of living in time (growing older) and with times (remembering and making memory). In other words, this edited collection considers the cultural stuff that ageing and memory are made of or, more precisely, the cultural practices and objects through which ageing and memory are made, experienced and interconnected in singular ways, for and by particular people, in specific socio-historical locations.

Memory and ageing are distinct cultural processes that, each in their own way, establish relationships with time that affect our ways of living in the present and for a future as we move through life. These relationships with time(s) take many forms, among them the multiple stories that tell of the changing weave of identities and people's often sinuous life paths; the care given to objects that are preserved for oneself or for others; and the traces, habits and rituals that continue to inhabit and mark bodies, places and our environments. Imprinting rhythms and cadences on experiences, and also highlighting durations as the (dis)continuities of practices, habits and relations, these relationships to time(s) express and mold the attachments that matter. The impression of an incessant acceleration of daily life has been amplified by digital technologies making possible the backup and the sharing through networks as well as near-instant access to personal archives. However, the opposite impression of running to a standstill, endlessly waiting and perpetually restarting is never far off, fueled in particular by the marked return of idols of yesteryear, new fashion trends straight out of the 1970s or 1980s, filters giving an "aged" finish to contemporary photos, not to mention the multiplication of "covers" and other forms of remake. Between these two distinct dynamics, how then are contemporary processes of memory and ageing constituted?

Memory and ageing are far from being uniform or universal cultural processes. They both participate in broader temporalities, politics of time structured and regulated by particular social, economic and political contexts (Sharma, 2014).[1] Through these politics of time, individual experiences are in a sense coordinated with and synchronized to those of other individuals, groups, institutions and technologies. We can think of the persistence of commonly shared expressions such as the *vieille fille* or "old spinster" that, in the Catholic and francophone world of Quebec before the Second World War, designated unmarried women of more than 25 years of age. Acting first and foremost as an offense that made female celibacy a site of articulation of heterosexist, economic and religious family policies, this pejorative social status was nonetheless highly visible thanks to its association with a calendar holiday – Saint Catherine's Day, celebrated November 25th. Year after year the holiday of "old spinsters" in Quebec has been "celebrated" with the production of confectionery, sold under the name *tire Sainte-Catherine* or "St. Catherine's taffy." Although today it is freed from the stigmas associated with it, the expression *vieille fille* continues to live through the traditional activity of candy-making still popular among many families or between friends. Other cultural processes of memory and ageing also configure experiences of time without necessarily being linked to categorizations based on age (generally approached in terms of cohort, generation, life stage, etc.) and memory. For instance, the current intensification of public calls for the duty of remembrance (*devoir de mémoire*), the increasing number of national anniversaries and commemorative mega-events, the multiplication of heritage initiatives as well as the rapid growth of souvenir economies bring forth the structuring power of the "politics of time" we live by as citizens or denizens.

Rife with various power relationships that shape them, the cultural processes of ageing and memory do not unfold in a unilateral way; even in similar places, experiences of time vary notably according to privileges, social inequalities and normative injunctions as well as the acts of resistance that shape them. The experiences of time constitutive of memory and ageing are multiple and variable depending on social, political and economic contexts, but also on the cultural forms and communities of belonging that orient their configurations.

Welcome to an exploration of subjects, citizens, technologies and cultural objects produced in and by temporalities, and to a series of critical reflections on the ways temporalities generate not only meanings, but also orientations, intensities and rhythms that matter. Welcome to a book that takes up the challenge of putting cultural processes of memory and ageing into relation, and advocates the importance and fruitfulness of their intersections, which unfold in their heterogeneity and various effects in the following chapters. Welcome to an exploration of some of the encounters, interlacings and tensions of memory and ageing that are at the heart of the lives of older adults and seniors.

A senior moment

Our focus on cultural mediations as actively shaping the contingent linkages and entanglements of memory and ageing sets this book apart. And so does our hijacking of the expression "senior moment." This expression is very commonly used in the English-speaking world. Two indications dated March 2020 are 1 110 million results of a simple Google search using these two words and the 875 books listed by Amazon that have "senior moment(s)" in their titles. Defined by online dictionaries as "an instance of momentary forgetfulness or confusion that is attributed to the aging process" (*Merriam-Webster's*) or as the act of "forget[ting] something in a way that is thought to be typical of people who are old" (*Cambridge Dictionary*), the expression tends to link ageing and memory within the same story, that of the weakening of human faculties caused by the passage of time.

Used to name, to warn of, but often also to laugh at the loss of memory that occurs with advancing age, this expression is part of a current politics of time dominated by biomedical discourse. The proliferation of methods and exercises intended to improve the neurocognitive capacities of older adults (Katz, 2012; Katz & Gish, 2015) – and thereby counteract or at least diminish the frequency of the senior moment – takes place within the hegemonic conception of the passage of time. From this perspective, ageing tends to be apprehended only through phases of growth (valued) and decay (denigrated), with which humans would be more or less universally and uniformly confronted. Ageing becomes synonymous with decline, a notion which, as Margaret Morgan Gullette (2011) claims, refers to the historical forces that have led to the "demonizing and commercializing of ageing-past-youth" (p. 8). From this perspective, memory would appear as a variable dependent on the ageing process: either lost or in the process of being lost or becoming more or less faulty due to the physiological ageing of the body that carries it, or on the contrary thickened and enriched thanks to accumulated lived experiences and the care taken to prolong its proper functioning.

Memory is consequently conceived in the image of a personal reservoir (Frow, 1997; Clermont, 2013) whose size varies over the course of a subject's life. The accuracy of its contents would also tend to weaken, since like a container filled with elements of the past, the memories it contains would be liable to disappear or crumble as time passes. The expression "senior moment" (and the biomedical discourses that subtend it) thus suggests a conception of memory understood as a human capacity modulated by the fluctuations of another irrevocable temporal process (e.g., ageing) which impacts on the presence or absence of memories, their accuracy or reliability.

We do not mean to deny or minimize the discomfort and anxiety that can accompany those moments where forgetfulness or some form of memory loss may become problematic, even traumatic, for those who experience it. In our societies where memory and personal identity have become so intrinsically bound to each other, the fear and the social consequences of Alzheimer's disease, the "master illness" (Goldman, 2017), and of various age-associated memory impairments are, not so surprisingly, on the rise. It is important for us, however, to highlight how the experiences of what is referred to, often negatively, as a "senior moment" are contingent on injunctions to age in the most "healthy" and "active" way possible in a context where population ageing remains a problem to be solved (Alftbert & Lundin, 2012; Boudiny, 2013; Moulaert, Carbonnelle, & Nisen, n.d.).

Despite the limits and discomforts it generates, the expression "senior moment" appeals to us. We turn to it not only to underline the articulation of ageing and of memory that it makes evident, but also to deliberately hijack it (*détourner*), to trouble the meaning of the terms that it brings together, as well as to multiply the tensions as much as the usual and expected intersections between the two cultural processes that it subordinates to one another.

We hijack the expression to mark the fact that this book constitutes a *moment* to question the experiences of ageing and memory that inform, among other thing, the lives of seniors and older adults. More than a collection of memories and testimonies of past generations, this book focuses on the contingent encounters of temporal processes and questions their multiple forms, their conditions and places of production as well as their different implications. The subjects of this book are at the center of various booming cultures of ageing and memorial practices, whether as members of commemorative media event audiences, users of technologies allowing for the archiving and preserving of artifacts, fans of cultural productions (including some that are "out of fashion"), art performers, consumers and collectors of commodities or memorabilia, or story producers. To dedicate a book to the exploration of memory and ageing through their cultural mediations thus becomes an opportunity to document and to analyze temporal processes whose interrelations and scope are little studied. While research on youth cultures or the primacy of youth in cultural milieus remains as abundant and popular as always, this book highlights other experiences and temporal relationships, often marginalized and seldom visible in the media.

The mandate of this book is to sketch out new avenues of problematization for thinking about ageing and memory together. Inspired by the notion of *problem-spaces* developed by David Scott (2004), our objective is "to think of different historical conjunctures as constituting different conceptual-ideological problem-spaces, and to think of these problem-spaces less as generators of new propositions than as generators of new questions and new demands"(p. 7). *Senior Moment: The Cultural Mediations of Ageing and Memory* approaches the cultural processes of memory and ageing *together* in an effort to understand them, to describe them, to analyze them in their heterogeneity and their complex entanglements. In proposing something other than the mere examination of essentially nostalgic feelings toward a lost youth, the exploration of processes of ageing and memory making focuses instead on the value given to the past *in the present and for the future* and on the ways of invoking it (or not), on the performative power of ageing and memory making as well as on the mobilized affects. How these two processes resonate together thus becomes a structuring question that lays the foundations of this problem-space (Scott, 2004).

The meeting of two temporalities ... and two fields of study

Memory and ageing are two semantically charged concepts, whose ontology remains the subject of debates and whose avenues of theorization and analysis turn out to be contrasted within memory studies and ageing studies. Many studies that have laid the groundwork for these fields during recent decades share a nonlinear or unequivocal approach to time and temporalities inspired by the complex temporal processes involved in storytelling, chronological reconstructions, artistic creations, performances, and discursive and audiovisual representations as well as practices of preservation, commemoration and conservation. They have contributed to opening up anti-essentialist conceptions of memory and ageing in which presumptions of universality or homogeneity are rejected. Anti-essentialist approaches leave aside a priori negative connotations and uncritical romanticization of the past, focusing rather on its often problematic incidences and contingent rearticulations in the present and for the future. Their interest thus lies in the present-pasts and in the becomings that temporal processes and practices trace and organize. In the field of ageing studies, anti-essentialist approaches put less emphasis on age as a stable marker and objective measure or as a step in the biological development of human beings, and more on the social relations of ageing and the varied experiences of ageing in their not-always-obvious connections with the historical and socio-economic contexts in which they live.

Since the beginning of the century, and as the field of memory studies increasingly consolidated, myriad works have questioned memory as a cultural, social, public or collective phenomenon. They have done so by focusing on public events (Casey, 2004); cultural phenomena (Sturken, 2008) and media productions (van Dijck, 2007; Garde-Hansen, Hoskins, & Reading, 2009; Garde-Hansen, 2011; Hoskins, 2011; Neiger, Meyers, & Zandberg, 2011). Memory issues have become a favored interpretation key for identity counter-histories (Bold, Knowles, & Leach, 2002) or a gateway to more intimately grasping traumatic political experiences (Allen, 2015). Despite the theoretical and methodological diversity of approaches and that of objects or sites of study, one constant is a conception of memory as a multifarious, heterogeneous, partial, mediated process, which cannot be reduced to some universal human faculty or to the mere content stored in one's brain.

"Memory works" (Kuhn, 2010), "memory acts" (Kuhn, 2002), "*technè* of memory" (Frow, 1997), *faire mémoire* ("memory making") (Valois-Nadeau, 2014) refer to some of the memory processes currently theorized. Distinct but convergent, relatively compatible without being interchangeable, these notions conceptualize memory as situated practice, rife with different power relations, the result of mediations and various apparatus (*dispositifs*). Each in their own ways, they criticize the notion of memory as a reservoir of contents already there and already constituted that would exist in and of itself, foregrounding the temporal dynamics at work in all practices and experiences of memory.

Processes of memory work to single out particular moments, to delineate periods and to sketch the temporal boundaries of events, weaving between them threads that signal ruptures, set up continuities, chant cycles or rhythms of return. As Annette Kuhn (2010) suggests, the memory work carried out starting from our own memories and archives allows us to revisit our personal trajectories, and to give them a particular direction or orientation. Our own experience of time can be grasped through, among other mnemonic techniques often learned from childhood (Frow, 1997), the reconstruction and the reorganization of sequences of events, the multiplication and juxtaposition of social statuses, the recounting of hardships and successes. But as well, because these temporal relations come into being and materialize in diverse ways, including cultural and artistic practices (Wakeling & Clark, 2015), memory work occurs through various mediations. As Kuhn (2002) argues, "[W]e cannot access the past event in any unmediated form. The past is unavoidably rewritten, revised through memory; and memory is partial; things get forgotten, misremembered, repressed" (p. 184). From this perspective, in being more than witnesses and clues of a history *already-there* to be revealed, the symbolic and material forms in which pasts are created and enacted matter. They matter for the directions that will be given to the stories and autobiographical trajectories at the heart of experiences of ageing.

Although several approaches to memory (and particularly those that approach it from a cultural perspective) concentrate on the effects *in the present* of these practices, *technè*, makings (*faires*), and acts of memory, the question of the authenticity of these pasts-made-present remains a recurrent issue within memory studies. Often presented as the counterpart of a history validated by different regimes of reliability (Nora, 1997), authenticity or trustworthiness (Morisset, 2009), memorial productions and practices are still questioned as to their capacity to accurately represent the past, and criticized for bringing a partial and incomplete vision of the past, deemed essentially subjective, and therefore, subject to alteration or manipulation (Frow, 1997). Forgetting, sometimes understood as inseparable from memory on both individual and collective levels (Ricœur, 2000; Augé, 2004), is portrayed as a key problem for contemporary societies suffering from amnesia (Huyssen, 1995, 2003; Méchoulan, 2008; Connerton, 2009).

The authenticity or accuracy of these pasts-made-present becomes particularly exacerbated when we are interested in the memory experiences of older adults and seniors and when we bring memory and ageing together. In today's neurocultures, forgetting constitutes a structuring problem of ageing that numerous supports, techniques and exercises seek to remedy by facilitating the retention of a maximum number of bits of information, of histories, of narratives, etc. (Katz, 2012; Williams, Higgs, & Katz, 2012). In forcing the juxtaposition of these two temporalities and fields of study, our objective is not to reintroduce these questions of authenticity and of forgetting that might be thought of as obvious, given the number of studies and massively consumed products that approach them in these terms. We are concerned instead with how and to what effects issues of authenticity and trustworthiness surface in certain situations and particular contexts of ageing, as well as how certain memory practices, in certain circumstances, call into question the presumed irrevocability and incontestability of ageing.

To approach memory as a mediated and mediatized process resonates with recent developments in ageing studies that address ageing as an assemblage of temporalities whose pace, frame and organization are shaped by economic, political and cultural contexts that these temporalities help constitute. Over the past two decades, ageing has also been increasingly apprehended as a heterogeneous process, which while happening throughout one's life from the moment of birth, is irreducible to physiology alone. Since the beginning of the 2000s in particular, a series of studies in the humanities and social sciences has undertaken to understand distinct experiences of ageing and to document concerns with ageism in order to offer something other than an interpretation of the disengagement or the decline of the ageing subject (Gullette, 2004, 2011; Lagacé, 2015). Ageing has thus been questioned in terms of materiality and embodiment (Dumas, Laberge, & Straka, 2005; Gilleard & Higgs, 2013; Katz, 2018). Ageing has also been considered through the emergence of "grey" commercial cultures (Sawchuk, 1995; Blaikie, 1999) and celebrity cultures (Jennings & Krainitzki, 2015; Marshall & Rahman, 2015; Dolan, 2017); the intensive commodification of retro cultures (Reynolds, 2011; Hogarty, 2016; Bauman, 2017); social politics (Biggs, 2001; Boudiny, 2013); cultural and media productions that represent ageing – and demonize it, especially when gendered and sexualized (Blaikie, 1999; Taylor, 2010; Bennett & Taylor, 2012; Bennett, 2013), to say nothing of relationships with technologies (Sawchuk & Crow, 2011; Gilleard, Jones, & Higgs, 2015; Martin & Pilcher, 2017) as well as with users and nonusers of digital media (Fernández-Ardèvol, 2016; Nimrod, 2016; Comunello, Fernández Ardèvol, Mulargia, & Belotti, 2017; Fernández-Ardèvol, Sawchuk, & Grenier, 2017). Through such studies the qualifiers of senior and older adults are understood as the result of identity processes, of belonging, of cultural practices, of narratives, of representations, of expectations and normativities, of particular social relations and interventions on bodies, which fluctuate according to political, economic, historical and cultural contexts.

Research has also contributed to a conception of ageing as a trajectory whose forms differ according to individual and collective pathways (Biggs, 2001; Gullette, 2004; Cruikshank, 2009). Ageing turns out to be thought of more as a plural experience than a state that would be triggered at a specific age (variable according to the society and the times), or even as a social category that would qualify (and immediately limit those concerned to) a group of individuals with attributes and issues that are supposed to be similar and homogeneous (in the same way as in childhood, youth and midlife). Though shaped and run through with similar politics, social norms and imaginaries, this experience of ageing is understood more through the prisms of duration, competing experiences and transformations rather than as an entry into a new social category. As Gullette(2004) points out, "[W]hile deconstructing stage and cohort differences, age studies could also emphasize a variety of connections and continuities"(p. 194). As we envision them, the cultural mediations of memory and ageing are one way in which these connections and continuities occur.

The cultural mediations of memory and ageing

Among all these recent theoretical developments and the debates that accompany them, one concern matters particularly for us – that of the relationships with time and temporalities through the prism of cultural mediations. We have chosen this particular focus because it offers many points of entry into the field, and, more specifically, into the objects, practices and the processes which make encounters between memory and ageing possible. Addressing cultural mediations of memory and ageing allows us to situate these temporal encounters first of all in artistic and entertainment environments, but also in cultural practices such as traditions or unique customs.

Above all, to question mediation, whether understood as an object or a process, leads us to reflect on several ways in which memory and ageing take shape. These include the artifact by which a particular memory resurfaces, acting as a trigger of the images and sensations that constitute a moment of one's past; the narration of a biographical story that retraces and constructs an individual's life course; the updating and preservation of certain memories via digital technologies and even the device that frames their production. Each of these objects or processes contributes in their own ways to mediate ageing and memory. This book brings forth mediations of different orders, registers and formats that continue to furnish the everyday lives of older adults and seniors, to stage particular experiences of time or to revisit them. The cultural mediations addressed in the following six chapters include a mainstream cinematic biopic retracing the life course of an important female political figure; relationships to ageing musical archives and to cherished vinyl records; a type of music scene specifically intended for and by seniors; the importance (greater or lesser) given to digitized photos, music and memories; the musical repertoire that becomes an integral part of one's life; as well as relationships with musical instruments played and mastered over decades.

Cultural mediations, we argue, play a crucial role in the forms taken by intersections of memory and ageing. In recognizing the constitutive role of *media* among different temporal and memory making practices (Valois-Nadeau, 2014), we share José van Djick's (2007) conception of "mediated memories," the potential of (trans)formations of technological devices, and more particularly the "mutual shaping" of technological and memorial devices. As van Dijck (2007) describes:

> Media technologies and objects, far from being external instruments for "holding" versions of the past, help constitute a sense of past – both in terms of our private lives and history at large. Memory and media have both been referred to metaphorically as reservoirs, holding our past experiences and knowledge for future use. But neither memories nor media are passive go-between: their mediation intrinsically shapes the way we build up and retain a sense of individuality and community, of identity and history. (p. 2)

Cultural mediations are thus more than neutral objects that act as reflections or signs of passing time. Taking inspiration both from Antoine Hennion's (2007, 2013) pragmatic critique regarding these objects that would be nothing but "passive intermediaries" and from the agency of the medium (Mitchell & Hansen, 2010), we have worked toward acknowledging their contributions to the configuration and the materialization of temporal relations. In a previous article, Line Grenier (2012) illustrated the performative aspect of different media, technologies and objects (ranging from a collection of cellular phones to meticulously maintained old fishing boats) with which some men age, continuing to establish and modify their relationships to the world. Echoing that project, this book further explores the performative character of mediations, so that those which connect and shape memory and ageing are seen as more than simple bridges to the past or closed and fixed indicators of a precise temporality. In the terms of a media ecology, we could say that they are the milieus, the means, the operators (Bardini, 2016).

Intersections of ageing and memory: Complex, textured and changeable temporalities

The chapters that follow present a diversity of intersections of ageing and memory,[2] but also of ageing *with* memory – the emphasis placed on one of the two cultural processes is not always the same, depending on the author's location, theoretical approach and groundings. A majority of the authors question these intersections as much as the cultural mediations that configure them via case studies, explorations or projects related to music, the object of a field of study in which time and temporality are of paramount importance to many researchers. Musical heritages, generations of audiences, ageing pop stars, the prevailing ageism within professional music environments, and the accumulation of media supports from different eras constitute avenues of problematization that have been developing within this field of study over the past 15 years. The concept of *musicking* (Small, 1998), which approaches music as a protean activity involving a wide variety of actors, is particularly relevant for exploring the multiplicity of mediations of music and, in their wake, the entangled practices and experiences of memory and ageing that they embody, perform and materialize. This attention to music is not, however, synonymous with a single "type" of ageing, nor with similar processes or practices of memory. Instead, it brings to the fore experiences of ageing that, though anchored almost exclusively in media cultures and Western contexts, are extremely varied.

The six chapters gathered here shed light on encounters between memory and ageing that are not always perfectly interwoven, nor necessarily essential or obligatory. By sometimes demonstrating the frictions and tensions that exist between the two cultural processes and their constitutive temporalities, and by identifying from an analytical perspective the moment when one seems to subordinate the other, it becomes possible to imagine different spaces and moments of struggle and resistance.

The following chapters bring to the fore different temporal experiences and relationships, which take shape within movements of migration, professional trajectories of women musicians, musical scenes and performances intended for seniors, but also through the chronology of biographization, film editing, transformations of archives and of musical instruments. Although the book places an emphasis on temporalities, the spatialization of memories and ageing that they inform appear in the background of many chapters, and allow us to think about how they define and anchor themselves according to relations to places and territory or territories.

The first chapter, "Remembering, Ageing and Musicking: Stories from the Archive," by Sara Cohen, focuses on musical archives and the relationships they generate among fans of popular music. In the wake of an important donation to the Institute of Popular Music (IPM) at the University of Liverpool, the author relates the experiences of participants of the project Music, Photographs and Stories from the Archives. In this project, the participants had access to the IPM archives, which were presented without prior organization to facilitate exploration and listening. The rediscovery of vinyl records, posters, cassettes or other media supports "from another time" was a great source of pleasure for the participants. A pretext for conversation and for the sharing of memories, the musical archive generated new relationships and exchanges among project participants. Visiting the Popular Music Archive also allowed participants to reinvent and reconstitute their own past, different stages of their life or even an era or a particular place, sometimes forgotten. For Cohen, the musical archive represents a rich entryway both for exploring the practices of storytelling and remembering that occur thanks to different objects, and for questioning the material forms of music as well as their effects on individual trajectories. By underlining the agency of the musical archive and the value placed on it by the participants, Cohen observes how the object "of yesterday" tells less about its own history than the recollected past of the individual to whom it is connected. These observations make it possible to account for how music becomes a key player in the ageing process, marking transitions and everyday moments, but also acting as a point of reference within personal trajectories.

The chapter "Soundtrack of My Life: Ageing, Autobiography and Remembered Music," by Ros Jennings, also investigates the relevance of music within individual trajectories and, more specifically, how it contributes to autobiographical memories. Highlighting a research device called the "soundtrack of my life," Jennings is interested in the ways in which identities are constructed, throughout life, through certain particularly significant musical works. This "soundtrack of my life," originally the title of a column in the British daily newspaper *The Guardian*, Jennings uses as an analytical tool for exploring autobiographical memories of celebrities who have contributed to this media column over the years, as well as for exploring the memories of other people she has interviewed using the same device. This work puts into relief the affective dimensions of music, the network of cultural references woven through time thanks to large-scale media coverage of certain musics, but also the ways in which this or that piece of music resonates (and continues to resonate) in bodies. Situated in time and space, the device and Jennings's analysis highlight the fluctuation, the maintenance of identities through time, as a form of "transageing." Autobiographical memories thus become a way to conceptualize ages and temporalities as fluid and variable, depending on the groups being interviewed.

The chapter "It's a Man's World for *The Iron Lady*: Truth, Prosthetic Memory and the Organized Forgetting of Feminism," by Josephine Dolan, consists of an analysis of Phyllida Lloyd's film *The Iron Lady*. This 2012 biopic, dedicated to the life of the former British prime minister Margaret Thatcher, brings a particular attention to the episodes of confusion that marked the end of her life. Dolan's chapter, which brings together the temporalities of the main character, a particular British political culture and the film itself, becomes the pretext for questioning different intersections of memory and ageing produced and diffused within Western cultural mega-productions. More specifically, Dolan highlights a film constructed from a stereotypical cultural imaginary of the "fourth age" (characterized by the decline of cognitive functions, frailty and confusion), a story dictated by flashback sequences and an editing style that plays with chronology, but also a genre of cultural production that performs and makes visible a homogeneous and consensual understanding of history. Understanding the film as prosthetic memory, a memory machine existing outside the human brain, Dolan questions how the meeting of these three temporal frames contributes to the constitution and regulation of a forgetful present, in which certain historical elements are repressed and others forgotten. But these omissions are far from fortuitous; this prosthetic memory, where power relations are articulated, contributes to the mediation of organized traumas and forgettings that silence certain voices – especially feminist voices and those associated with counter-narratives. Putting in tension the truth effects produced by the biopic genre and the representations of episodes of confusion linked to human ageing, Dolan underlines issues of truth, fictionalization and dramatization that color the meeting up of memory and ageing.

In the next chapter, entitled "Ageing with Waves: The Im/material Worlds of Two Quebec Ondists," David Madden continues the exploration of the reciprocal formation of memory and ageing within the trajectories of ageing women, here musical interpreters of the ondes

Martenot. Tracing a feminist microhistory of this instrument and its contribution to electronic music while also exploring the affective relations and attachments of these two ageing musicians to their instrument, Madden is interested in the points of encounter between the temporalities of objects and the subjects who bring them to life. The ondes Martenot thus becomes a privileged site for questioning a unique register of temporalities, plus the tensions between the material and the immaterial that vibrate or resonate within a particular cultural milieu. The instrument also embodies the mediation of artistic trajectories of its interpreters, sociocultural contexts in which a certain electronic music has developed, and everyday forms of companionship that have been woven over time. With the help of semistructured interviews and periods of artistic co-creation, Madden explores how these two creative interpreters have enabled this old instrument to last, making its preservation possible through its continuing to be played (sometimes) and not only museified. Equally, Madden explores how the instrument continues to live by these musicians' side, at the heart of their own experience of ageing. Madden thus emphasizes their relationship with the instrument through time and the transformations that modulate it, affective stories told in an intimate and personal style, shared memories and ongoing stress as co-constitutive of the musicians' experience.

Helmi Järviluoma questions the ways in which issues of memory and ageing are articulated in a framework of international mobility. In " 'Displacement,' Ageing and Remembering: Case Study of a Transnational Family," Järviluoma follows the daily life of a Pakistani family who have requested asylum in Finland, thereby showing how individual memories are articulated with cultural practices marked by international displacements. This ethnography allows Järviluoma to approach experiences of ageing as being shaped by multiple attachments and detachments involving both places and different mobile "media of memory." What is preserved through the years and multiple moves? How do immigrants maintain and create links with their country of origin and cultures of belonging? And how do these links comingle within different generations of the same family? These are the questions addressed in this chapter. Järviluoma's ethnographic work also brings into light the cultural embedding of "media of memory." Using the example of taking photos, she discusses the meanings given to different forms of forgetting, of memory, of preservation of artifacts, which sometimes differ from those that can be glimpsed by dominant practices in Western contexts. This putting into perspective is also the occasion to take into consideration "media of memory" that exist "under the radar" of research on memory in a Northern occidental context. By proposing, for example, that the family unit comes to function as a medium of memory, Järviluoma then proposes a conception of mediation as being not exclusively about objects and technologies, but also encompassing human bodies, groups and the family. As she puts it, "I am assuming a definition of mediation that goes beyond technical media: present moments of bodies and minds are always-already mediated, delineated and enriched by the past." This chapter invites us therefore to think of memory, ageing and place attachment outside of settled, already agreed upon spaces and objects of memory, and to imagine the coexistence of complex spatio-temporal relations within the same family – relations of which we would be mistaken to presume uniformity, if not the relatedness of memories and ageings.

Finally, in their chapter entitled "Resoundingly Entangled: Ageing and Memory in Étoile des aînés in Québec," Line Grenier, Kim Sawchuk and Fannie Valois-Nadeau offer a theoretical and empirical exploration of the articulations of memory and ageing. Drawing from the ethnographic study they conducted of a musical competition for seniors, the authors undertake a detailed analysis of a particular moment of musicking involving the vocal rendition of "Climb Ev'ry Mountain" from the 1965 American musical drama film *The Sound of Music*. The emancipatory meaning of the tune and its public performance by the contestant, the judges' comments on the performance, as well as the sociocultural contextualization of that hit song become different points of entry into the entanglements of memory making and ageing. More specifically, by structuring their analysis around two prepositions ("aside" and "with"), the authors highlight two specific modes of entanglement through which individual and collective experiences are made to resonate. How do specific moments of musicking come to interweave different life trajectories? How do they connect individuals within the same time-space and allow them to "travel" together, to make relevant today the musical repertoires and sounds associated with a particular epoch, and become an instantiation of a specific politics of ageing? By addressing such questions, Grenier, Sawchuk and Valois-Nadeau provide analytical and conceptual tools that help us better understand the different registers of co-presence through which ageing and memory making come to inform each other. Their critical discussion of a particular moment of musicking also shows how cultural mediations become temporal and spatial markers, points of bifurcation and conjuncturally political resonance.

Notes

1. As suggested by Sarah Sharma (2014), temporalities express "how individuals and groups synchronize their body clocks, their senses of the future or the present, to an exterior relation – be it another person, pace, technology, chronometer, institution, or ideology" (p. 18).
2. The subtitle of this section is inspired by Emily Keightley (2012), who, presenting a similar yet different argument than the one we make here, writes: "[M]edia texts and technologies in their situated contexts of use support a context, textured and changeable temporality" (p. 221).

References

Alftbert, Åsa, & Lundin, Susanne. (2012). 'Successful ageing' in practice: Reflections on health, activity, normality in old age in Sweden. *Culture Unbound: Journal of Current Cultural Research*, 4, 481–497.

Allen, Matthew. (2015). *The labour of memory: Memorial culture and 7/7* (Palgrave Macmillan Memory Studies). London: Palgrave Macmillan.

Augé, Marc. (2004). *Oblivion* (Marjolijn de Jager, Trans.). Minneapolis: University of Minnesota Press.

Bardini, Thierry. (2016). Entre l'archéologie et l'écologie médiatiques: Une perspective sur la théorie médiatique. *Multitudes, 62*(1), 159–168. https://doi.org/10.3917/mult.062.0159.

Bauman, Zygmunt. (2017). *Retrotopia*. Cambridge: Polity.

Bennett, Andy. (2013). *Music, style, and aging: Growing old disgracefully?* Philadelphia: Temple University Press.

Bennett, Andy, & Taylor, Jodie. (2012). Popular music and the aesthetics of ageing. *Popular Music, 31*(2), 231–243. https://doi.org/10.1017/S0261143012000013.

Biggs, Simon. (2001). Toward critical narrativity: Stories of aging in contemporary social policy. *Journal of Aging Studies, 15*(4), 303–316. https://doi.org/10.1016/S0890-4065(01)00025-1.

Blaikie, Andrew. (1999). *Ageing and popular culture*. Cambridge: Cambridge University Press.

Bold, Christine, Knowles, Ric, & Leach, Belinda. (2002). Feminist memorializing and cultural countermemory: The case of Marianne's park. *Signs: Journal of Women in Culture and Society, 28*, 125–148.

Boudiny, Kim. (2013). 'Active ageing': From empty rhetoric to effective policy tool. *Ageing and Society, 33*(6), 1077–1098. https://doi.org/10.1017/S0144686X1200030X.

Casey, Edward S. (2004). Public memory in place and time. In Kendall R. Phillips (Ed.), *Framing public memory* (Rhetoric, Culture, and Social Critique, pp. 17–43). Tuscaloosa: University of Alabama Press.

Clermont, P. (2013). *De la mémoire au mémoriel: Maurice Richard et Janette Bertrand comme personnalités publiques au Québec*. Montreal: Nota Bene.

Comunello, Francesca, Fernández Ardèvol, Mireia, Mulargia, Simone, & Belotti, Francesca. (2017). Women, youth and everything else: Age-based and gendered stereotypes in relation to digital technology among elderly Italian mobile phone users. *Media, Culture and Society, 39*(6), 798–815. https://doi.org/10.1177/0163443716674363.

Connerton, Paul. (2009). *How modernity forgets*. Cambridge: Cambridge University Press.

Cruikshank, Margaret. (2009). *Learning to be old: Gender, culture, and aging* (2nd ed.). Lanham, MD: Rowman & Littlefield.

Dolan, Josephine M. (2017). *Contemporary cinema and 'old age': Gender and the silvering of stardom*. London: Palgrave Macmillan.

Dumas, Alex, Laberge, Suzanne, & Straka, Silvia M. (2005). Older women's relations to bodily appearance: The embodiment of social and biological conditions of existence. *Ageing and Society, 25*(6), 883–902. https://doi.org/10.1017/S0144686X05004010.

Fernández-Ardèvol, Mireia. (2016). An exploration of mobile telephony non-use among older people. In Emma Domínguez-Rué & Linda Nierling (Eds.), *Ageing and technology: Perspectives from the social sciences* (Aging Studies, vol. 9, pp. 47–65). Bielefeld, Germany: transcript-Verlag.

Fernández-Ardèvol, Mireia, Sawchuk, Kim, & Grenier, Line. (2017). Maintaining connections. *Nordicom Review, 38*(s1). https://doi.org/10.1515/nor-2017-0396.

Frow, John. (1997). *Toute la mémoire du monde*: Repetition and forgetting. In *Time and commodity culture: Essays in cultural theory and postmodernity* (pp. 218–246). Oxford: Oxford University Press.

Garde-Hansen, Joanne. (2011). *Media and memory* (Media Topics). Edinburgh: Edinburgh University Press.

Garde-Hansen, Joanne, Hoskins, Andrew, & Reading, Anna (Eds.). (2009). *Save as... digital memories*. Basingstoke, UK: Palgrave Macmillan.

Gilleard, Chris, & Higgs, Paul. (2013). *Ageing, corporeality and embodiment*. London: Anthem Press.

Gilleard, Chris, Jones, Ian, & Higgs, Paul. (2015). Connectivity in later life: The declining age divide in mobile cell phone ownership. *Sociological Research Online, 20*(2), 1–13. https://doi.org/10.5153/sro.3552.

Goldman, Marlene. (2017). *Forgotten: Narratives of age-related dementia and Alzheimer's disease in Canada*. Montreal: McGill-Queen's University Press.

Grenier, Line. (2012). Ageing and/as enduring: Discussing with "Turtles [that] don't die of old age." In Guillaume Latzko-Toth & Florence Millerand (Eds.), *TEM2012: Proceedings of the Technology and Emerging Media Track, annual conference of the Canadian Communication Association* (pp. 1–12). http://www.tem.fl.ulaval.ca/www/wp-content/PDF/Waterloo_2012/GRENIER-TEM2012.pdf.

Gullette, Margaret M. (2004). *Aged by culture*. Chicago: University of Chicago Press.

Gullette, Margaret M. (2011). *Agewise: Fighting the new ageism in America*. Chicago: University of Chicago Press.

Hennion, Antoine. (2007). *La passion musicale: Une sociologie de la médiation* (Rev. ed.). Paris: Editions Métailié.

Hennion, Antoine. (2013). D'une sociologie de la médiation à une pragmatique des attachements [From a sociology of mediation to a pragmatism of attachments]. *SociologieS* [Online], Théories et recherche. http://sociologies.revues.org/4353.

Hogarty, Jean. (2016). *Popular music and retro culture in the digital era* (Routledge Advances in Sociology). New York: Routledge.

Hoskins, Andrew. (2011). Media, memory, metaphor: Remembering and the connective turn. *Parallax, 17*(4), 19–31. https://doi.org/10.1080/13534645.2011.605573.

Huyssen, Andreas. (1995). *Twilight memories: Marking time in a culture of amnesia*. New York: Routledge.

Huyssen, Andreas. (2003). *Present pasts: Urban palimpsests and the politics of memory*. Stanford, CA: Stanford University Press.

Jennings, Ros, & Krainitzki, Eva. (2015). "Call the celebrity": Voicing the experience of women and ageing through the distinctive vocal presence of Vanessa Redgrave. In Deborah Jermyn & Su Holmes

(Eds.), *Women, celebrity and cultures of ageing: Freeze frame* [E-book] (pp. 178–196). Consulted at http://public.ebookcentral.proquest.com/choice/publicfullrecord.aspx?p=4322604.

Katz, Stephen. (2012). Embodied memory: Ageing, neuroculture, and the genealogy of mind. *Occasion: Interdisciplinary Studies in the Humanities, 4*, 1–11.

Katz, Stephen (Ed.). (2018). *Ageing in everyday life: Materialities and embodiments*. Bristol, UK: Bristol University Press.

Katz, Stephen, & Gish, Jessica. (2015). Aging in the biosocial order: Repairing time and cosmetic rejuvenation in a medical-spa clinic. *Sociological Quarterly, 56*(1), 40–61.

Keightley, Emily (Ed.). (2012). *Time, media and modernity*. Basingstoke, UK: Palgrave Macmillan. https://doi.org/10.1057/9781137020680.

Kuhn, Annette. (2002). *Family secrets: Acts of memory and imagination*. New York: Verso.

Kuhn, Annette. (2010). Memory texts and memory work: Performances of memory in and with visual media. *Memory Studies, 3*(4), 298–313. https://doi.org/10.1177/1750698010370034.

Lagacé, Martine. (2015). *Représentations et discours sur le vieillissement: La face cachée de l'âgisme?* [E-book]. Quebec City: Presses de l'Université Laval. Consulted at http://proxy.lib.sfu.ca/login?url=http://books.scholarsportal.info/viewdoc.html?id=/ebooks/ebooks3/upress/2015-10-02/1/9782763723921.

Marshall, Barbara L., & Rahman, Momin. (2015). Celebrity, ageing and the construction of 'third age' identities. *International Journal of Cultural Studies, 18*(6), 577–593. https://doi.org/10.1177/1367877914535399.

Martin, Wendy, & Pilcher, Katy. (2017). Visual representations of digital connectivity in everyday life. In Jia Zhou & Gavriel Salvendy (Eds.), *Human aspects of IT for the aged population: Applications, services and contexts*(Lecture Notes in Computer Science, vol. 10298, pp. 138–149). Cham, Switzerland: Springer.

Méchoulan, Éric. (2008). *La culture de la mémoire ou comment se débarrasser du passé?* Montreal: Presses de l'Université de Montréal.

Mitchell, W. J. T., & Hansen, Mark B. N. (Ed.). (2010). *Critical terms for media studies*. Chicago: University of Chicago Press.

Morisset, Lucie K. (2009). *Des régimes d'authenticité: Essai sur la mémoire patrimoniale*. Rennes, France: Presses Université de Rennes.

Moulaert, T., Carbonnelle, S., & Nisen, L. (N. d.). *Le vieillissement actif dans tous ses éclats* [E-book]. Consulted at http://pul.uclouvain.be/fr/livre/?GCOI=29303100620490.

Neiger, Motti, Meyers, Oren, & Zandberg, Eyal (Eds.). (2011). *On media memory: Collective memory in a new media age*. Basingstoke, UK: Palgrave Macmillan.

Nimrod, Galit. (2016). The hierarchy of mobile phone incorporation among older users. *Mobile Media and Communication*, 4(2), 149–168. https://doi.org/10.1177/2050157915617336.

Nora, P. (1997). Entre mémoire et histoire: La problématique des lieux. In P. Nora (Ed.), *Les lieux de mémoire* (vol. 1, p. 23–43). Paris: Gallimard.

Reynolds, Simon. (2011). *Retromania: Pop culture's addiction to its own past*. New York: Faber & Faber.

Ricœur, Paul. (2000). *La mémoire, l'histoire, l'oubli*. Paris: Éditions du Seuil.

Sawchuk, Kimberly A. (1995). From gloom to boom: Aging, identity and target markets. In Mike Featherstone & Andrew Wernick (Eds.), *Images of aging: Cultural representations of later life* (pp. 116–134). London: Routledge.

Sawchuk, Kim, & Crow, Barbara. (2011, Spring). Into the "grey zone": Milieus that matter. *Wi: Journal of Mobile Media*. https://wi.mobilities.ca/into-the-grey-zone-seniors-cell-phones-and-milieus-that-matter.

Scott, David. (2004). *Conscripts of modernity: The tragedy of colonial enlightenment*. Durham, NC: Duke University Press.

Sharma, Sarah. (2014). *In the meantime: Temporality and cultural politics*. Durham, NC: Duke University Press.

Small, Christopher. (1998). *Musicking: The meanings of performing and listening*. Middletown, CT: Wesleyan University Press.

Sturken, Marita. (2008). Memory, consumerism and media: Reflections on the emergence of the field. *Memory Studies, 1*, 73–78. https://doi.org/10.1177/1750698007083890.

Taylor, Jodie. (2010). Queer temporalities and the significance of 'music scene' participation in the social identities of middle-aged queers. *Sociology, 44*(5), 893–907. https://doi.org/10.1177/0038038510375735.

Valois-Nadeau, Fannie. (2014). *Un centenaire, des faire mémoire: Analyse des pratiques de mémoire autour du Canadien de Montréal*. Unpublished doctoral dissertation, Université de Montréal, Montreal. Consulted at https://papyrus.bib.umontreal.ca/xmlui/handle/1866/11634.

van Dijck, José. (2007). *Mediated memories in the digital age*. Stanford, CA: Stanford University Press.

Wakeling, Kate, & Clark, Jonathan. (2015). Beyond health and wellbeing: Transformation, memory and the virtual in older people's music and dance. *International Journal of Ageing and Later Life, 9*(2), 7–34. https://doi.org/10.3384/ijal.1652-8670.15262.

Williams, Simon J., Higgs, Paul, & Katz, Stephen. (2012). Neuroculture, active ageing and the 'older brain': Problems, promises and prospects. *Sociology of Health and Illness, 34*(1), 64–78. https://doi.org/10.1111/j.1467-9566.2011.01364.x.

Chapter 1: Remembering, Ageing and Musicking
Stories from the Archive

Sara Cohen

At the University of Liverpool, a vast amount of material has been gifted to the Institute of Popular Music (IPM) since it was established in 1988. This material includes photographs and music magazines, the personal collections of music writers and industry professionals, and sound recordings in various formats. Among these recordings are over 50,000 vinyl records, thousands of reel-to-reels, and cassette tapes, CDs and DVDs crammed into large cardboard boxes. The materials date from the birth of recorded sound, hence the inclusion of cylinder discs, but most items originated between the 1950s and the 1980s. They are stored in boxes stacked floor to ceiling in a suite of upper-floor rooms and on racks of shelving in two large basement rooms. The materials constitute a substantial Popular Music Archive that has no dedicated archivist or listening facilities and is currently not publicly accessible or cataloged. It nevertheless offers a rich and fascinating resource for research on music, and its materials inspired this chapter, which explores the relationship between music and ageing.

There exists, as yet, only a small, emerging body of scholarship that relates music to a concern with ageing as a culturally informed experience, a conceptualization of ageing developed by social anthropologists such as Margaret Clark (1967), Sharon Kaufman (1986) and Barbara Myerhoff (1992). This scholarship includes seminal studies of ageing youth cultures, most notably ageing punk rockers in the United Kingdom and Australia (Bennett, 2013), and of age and ageing in US hip-hop culture (Forman, 2016), as well as studies of well-known musicians, whether the "late voice" of well-known singer-songwriters such as Leonard Cohen (Elliott, 2015), or the strategies employed by Madonna and other celebrated female musicians to engage with issues and debates related to public ageing (Jennings & Gardner, 2012).

This chapter also explores ideas and experiences of age and ageing through a focus on music, but considers how they emerge through people's interaction with archival materials, particularly through the acts of remembering that these materials enable. The chapter is informed by the activities of a group of people who visited the Popular Music Archive to engage with its materials, and by anthropological approaches that attend to the social practices of music, memory and age. With regard to music, the ethnomusicologist Christopher Small (1998) introduced the verb "musicking" to argue that music is a practice rather than a thing. He applied this verb to all aspects of music performance, whether performing live or rehearsing, listening to Muzak in an elevator, selling tickets for a performance or cleaning up after the audience has gone. People also engage with music through storytelling and remembering – practices that have been a long-standing concern for social anthropologists.

Although memory is a broad concept defined in various ways and encompassing discourses that are multiple and diverse, for many anthropologists it is a social activity through which people engage with historical events and experiences. The anthropologists Paul Antze and Michael Lambek (1996), for example, make a strong case for moving away from theoretical and political discourses on memory, in order to adopt a more grounded approach that focuses on memory as a lived, embodied and everyday practice. Through ethnographic research on symbols, myths, rituals and narratives, they and other anthropologists have also drawn attention to the "work" of memory. Whether involving the efforts of the individual or the collective, it is through such work that the past is made present and meaningful, and strategically or unwittingly forgotten. Focusing on the work of remembering, this chapter considers what this work reveals about age and ageing, and once again the emphasis is on praxis, and on ageing as a social as well as a biological process.

Most studies of music and memory are not concerned with the social practice of remembering. Those that are tend to prioritize the sonic when discussing memory, rather than discussing it in relation to music materials more generally, with exceptions including my own research on music and cultural memory (Cohen, 2014, 2016) and that of Andy Bennett and Ian Rogers (2016), and Michael Pickering and Emily Keightley's (2015) reflections on photography, music and memory in everyday life. Although music is commonly considered to be intangible, as sound it has tangible and corporeal effects, and there are also the "material extensions" of music discussed in this chapter, defined by Will Straw (2003) as "the range of material forms (the objects and technologies) through which music is performed, received, collected and rendered mobile" (p. 229). The first of the chapter's three parts describes how people engage with such music materials through practices of remembering, and how these materials encourage the telling of stories about the autobiographical past, as well as about the present and future. In doing so, it shows that by enabling people to situate themselves and the materials in passages of time, these practices of remembering prompt reflection on age and ageing.

This discussion provides a basis for the second part of the chapter, which highlights two ways in which music materials offer a resource for research on ageing. First, it discusses the ageing of people and considers what people's encounters with music materials suggest about how this process is experienced and thought about. Second, drawing on work in anthropology and archaeology concerning the interdependency of people and the material world (Bourdieu, 1972/1977; Graves-Brown, 2000; Pearson & Shanks, 2001), it discusses how people engage with materials that are also ageing, and the ideas and experiences of age and ageing that emerge from this process. Bringing together and developing the threads running through parts one and two, the third and final part of the chapter argues that music's distinctive influence on how people remember makes it a productive resource for research on their experiences of age and ageing, and the chapter concludes by considering the significance and potential benefits of such research.

Engaging with music through storytelling and practices of remembering

Music, Photographs and Stories from the Archives was a four-month project that ran in 2016. It was established to enable staff from the University of Liverpool to engage with local cultural organizations and the wider public, and to provide training in cultural engagement for an early career researcher. The project involved collaboration between the Institute of Popular Music (IPM) and the Open Eye Gallery (OEG), and one of its main aims was to engage the public in the significant but underutilized archives of both organizations. Based in one of Liverpool's most prestigious and prominent new architectural developments, the OEG is a purpose-built gallery positioned at the heart of the city's regenerated waterfront. It houses 1800 photographs from the 1930s to the present day, all carefully stored and documented but with little contextual material. The focus of this chapter, however, is on how members of the public engaged with the Popular Music Archive of the IPM and the University of Liverpool.

Engaging with music through storytelling

The basic idea behind Music, Photographs and Stories from the Archives was to enable people to visit each archive and select materials, some photographic and some audio, that resonated with their lives and personal experience. They would then put together a photo story and a music story based on these materials. The process was somewhat similar to the ways in which people document their lives and craft portraits of themselves through Instagram and other forms of social media, whether they do so "on the go," as events unfold, or retrospectively. These stories formed the basis of a modest, temporary and publicly accessible exhibition staged at the Open Eye Gallery in conjunction with a concert organized in collaboration with Liverpooljazz, an organization working to raise the profile of jazz performance in Liverpool. Members of the public could thus engage with the stories while listening to live performances of repertoire related to the archival materials. Public feedback on the exhibition was an important aspect of the project plan, enabling a wider audience to have input into the project and share stories of their own.

Although a rather experimental project, Music, Photographs and Stories from the Archives was nevertheless underpinned by extensive research that I had conducted previously. In 2014, for example, I undertook research on the materials of the Popular Music Archive as part of a major exhibition project (Cohen, Jones, & Sillitoe, 2014). Previously, I was part of a three-year project on popular music heritage, cultural memory and cultural identity in Europe involving investigation into not only official and collective memory, but also the vernacular, autobiographical memories of music audiences.[1]

Through the efforts of the Institute of Popular Music, the Open Eye Gallery and Liverpooljazz, about 50 project participants were recruited, from various social backgrounds, who had different interests and degrees of involvement in music. They included a group of male jazz musicians and fans over 50 years of age, while the rest of the participants were men and women aged between 20 and 75. These participants were to co-curate their music and photo stories through collaboration with the early career researcher appointed to the project. The researcher was the core member of two small teams based at each organization. At the Institute of Popular Music, the other team members were me as the project leader and IPM director, and a couple of university colleagues who could be consulted on certain aspects of the project, while the team at the OEG consisted of the gallery's director and staff.

Initial small-group sessions were held in each archive to introduce participants to the archival materials. At the university, a colorful assortment of materials was piled onto central tables where participants could congregate and rummage through the materials before being guided around the archive. Although a few visitors were rather shy and quietly hovered at the back of the group, others would catch sight of a flexi disc, songbook or concert program and immediately launch into a story related to it. These stories flowed thick and fast, making it difficult for members of the project team to interrupt and move things on, but eventually participants encountered other materials that attracted their interest and were located elsewhere in the archive. Adam and Ben, two friends in their twenties, quickly became engrossed with the vinyl records, especially the collections of "library music" albums[2] and African music, and asked if they could bring their decks in and sample or remix them. Wallace, a jazz musician in his seventies, inspected the shelves of 78s before offering to bring in *his* deck so that he could play and talk about his mother's favorite records. Victor and Michael, best friends since childhood, examined the jazz programs, and Michael told us about a program he had carried around with him since 1958, when he had purchased it at a Buddy Holly and the Crickets concert. He fished it out of his bag to show us while Victor explained that unlike Michael, he had been prevented from going to the concert by his father, who had insisted that he had schoolwork to attend to.

Isabel, a young Spanish woman, described an interest in British music that had come from her father, who had been based in Liverpool as a sailor during the 1950s, and her passion for David Bowie and Queen when growing up. We hunted through the archive for relevant materials to present her with, including a magazine featuring a review of Queen's 1981 Latin America tour. The review reminded her, she told us, of how she had felt as a teenager hearing Freddie Mercury, a performer she so admired, sing a song in her mother tongue. While searching for relevant materials we also found photographs of women punk musicians for Jill and a selection of fanzines for Anne. This, then, is how the weekly sessions progressed, with materials prompting stories that directed the project team to additional materials prompting further stories, and so on. As expected, some participants dropped out of the project due to competing pressures on their time, but others became regular visitors, spending time in the archive between the weekly sessions. In fact, Adam and Ben spent days on end hunched over their decks in the basement creating new compositions through sampled sounds, and reading up on African musicians featured on albums recorded in the 1970s.

Participants also invited me and other members of the project team to meet with them away from the archives and attend various events they were involved with. Some offered the team additional opportunities for public engagement, and among other things we broadcast a weekly Stories from the Archive session on the regional BBC radio station. This involved choosing an item from the archive that we could take down to the BBC studios every Tuesday and talk about on air for ten minutes or so, along with a musical excerpt that could be played and related to this item. Word about the project spread and we were soon inundated with further invitations, offers and requests. Eventually, a selection of music and photo stories was exhibited in a large public atrium on a sunny Saturday afternoon. As participants and visitors perused the exhibition, they were entertained by a live jazz band and recorded sounds from the archive deejayed by Adam and Ben.

Engaging with music through remembering

Throughout the Music, Photographs and Stories from the Archives project, materials from the music archive were looked at, listened to, touched and smelled. Inevitably, some materials were not much attended to, but there were also others that the participants found particularly interesting or meaningful. Getting participants to stick to the project brief was not always easy, however, and some were clearly more interested in telling a story about the musical materials rather than in using these materials to tell a story about themselves. Most nevertheless found it quite easy to locate materials they could attach to their own personal experience and autobiographical past, and to engage with the archival materials through practices of remembering. In fact, the project suggested that music is particularly good to remember with, something that can be illustrated through the activities and stories of a group of participants who were in their fifties and had strong and long-standing interests in music and music-making. One of them, Paul, was waiting outside the building for the project team to arrive for the first archive session. Dressed in black and clutching a leather briefcase, he looked rather businesslike and apprehensive. We introduced ourselves and he began to explain that he was a teacher but was interrupted by the arrival of Ian, a confident singer-songwriter with wild curly hair who exuded energy. Ian had brought along his friend James, a tall, broad-shouldered man who smiled at us quietly and let Ian do all the talking. After these introductions, we led Ian, James, Paul and a few others up to the archive, where the conversation began to flow more easily as they inspected the materials we had laid out.

Eventually all of us made our way over to the sound recordings, which include a collection of BBC reel tapes from the 1980s featuring interviews with, and live performances by, many Liverpool-based rock bands, although Liverpool-related materials comprise only a small proportion of the archive. For Paul, Ian and James, who had been involved with Liverpool rock culture at that time, stumbling across these tapes was like discovering gold. Together they examined the flat square boxes in which the reel tapes were stored, reading out the titles of the recorded tracks scribbled on the box covers. They pored over the accompanying catalog, comprising a list of band names and song titles typed on a sheet of paper. Pointing out names and titles they recognized, they reminded each other of the musicians and bands involved, what had happened to them and what they were up to now, how their songs had sounded and whether they had been commercially released. They also shared experiences of the bands they had been in themselves or had hung out with, and Paul mentioned some interviews he had recently conducted with musicians from the same period for a local television channel. They chatted about these musicians until James realized that he was late for an appointment and had to rush off. As he was leaving, he told members of the project team that he was due to retire in three weeks' time and that this had been one of the best days of his life. He now wanted, he added, to devote his retirement to helping us sort out the archival materials while also resuming his involvement with local music-making. So he left us his card, which identified him as a high-ranking law enforcement official, and during the remaining weeks of the project, he became a regular visitor to the archive.

Every now and then, James and other project participants related particular archival materials to "a memory" they "had," as if memory were a thing to be stored and retrieved. Citing Paul Antze and Michael Lambek's (1996) summary of memory studies, Gable and Handler (2011) point out, "It has long been recognised that in modern consumerist societies [. . .] 'memory' is conflated with 'experience' and both are imagined as things to be possessed" (p. 39). Yet encounters like the one involving the BBC tapes show how the archival materials inspired various practices of remembering, and suggest that memory can be more productively conceptualized as a process rather than a thing. These encounters therefore highlighted the doing of memory but also what memory does in specific situations and contexts. Sometimes, for example, the archival materials prompted project participants to remember in ways that caught them by surprise and triggered particular emotions, much like the "spontaneous memory" discussed by Tia DeNora (2000, p. 63) and prompted by the sound of music, or the "involuntary memory" described by the novelist Marcel Proust (1913/2011) and provoked by the taste of madeleines.

One example of this occurred during a filmed interview with James when he selected at random a 1981 issue of the Liverpool fanzine *Merseysound* to talk about on camera. "It was like your bible if you were into music at the time," he explained, pointing out that the fanzine cost only 20 pence per issue. Flicking through the pages, he pointed out articles providing guidance on how to write a song, make your own demo tape, and form or manage a band. "It told you everything," he continued, "and it had just about everything, including interviews with local bands." Stabbing a finger at the photographs accompanying such interviews, James named the musicians and bands involved and provided details on what they went on to do, what records they had out, who ended up being in a band with whom, what they were up to now, and so on, while also naming the journalists who had interviewed them. Turning the pages, he commented, "Even now I can remember all these bands. I can remember the gigs. I mean, it was just amazing." The reviews, advertisements and announcements prompted further comments on the events, venues and services involved, and as James came to the readers' letters page, he was about to add something ("and also –") when he was suddenly stopped in his tracks. "I can't believe this," he said. "This is a reply to a letter I wrote in about visual aids. I literally just can't believe this . . ." Reminded of his letter, he was about to explain what had prompted him to write it but then blushed, held his head in his hands and began to stutter before beaming up at the camera operator and members of the project team. "Genuinely, I didn't know it was there," he proclaimed in reference to the editor's reply. "That's made me really smile."

Besides such instances of involuntary or spontaneous memory, there was also the more voluntary and concerted effort or "work" of remembering (Litzinger 1988; Krause 2005) as participants circulated and shared reminiscences with others through conversation, filmed interviews and various media technologies. Through these practices the past was invented or reinvented, recalled or forgotten. As pointed out by scholars such as Michel-Rolph Trouillot (1995) and Andreas Huyssen (1995), remembering is a selective practice, and understanding it demands attention not only to what is remembered, but also to what is not. During conversations in the archive, for example, project participants sometimes related music to negative aspects of the past and some of the bad things they had experienced. The stories they fashioned for public display, however, tended to dwell on the positive. James and Paul certainly responded positively to the Liverpool-related materials they came across, and during his first visit to the archive, James used his mobile phone to photograph a flyer advertising a local club from the 1980s. He posted the image to a Facebook group devoted to Liverpool's independent rock culture where images of 1970s and

'80s memorabilia were exchanged regularly. Site posts also included those featuring photographs of the group's members both then and now, memories of the local musical past, and information on contemporary events. The project team discovered James's post after someone emailed us to ask about the item, having seen it on the Facebook site, and we subsequently became members of the group ourselves.

Paul, meanwhile, asked if he could make a film about our Stories from the Archives project with the local television channel he had been working with. We were approaching the end of the project and had been making our own modest, in-house film about it, but Paul's connection with this television channel offered us a welcome opportunity to collaborate on the production of a film that would engage a wider public in the work that we were doing. Paul invited ten or so people to take part in the film. All of them had been involved with 1980s Liverpool rock culture in some way, whether as journalists and radio broadcasters, record label and record shop owners, musicians or fans. Most had taken on more than one of these roles, often simultaneously, which is very much in keeping with the conventions of "indie" or "alternative" rock culture. The camera crew arrived and was dispatched to the café next door while everyone else milled around the archive, chatting and exploring the materials. The atmosphere was friendly and relaxed, and every now and then Paul appeared to usher people one by one into the café to be filmed along with the materials they had chosen to talk about. For these participants the archive, particularly the Liverpool-related materials, provided a rich resource for remembering. Ana from the Philippines told us about her love of 1980s Liverpool rock bands, which is why she had ended up moving to Liverpool two decades earlier. Denise, whom I recognized as a central contributor to the above-mentioned Facebook group, described her own personal collection of 1980s music memorabilia while her husband, John, related stories about concerts in the 1980s that he had either organized or reviewed. The film crew was delighted when the two of them turned up for their interview with an article they had found about the concert at which they first met.

In these and other ways, the project generated connections between autobiographical and collective remembering. The making of the documentary film, for example, depended on collaboration between project participants and the sharing of stories about the local musical past, including stories that were subsequently shared through social media. Those participating in the filmmaking either voluntarily related materials to stories about their own personal past and used them as a resource for autobiographical remembering, or the materials prompted such stories in a more serendipitous way. Music materials that were investigated and selected for the film were also related to a remembering that was collective as well as personal, because it involved events from the past that the participants had shared knowledge or experience of. Similarly, through spoken anecdotes and storytelling, James, Ian and Paul attached the BBC tapes they selected from the shelves to their own lived memories of 1980s Liverpool rock culture that they swapped with each other, using the tapes to establish connections and generate a sense of the past that was collective and shared. The young artist-deejays Adam and Ben, in contrast, were engaged in remembering of a rather different kind – exploring, sampling and combining sounds from the archives, such as those from 1970s Africa, and conducting their own research on these sounds so they could attach them to the histories and lived experiences of others.

Situating music in time through storytelling and remembering

For those participating in Music, Photographs and Stories from the Archives, the archival materials provided a focus for the telling and sharing of stories, and for forms of remembering that could be described as voluntary or involuntary, autobiographical or collective. Through these practices the materials were not simply related to the past, but also forged relations between past, present and future, enabling both materials and participants to be situated in time passages. In fact, one of our project participants even made a passing reference to the archive as a collection of "time capsules."

To begin with, the materials prompted practices of remembering that took place in the present and enabled relations to be established between then and now, and between current and former selves. For James, coming across the reply to his letter in *Merseysound* brought an unexpected encounter with his younger self. Paul was likewise taken by surprise when presented with the reel-to-reel tape featuring him and his band that the project team had managed to find in the local BBC tape collection. Lying flat at the bottom of the box was a sealed envelope featuring a handwritten address and containing the letter Paul had sent the BBC in 1982 requesting that his tape be played on air. Using mobile phones, we were able to capture on film the moment when Paul spotted his own handwriting, opened the envelope, and read out his own letter written 34 years previously.

In addition to unexpected encounters like this, project participants were commonly attracted to materials that they could deliberately use to make sense of events in the past and how things had subsequently unfolded. Again, these materials commonly generated comparisons between then and now. Holding up the sleeve of a David Bowie album, Isabel explained that she used to spend all her pocket money on materials related to Bowie and Queen, which meant not only "having no money for a month," but also, given that this predated online streaming, time spent visiting record shops and rummaging through their stock. For Victor and Michael, going through a Buddy Holly concert program and reading out the printed itinerary prompted reflection on changing conventions in live music. At the age of 15, Michael used to impersonate Buddy Holly and invite school friends over to his house to listen to Holly's latest single. He remembered how at concerts in the mid- and late 1950s, fans would have to sit through a host of variety acts and an intermission before they got to see a short set from the headline star performer, and how at the end of the performance everyone would stand up for the national anthem. James used an issue of *Merseysound* to tell the project team about his experiences of music in the early 1980s, and also about the importance of such cheap, DIY publications in the pre-digital era.

The archival materials allowed project participants to not only draw comparisons between then and now, but also to map their life stories. Inevitably, this mapping revealed differences between these participants in terms of their music activities and experience. One or two participants, for example, described how they enjoyed listening to music but were not especially interested in it, while others had been actively involved with music, whether as audience members or musicians. Music had nevertheless accompanied most of them throughout their lives and they were therefore able to relate the archival materials to a series of autobiographical events, and to narratives of time and a sense of time passing. Research with audiences in England (Cohen, 2016) likewise highlights music's role and significance in the mapping of autobiographical memory, with individuals able to chart different stages in their lives through particular songs and albums or musical places and spaces, hence the common association of childhood with music listened to in the family car and other domestic spaces, young adulthood with clubs and festivals, and so on. As Andy Bennett (2013) writes, "Embedded in memory and embodied through reflection on their relation to individual biography, popular music can thus become an important source of life-mapping for ageing popular music fans" (p. 48), while Lauren Istvandity (2014) describes music as a "lifetime soundtrack."

The stories of some project participants showed how music accompanies people throughout their lives while also offering them a pathway through life (Finnegan, 1989). Like Paul and James, some project participants had dipped in and out of music-making due to competing family and work commitments. Others, like Pete and Matt, had experienced almost a lifetime of continuous and active involvement in music-making. Coming across the names and photographs of the musicians and bands featured in the *Merseysound* fanzine prompted James to trace their musical pathways, noting the bands that had broken up or reformed and the musicians who had moved in and out of these bands over the years, much like Pete Frame's (1983) diagrams of rock bands as family trees. Inspecting the BBC reel-to-reel tapes from the 1980s featuring performances by Liverpool bands, Paul observed that some of these bands had recently released albums of the analogue material that they had first recorded or performed 30 years previously. He and his fellow band member Carl then told us the story of their own band: how it had formed and developed and the unexpected twists and turns along the way. They showed us an image of the band's 45 single that had been released by a German label some time ago. The band had subsequently broken up, but little known to them, the record became a hit in the Philippines, a country they had never visited. They found out about this in 2007 when they established a page for their band on MySpace and were suddenly besieged by messages from fans in the Philippines stating, "We found you! Where've you been?" It turned out that mobile deejays working for an independent radio station in the Philippines had played their record but used to black out the label and sleeve of all the records they played, retitling the songs and renaming the bands. One explanation for this, according to Paul and Carl, was that the deejays wanted to keep the sources of their playlist secret so that competitor stations owned by the Marcos regime would not be able to identify and monopolize them. Once the band's MySpace page was set up, however, and fans from the Philippines recognized their song, Paul and the others discovered their overseas fame and decided to re-form the band.

When Matt came across an album he had once featured on, it likewise prompted him to reflect on his music and performance style at the time the album was recorded, and how it had since developed. Over the years, he mused, there had been changes in what he chose to write songs about, as well as in his music tastes and also his voice, with age, he joked, lending his vocals greater gravitas. He subsequently took me on a tour of Liverpool and places connected to his musical past, and to materials he had come across in the archive, showing how musicians weave their musical memories and biographies through the urban landscape (Cohen, 2012). During this tour he dwelt on the city's changing places of music, including sites that had once hosted music venues and sites where a venue had once stood but had subsequently vanished.

UK cities typically have a high turnover of such places, partly due to the general instability of small music businesses, fast-changing trends in live music and dramatic urban transformations. The landscape of cities such as Liverpool has, over the past few decades, experienced fluctuating economic fortunes and intense programs of physical regeneration. What struck me when walking around the city with Matt was how the urban landscape provides, much like the university-based archive, a tangible, material resource for remembering, particularly for those, like Matt, who had lived in the city for some time. For him, and occasionally for me too, some of the buildings we passed provided physical reminders of a former self, of times and venues gone by, of musical places that had been lost. Many of our project participants had lived in the Liverpool region all or most of their lives, so during the project they too were able to exchange stories about the local music clubs and venues in which they had either played music or seen others play.

By associating certain buildings in the city with particular music groups and events, such as a hotel that had once been a focal point for those involved with the city's 1970s rock "scene," Matt suggested, through his storytelling and remembering, that places can be experienced as reflecting the values and lifestyles of certain generations over others, and therefore as "generationed" (May & Muir, 2015). The same point could be made about the materials in the Popular Music Archive and how they forged relations within and across generations. Among them were materials that drew the attention of the group participating in the television filming session and made connections between members of the group quite visible. The conversation prompted by an issue of *Merseysound*, for example, a fanzine that ran for only three years or so, revealed that one member of the group had edited it while others in the group had either published articles or reviews in it, been interviewed or reviewed for it, run a business that was advertised in it or, like James, had been its avid readers and letter-writers. A concert program revealed similar connections, since among the group were those who had promoted, reviewed and performed at the concert, and designed the poster for it. In this way the production of the film, and our project more generally, enabled materials to become attached to experiences shared by a group of peers from a particular generation, while depending on intergenerational collaboration.

The archival materials were embedded in relations between generations in other ways too. For example, the materials prompted narratives and autobiographical remembering that involved tracing the influence of parents or children on participants' lives and music tastes. While Wallace had wanted to play us his mother's favorite records, Isabel's father loomed large in her story. Having been struck by the Britishness of some of the materials in the Popular Music Archive, she remembered her love of Bowie and other British performers as a young Spanish girl, and her father's stories of traveling to Britain as a sailor and the music venues he frequented during visits to Liverpool. These recollections made her reflect on how she had eventually come to live in Britain herself and the influence of music and her father on this move. By inspiring these kinds of stories about the transfer of influences or objects from one generation to another, the archival materials raised notions of inheritance and legacy.

Similarly, for most of the project participants the archive was not only a repository of materials, but also a place where the materials would be respected and cared for. Consequently, throughout the project we were offered donations of archival materials or introductions to individuals who had materials to donate. They included offers from the children of a recently deceased jazz fan who wanted their father's vast CD collection to go to a good home, and from a musician in her seventies who had a wealth of personal materials and music industry experience that she desperately wanted younger generations to benefit from. Legacy was something that Paul was also concerned with. For him, inviting those who had been involved with 1980s Liverpool rock culture to participate in the project and the making of a television documentary about it was not simply an exercise in nostalgia but about highlighting their ongoing creative practice and influence, thereby gaining recognition for the period and the musical creativity it had given birth to.

Music as a resource for research on age and ageing

Through practices of remembering that situated the archival materials in time, those participating in Music, Photographs and Stories from the Archives moved back and forth between then and now, mapping the journeys in between and those going forward and into the future. Their stories of particular times and events in the past were told and experienced in the present, and they shared thoughts about legacy and inheritance and a musical past that lived on, evolving across the generations. Often, the materials evoked a sense of time passing that was redolent with emotion. It occurred to me, therefore, that because the archival materials worked so effectively to prompt storytelling, remembering and journeys through time, these materials could provide a productive and unique resource for research on age and ageing. This section outlines two possible, intersecting paths for this research, which together highlight the potential for investigating ideas and experiences of ageing generated through the interaction between people and music materials.

Research on the age and ageing of people

First, Music, Photographs and Stories from the Archives was a project focused on public engagement rather than research, but it nevertheless suggested that music materials provide a rich resource for research on human age and ageing. This research could explore how such materials accompany people as they age, as well as what they reveal about people's ideas and experiences of age and ageing. To begin with, the archival materials "aged" the project participants, linking them to certain age groups or generations. This was particularly evident when these materials were connected to lived memories of particular events, whether 1980s Liverpool rock culture or a 1958 Buddy Holly concert, or to music technologies associated with particular times and eras, such as a parent's 78 records. When walking around the city with Matt, I was likewise struck by how a city can seem not only a place that people age in but, as with the archival materials, one that "ages" them. The two of us knew something about the hidden music history of various buildings encountered during our walk, and how over the years these buildings had been adopted and adapted, used and reused as music venues. This knowledge fixed us to particular times in the city's past while also enabling us to share experience and establish some common ground. Moreover, as we walked around the city, some of the buildings we encountered reminded Matt of particular events, prompting stories of his experiences as a musician and how his music and music-making had developed over the years.

As discussed in the previous section, the materials in the Popular Music Archive likewise facilitated autobiographical narratives, enabling the project participants to tell a story about who they are, where they have been and how their lives have changed over the years – and to trace events and influences back and forth across past, present and future. By showing how music had accompanied participants throughout their lives, sometimes providing them with a "pathway" through life (Finnegan, 1989), these narratives revealed something about how people age with music. In his book on ageing fans, Andy Bennett (2013) explains how "for many ageing followers of rock, punk, dance, and other contemporary popular music genres, the cultural sensibilities they acquired as members of music driven youth cultures have remained with them, shaping their life courses and becoming ingrained in their biographical trajectories and associated lifestyle sensibilities" (p. 2). For some of the older fans he interviewed, their long-term interest in music had led them to pursue music-related careers that allowed them space and flexibility for music, and to "become proactive in the preservation of particular music genres or in the dissemination of musical skills" (p. 7). This could certainly be said of Paul and Carl, who used materials from the archive to help them recount the story of their band. It was obviously a story they had recounted many times, but it helped, as did Matt's stories and anecdotes, to illustrate the twists and turns in the musical careers or trajectories of amateur and semiprofessional musicians, and the various challenges and opportunities encountered along the way.

The story of this band suggested that for project participants like Paul and Carl, engaging in music practice over the years, whether as a musician or a fan, had involved negotiating changes in musical styles and scenes, in technologies and industries, and in places of music. They had also experienced and negotiated changes in their personal and domestic lives, including those attributed to age. Occasionally project participants also offered a sense of themselves as ageing, as when Matt encountered one of his early recordings in the archive and described his voice as a younger musician, and how it had subsequently matured. Another participant likewise spoke of the growing maturity of his music. Now that he was not so anxious for commercial success and a music career, he told us, he could explore diverse styles and become more experimental with his songwriting: "When you reach a certain age you can please yourself and become more selective about what you play and where," he said. The autobiographical accounts of Matt and other musicians who participated in our project suggested musical paths that had often taken unexpected or unconventional directions; these paths bore little resemblance to stereotypical UK media images of ageing rockers (such as Keith Richards) or of middle-aged talent show contestants desperate for their one last chance at commercial success (as seen on the British reality show *The X Factor*). Moreover, the conversations of Paul and others about their experiences of 1980s rock culture challenge the widespread assumption that the memory practices of ageing music audiences are always and inevitably nostalgic, thereby supporting the findings of Andy Bennett (2013) from his research on ageing youth cultures.

By enabling project participants to map their life histories and trajectories, the archival materials also enabled stories of ageing with music and of age-related experiences, whether moments of childhood or later-life transitions, such as retirement. In addition, the materials prompted participants to compare their experiences at different ages. This sometimes involved reflection on differences between then and now, or between younger and older selves, which can be illustrated through my own personal experience of the project. As director of the project, I not only oversaw and observed project activities, but also participated in them. Yet when writing about such projects, it can be tempting to concentrate on the experiences of the other participants, neglecting to report on those of the project team. In fact, through the television filming session in the archive, I became reunited with a few people and materials I myself had encountered during the mid-1980s, when I spent a year living in Liverpool and studying its rock culture as part of my doctoral research (Cohen, 1991).

The filming session was the first time I had seen Pete, for example, since 1986, when he was a young teenager and the lead guitarist and vocalist with a band he had formed with his friends. He had since gone on to develop a successful career as a professional musician, and during the filming he invited me to the launch of an album by his son, who was now also in a band. Pete was one of the group of people Paul had invited to be interviewed for the film, and as they explored the archive, members of the group selected materials to talk about that related to Liverpool's 1980s rock culture. Among these materials were fanzines, recordings and concert posters that were familiar to me, since I had been involved with the musical life of the city at that time, so I was able to relate them to personal experience. Inevitably, perhaps, becoming reunited with people and materials from the past prompted me to reflect not only on the passing of time, but also on my own advancing years. Moreover, as I joined the group participating in the filming session and gathered around the table, we all sifted through materials piled on top of it, coming came across items connected to our lived experience of 1980s Liverpool, and the ensuing conversation inspired a sense of ageing together. In this and other ways, the music materials not only enabled relationships between people from the same or different age groups and generations, but also facilitated the construction of identities that were sometimes associated with age.

While the archival materials encouraged the telling of stories about the past and present, they also prompted reflection on future developments and older selves. This was suggested by the discussions about legacy and inheritance, which occasionally touched on the issue of mortality. Some of the collections in the archive had been put together by people who had subsequently died and whose collections had been donated to us by their relatives. Explaining this to project participants led to conversations about the music materials that they had collected themselves or the music collections of their friends, relatives and acquaintances. In his book entitled *Stuff*, the anthropologist Daniel Miller (2009) eloquently discusses the importance of material objects and possessions for people engaging with death, and experiences of bereavement and illness, along with a sense of getting older, had clearly made one or two of our project participants think about their own music "stuff" and what might happen to it. In this sense, music materials prompted questions about what it means to grow old and what happens when people die. For those participating in the filming session, coming across materials related to a local musician they had been familiar with and who had recently died evoked a particularly poignant sense of time passing. So, too, did materials related to the recently deceased David Bowie, at least for me, who, like Isabel and so many others, had grown up with Bowie's music.

These and other encounters in the archive showed how the stuff of music, mediated by memory, enables ideas concerning age and ageing to be imagined, experienced and interrogated. Referring to Joseph Kotarba's work on songs, Stephen Katz (2014) points out that music can help people to make sense of their lives as they age:

> While certain songs may freeze moments in time, such as a couple's wedding song or the graduation song of a certain class cohort, music also extends the self into time (Kotarba 2013). According to Kotarba, not only can "our song" provide "meaning for benchmark events in the relationship," it also "can help the person feel like a lover" throughout the history of their relationship (Kotarba 2013, 22). Thus music and identity can be artfully and biographically navigated as meaningful

patterns of growth, apart from a commercialized culture of nostalgia. (p. 99)

Materials in the IPM's Popular Music Archive are connected to a multitude of songs and compositions, offering a productive resource for exploring contemporary and historical ideas and attitudes concerning age and ageing, whether through analysis of lyrics, voice and vocal performance, sounds and related visual and moving images, and so on.

Research on the age and ageing of music materials

Besides research on human age and ageing, the Music, Photographs and Stories from the Archives project suggested the potential for research that explores how people engage with music materials that are also ageing. Stephen Katz (2005) notes, "[Ho]w much our ideas, metaphors, and meanings of ageing are materially inscribed, yet how so little account we take of the material life of ageing around us and outside of our particular human experience of it" (p. 233). Referring to the materials of everyday life, Line Grenier (2012) states that her interest is not so much in the meaning or function of such materials as in their productive power. "What do these objects do?" she asks. "What do they enable? What is done through them, and on their behalf?" (p. 5).

As illustrated above, materials in the Popular Music Archive affected project participants in physical and emotional ways; they provided a resource for autobiographical narratives of time and ageing, and for collective remembering and conversational exchange; and they forged relationships between people from the same or different generations. As part of this process, the materials developed and cemented relationships between friends (Victor and Michael), partners (Denise and John), relatives (Isabel and her dad), and peers (those sharing a history of the 1980s Liverpool music scene). The materials also established bonds between project participants who had not previously met (as illustrated by Paul's encounter with Ian and James). Music materials are therefore social agents that enable things to happen and influence ideas and experiences. At the same time, however, these materials are significant not only as prompts, props and enablers, but also as objects in their own right, with their own particular look and feel. In fact, the tangibility of such materials might partly explain why project participants were attracted more to the music archive than to the archive of the Open Eye Gallery. Sessions at the latter had to be booked in advance to search the catalog via an in-house computer, while the printed photographs were carefully stored elsewhere and not readily available for scrutiny. The significance of music's tangibility is likewise suggested by the central character in Nick Hornby's (1995) novel *High Fidelity*, whose records were closely connected to his autobiographical remembering of past events and relationships. "Tuesday night," he declared, "I reorganized my record collection. I often do this at periods of emotional stress. There are some people who would find this a pretty dull way to spend an evening, but I'm not one of them. This is my life, and it's nice to be able to wade in it, immerse your arms in it, touch it" (p. 54).

Concentrating on the materiality of the archival materials reveals certain parallels between the ageing of these materials and the ageing of people. During their visits to the Popular Music Archive, some participants stumbled across materials they recognized and seemed surprised to find that these materials were not only still around and had been enjoying a parallel existence to themselves, but had been deliberately collected and stored. Matt told us that seeing the local flyers and fanzines from the 1980s "in the flesh," as it were, provided "physical proof of my past existence and experience." The archival materials had nevertheless changed over time and with use, undergoing transformations in their shape and appearance, feel or smell. Many reached the university having been well kept and loved, as shown by the sound recordings displayed in protective sleeves and leather-bound cases, and the handwritten catalogs and scrapbooks meticulously documented and rich with ink. Yet many also displayed signs of age and deterioration, such as the well-thumbed books and magazines and cracked plastic cassette covers, or the creased photographs and faded posters with yellow stains and frayed edges. Some of these ageing objects were in desperate need of specialist attention, including the singles that had warped and buckled, and the albums sprouting spores of white fungus from their grooves and a milky film spreading out across black vinyl. Many items were palimpsests revealing aspects of past use and ownership, such as the record sleeves adorned with layers of stickers and printed or handwritten labels.

For Mike Pearson and Michael Shanks (2001), "The decay of an artifact is a token of the *human* condition. The fragment, the mutilated and incomplete thing from the past, brings a sense of life struggling with time: death and decay await us all, people and objects alike. In common we have our materiality" (p. 93). Similarly, Tim Dant (1999) notes that material objects are "products of their time, bearing the style of their production and the aesthetic of their design under the patina of age much as humans bear the style of their education and their formative experiences under ageing skin" (p. 151). As objects of their own time, the materials of the Popular Music Archive are ageing according to how they were made and what they were made of. The singles and albums, for example, show signs of age and damage on the surface of recordings made of vinyl and polystyrene, while earlier recordings made from shellac or acetate have been even more vulnerable to decay. Meanwhile, the reel tapes vary in size and the tape machines are limited in terms of the sizes they can play, with more specialized machines being quite difficult or expensive to procure. Some of the archival materials have therefore become obsolete as well as damaged, linked to music technologies that have become outdated and replaced by their successors. Like humans, all of these archival materials have their own biographies and life histories (Kopytoff, 1986), so explaining to project participants how particular items ended up in the archive meant sharing stories about their provenance: how the items came to be made, collected and subsequently passed on to us, and the chains of ownership involved.

A considerable body of scholarly literature explores the social life and mobility of things, and how they circulate through different hands, contexts and uses, and along specified paths. Arjun Appadurai (1986), for example, focuses on the paths of commodities, which he defines as "not one kind of thing rather than another, but one phase in the life of some things" (p. 17). Many, though by no means all of the materials in the Popular Music Archive had a previous life as commodities embedded in circuits of trade but subsequently became what Will Straw (2000) terms "exhausted commodities." Drawing on the work of Walter Benjamin and Michael Thompson, Straw refers to musical recordings, books and other objects whose economic value has often withered, highlighting the disjunction between economic decay and physical decay. He situates these objects in time, highlighting the processes through which they become cultural waste as their meanings and value are exhausted, but how they can nevertheless be recycled, retrieved, revived and revalorized. Vinyl recordings, for example, were once thought of as an outdated technology, but subsequently became a focus for new businesses, practices and scenes. Straw also considers how exhausted commodities are spatially situated, describing objects that pile up like sediments and the retail sites and other institutions that have evolved to house them.

In this sense, therefore, a pile of tired old materials had accumulated at the University of Liverpool – materials that no longer served much purpose and raised questions about whose "stuff" goes where and why, and what should or should not be done with it. Knowing how best to care for these materials had presented university staff with quite a problem, just as media and policy discourses have presented ageing populations and their care as a problem for countries like Britain, where people are generally living longer. In fact, the materials had been caught up in a complex and long-running politics of space tied to notions of value. They had not, for example, been cared for as part of the Special Collections housed in the university's central library, despite long-standing efforts to explain their significance to senior librarians. Furthermore, although the archive had recently attracted support from senior university managers, for years its materials had been relocated from one part of the university to another, with items sometimes deliberately thrown out. As noted by scholars engaged in research on contemporary popular music archives (Baker & Huber, 2014; Baker & Collins, 2016), the association of popular music with mass culture has commonly imbued its material extensions with a sense of "disposability," which is why people without an intimate attachment to such materials may see no value in retaining them, whether those people are members of a public institution or family members dealing with the collection of a dead relative.

The people who participated in our project brought alternative perspectives regarding the value of the Popular Music Archive, and for most this lay in the ability of its materials to prompt stories and become attached to experience. Inevitably, many of the project participants were nevertheless drawn to the archive's rarer items, such as some original Bob Dylan posters, but all of them were impressed by the sheer size and scale of the archive, underscoring Straw's (2000) point that the bulky presence of materials as cultural waste can contribute to a sense that they nevertheless have value and coherence. Moreover, the fact that the archival materials were not catalogued or publicly accessible undoubtedly enhanced their value for some project participants, contributing to a sense of discovery. Again, this observation is supported by the work of Straw (2000), who argues that the inaccessibility of exhausted commodities can contribute to their status as fetish objects, as with the fetishization of vinyl records in the digital era.

Materials in the Popular Music Archive also attracted the interest of archivists and museum staff who had heard about the project, and who visited the archive to find out more. Given that the materials had not been under the care of a dedicated archivist, these visitors advised us on specialist techniques that would enable them to be preserved in their current state or conserved. Their main concern, therefore, was to either take the materials back in time by removing the effects of ageing, as with the use of plastic surgery on humans, or to extend their life. One of these visitors was the curator of a gallery associated with the university, who was concerned about the visible signs of damage and ageing on the materials, and the negative message they would convey about the university and its lack of care for the archive. For other project participants, however, the signs of age on such objects were clearly regarded as part of their character or aesthetic appeal, helping to authenticate them and give them value.[3] One member of the public visiting the exhibition connected with the project told the project team that he had seen a recent photocopy of one of the fanzine issues on display but that it was nice to see the original, an object displaying obvious signs of wear and tear that had itself been a photocopy in the first place. A couple of other visitors read out to each other the words written on various labels glued on top of one another on the sleeves of albums that Adam and Ben had selected to play, clearly interested in the stories that this montage of labels told about the albums' past lives. In these and other ways the project revealed positive attitudes toward ageing materials, something also suggested by the labeling of objects as "antique," "retro" or "vintage" in British popular culture.

The project also revealed positive attitudes toward the archival materials more generally, which suggests that interest in the material cultures of music has not waned in the digital era. On the contrary, the emergence of digital technologies and social media has, somewhat paradoxically, fueled interest in material music objects and their curation, storage and preservation, and it has provided new, virtual opportunities for remembering with such materials. For example, Paul's involvement with the project led to the making of a documentary film about it, which brought to the university archive members of a Facebook group who shared reminiscences about Liverpool's post-1970s independent music scene online, and in doing so encouraged collective interest in materials related to the scene. The ways in which the mass media and digitization have fueled interest in memory and material culture have been discussed by scholars such as Andreas Huyssen (1995), and this trend is illustrated by the expanding scholarship on music and materiality (Roy, 2015; Hogarty, 2015). The work of Anne-Kathrin Hoklas (2014) and Caroline O'Sullivan (2016) suggests that older people are more orientated toward music's material culture than members of the "digital generation," but this was not evident in our project, which suggested that the material cultures of music continue to attract people of all ages. Ours is a finding also evident in Paolo Magaudda's (2011) research with young Italian and Irish audiences, which suggests that the material stuff of music is becoming more rather than less crucial in shaping consumer practices, and in the work of Jean Hogarty (2015), who argues that despite the widespread use of immaterial formats such as streams and downloads, younger music audiences prefer material music formats, "believing them to function as stronger repositories of memory" (p. 148).

Meanwhile, research on diverse music audiences in England and Australia shows how people of different ages curate their memories through songs via YouTube, Spotify, mixtapes, and so on, while at the same time keeping, collecting and displaying items of music memorabilia, such as ticket stubs from concerts they have attended (Cohen, 2014; Bennett & Rogers, 2016). Reflecting on his own collection of tickets, a London-based businessman in his fifties explained: "The different shapes, sizes and colours, the logos, the fonts, the quality of the paper all start to trigger more thoughts. The escalating price of tickets over the years. The venues: the dives that remained and the palaces that were closed" (quoted in Cohen, 2014, p. 135). As noted by Andy Bennett and Ian Rogers (2016), such reflections illustrate

> a richness of detail to the stories told when they were reiterated *through* a material item. By focusing our attention on memory and the means by which it is recalled, we have successfully found occasions and examples that speak to the immense effectiveness of the material as a means to access some of music's core attributes, namely affective experience and the memory traces that enable listeners to narrate these experiences to others [. . .] Among our interviewees, there was a reported tendency to align materiality with narratives of youth and ageing, to signpost a life by cycles of engagement with music's physical extensions. (p. 39, original emphasis)

These "physical extensions" are examples of the many "mediations" through which music exists (Born, 2010). Rather than entertain a notion of "the music itself," scholars engaged in empirical research on music have tended to focus instead on the practices, processes and mediations of music, and on what music does rather than what it is or means (e.g., Blacking, 1973; Small, 1998). This focus has helped them to show how music "affords" social activity (DeNora, 2000). In fact, social theorists have had a long-standing interest in the "affordance" of materials (Gibson, 1977) and how things make people just as people make things, as illustrated by research on clothes, tools, buildings and other things in social anthropology and archaeology (Bourdieu, 1972/1977; Graves-Brown, 2000; Pearson & Shanks, 2001). Materials "make people" in accordance with their physical properties (shape, quality, and so on), and research with ageing music materials could explore this process further. It could examine, for example, how people engage with the materiality of such materials, including older audiences for whom the significance of these materials might have changed over time and as they, too, have aged.

The specificity and contexts of remembering and ageing with music

The Music, Photographs and Stories from the Archives project showed that music offers a productive resource for storytelling and remembering, and for research on age and ageing. The project drew attention to human ageing through the practices of remembering it inspired, and it also raised questions about the ageing of the archival materials. This suggests that while music materials provide a resource for research, it is important to consider the agency of these materials and their physical properties or materiality. The project also highlighted the importance of attending to the specificity of music as a cultural form and the specific contexts of musicking, remembering and ageing. These points are developed in this final part of the chapter, which builds on and refines the argument that has been made so far by asserting that music is a particularly productive resource for research on ageing because of its distinctive influence on how people remember.

Andy Bennett and Jodie Taylor (2012) argue that little is known about how healthy and independent ageing subjects use music in their everyday lives. By attending to the influence on memory of music as sound, the work of Tia DeNora (2000) nevertheless points to music's significance as part of the daily lives and biographical trajectories of a particular group of British women. Music, particularly popular music, was certainly woven through the memories and biographical trajectories of everyone who participated in our project. Even those who told us they were not particularly interested in music were able to remember with music, and for all of the project participants, music had crossed over into different domains of everyday activity and become associated with experiences that had accumulated over the years. The songs of Bowie and other popular musicians have engaged and connected audiences from the same or different generations and become embedded in the soundtrack of so many lives. Partly because it accompanies people throughout their lives, music inspires narratives of time and remembering. Audiences can also engage with music almost anywhere and at any time, and given this ubiquity and portability, music provided project participants with a focus and frame for remembered events – events that could be both deeply private and highly public.

Music also has a peculiar ability to prompt memories that can be intensely emotional and visceral, something that was noted by at least one of our project participants. As sound, music certainly has a powerful ability to evoke emotions connected to people and events from the past. The journalist Laura Barton (2014) captures something of this in her moving account of how music can provoke experiences of grief and loss that can be intensely physical and overwhelming. Similar examples of involuntary memories and feelings prompted by musical sounds are described by DeNora (2000), while Michael Pickering and Emily Keightley (2015) identify "photography and recorded music as the most salient media of remembering in everyday life" (p. 24). The latter argue, however, that while music and photography work in partnership as vehicles for remembering, they differ in terms of their formal characteristics and their relationship to time and memory. Echoing a point made by DeNora (2000, p. 67), they write:

> [P]hotographs are commonly considered as freezing specific moments and in that sense snatching them out from the temporal flow in which they were once immersed, whereas music occurs within this flow and seems intrinsic to it even when recorded and then listened to at a later time. These contrary modes of signification and representation directly and indirectly affect the ways they act in remembering practices and in the ways they activate the mnemonic imagination. (Pickering & Keightley, 2015, p. 181)

Some of our project participants were clearly invested in music as musicians or as music fans, but for most people music can activate memories and the imagination, often in ways that can be difficult to put into words. For 88-year-old Jack Levy, whom I met while working on a previous project and used to visit regularly (Cohen, 1995), the mere mention of a Liverpool dance hall from the 1930s to 1950s would prompt memories of the music he had danced to as a young man. Now living in a care home for the elderly, he was unable to go out anywhere and had no friends or family who could visit. His room was dark and dingy, with a faded carpet and a brown patch on the armchair marking the spot worn by the habitual pressure of his head. Sitting in this chair, he would identify the exact location of each of the dance halls he visited and how he used to get there, the names of the bandleaders and musicians who performed there, the groups and communities the hall supported, and the many women he danced with and courted. Closing his eyes and swaying his arms and torso, he would recall the glamor and swirl of the dresses and richness of decor, the spring and shine of the dance floors, the sounds of the bands and the sheer exuberance of the dance. For Jack, therefore, even when music was not being listened to or heard, it was nevertheless related to "embodied memory" (van Dijck, 2007, p. 78). Moreover, my conversations with a group of residents in another care home prompted the staff member present to note how the subject of music seemed to facilitate memories about all sorts of things that the residents did not usually discuss, and things that did not necessarily concern music.

Like Jack, those who participated in Music, Photographs and Stories from the Archives were all able to relate music to memory and a sense of time passing, and of being a certain age and growing older. These participants nevertheless differed in terms of age and social background, and they engaged and remembered with the archival materials in diverse ways. The creative practice of Ben and Adam, and their exploration and sampling of music history through sound, was not the same as the memory practices of Denise, who had cultivated a collection of music memorabilia related to her own lived experience. An autobiographical memory prompted by a music fanzine, recording or letter was not the same as the collective and collaborative work of online remembering conducted through a group of Facebook "friends." Comparative research on how people remember with the stuff of music could reveal experiences of age and ageing that are likewise diverse, attending to the contexts that shape such practices and how particular experiences are related to more general trends. This would help to show that experiences of age and ageing can be diverse but also highly structured, and that the process of remembering with music is rarely straightforward and often contested.

Studies of music and autobiographical memory have produced valuable insights by attending to the firsthand accounts of listeners and audiences (DeNora, 2000; van Dijck, 2007; Istvandity, 2014), yet they sometimes neglect to provide information on what the people involved do as well as what they say they do, or on the social situations and interactions involved. This chapter has described the Music, Photographs and Stories from the Archives project and the Popular Music Archive in order to establish a context that undoubtedly influenced the participants' memory practices and the stories they produced. The opportunity to explore a dedicated, university-based music archive seemed to frame participants' engagement with the archival materials in particular ways, although project activities and memory practices also extended beyond the archive and across other sites. Some participants told us how important they thought it was that an archive like ours existed, and all of them knew that the project was part of our efforts to develop the archive. Their response to the project was therefore overwhelmingly positive, and throughout the project there was a sense that for them, a resource like the Popular Music Archive served to validate their stories and experiences, and lend the music materials status. Participants were also guided by the idea of curating a story and self-portrait for public display and through collaboration with others, which might have constrained their storytelling in particular ways, perhaps encouraging, for example, stories dwelling on positive rather than negative experiences.

As well as being informed by these various contexts, the remembering of our project participants was shaped by their journeys through the archive and their encounters along the way, journeys that had different starting points and took different directions. Paul's encounter with James and Ian by the collection of BBC Radio Merseyside tapes, for example, generated particular memories and shared experiences of Liverpool bands and music-making during the 1980s. Moreover, these memories and experiences were clearly influenced by the conventions of alternative rock, with its emphasis on DIY culture, authenticity and preservation (Bennett, 2009). Practices of autobiographical and collective remembering are therefore shaped by particular social and cultural contexts, including genre-based cultures, as are ideas and experiences of age and ageing. The relationship between music, memory and ageing in Liverpool's alternative rock culture has certainly been rather different from that evident in the city's country music scene, which has been informed by traditional country music and its conventional emphasis on nostalgia, age and experience (Cohen, 2005), and also different from narratives of memory, age and ageing conventional to North American hip-hop (Forman, 2016). Engaging with music through autobiographical memory can likewise be highly conventional. The autobiographical remembering of Liverpool-based rock and hip-hop musicians, for example, has been shaped by cultural contexts involving particular relations and inequalities of class, race, gender, and so on (Cohen, 2014), as well as by dominant images and biographical accounts of musicians featured in published interviews and documentary film.

Memory is thus situated and can also be highly localized while at the same time influenced by broader contexts and trends, as are experiences of age and ageing. The Popular Music Archive at the University of Liverpool is based in a well-known "city of musical memory" (Waxer, 2002) where the interplay between official and vernacular memory can be quite evident, showing how memory can involve negotiation and struggle over what will be remembered and what forgotten. Efforts to commemorate 1980s Liverpool rock culture have been prompted in part by the dominance of Beatles heritage and tourism in the city, and the notoriety of the city's rock scene of the 1960s. This promotion of rock as heritage over the past two or three decades, not just in Liverpool but across other UK cities, has been fueled by various factors (Cohen, 2007; Bennett, 2009) and fiercely critiqued. Simon Reynolds (2012), for example, bemoans what he describes as a contemporary music "retromania" that has killed off musical innovation and involves, among other things, 1980s rock tours, tribute performances, television documentaries, and so on. As illustrated above, however, for those participating in our project, music was embedded in vernacular memory in ways that were not necessarily nostalgic or tied to the past, and there was little indication of music being thought of as "heritage."

Conclusion

Focusing on a public engagement project that brought 50 people to a university-based music archive, this chapter has made a case for research that investigates the relationship between music and ageing by examining practices of remembering and the contexts involved.

The chapter began by describing how music materials in the university archive provided a stimulus for the remembering and storytelling of the project participants. Through these practices they constructed the past in the present and contemplated not only where they had come from, and where they were at or heading to, but also their hopes or fears for the future. In doing so they showed how music enables a form of time travel, prompting reflection on the journeys or pathways that people have taken in life and consequently on questions of age and ageing. The second part of the chapter discussed the ideas and experiences of age and ageing that emerged through this process, focusing on the ageing of not only people but also music materials. This discussion pointed to the significance of music's materiality for understanding the relationship between music, remembering and ageing. The final part of the chapter turned to music's specificity as a cultural form, arguing that this makes it a particularly productive resource for research on social remembering and ageing.

Throughout the Music, Photographs and Stories from the Archives project, I was struck by what the archival materials suggested about the special qualities of music, and how much it matters to people. Even those participants who described themselves as not deeply interested in or knowledgeable about music could quite easily attach it to stories of events from the past that were mundane or exceptional, and to the people and relationships involved. Yet my involvement with interdisciplinary projects and committees at UK universities over the past three decades has shown me that scholars who are based in other areas of the humanities and social sciences still tend to regard music as a relatively closed and inaccessible subject, and one they associate largely with vocational training in live performance and instrumental tuition, or with the study of famous musicians and composers. Its relevance for strategic research collaborations and themes (such as "healthy ageing") is therefore not generally or immediately recognized. Yet music offers a rich resource for research exploring people's practices of remembering in everyday life and diverse experiences of age and ageing. Apart from the seminal studies of music and ageing referenced in this chapter, popular music studies have largely focused on younger audiences and music-makers, and there has been a dearth of research on music and cultural ageing more generally. Such research could help to deepen understanding by countering narrow media images and popular stereotypes of ageing, and negative media and popular discourses concerning ageing as a problem to be solved.[4]

The Music, Photographs and Stories from the Archives project also demonstrated how the "stuff" of music could help to engage the public in such research. Members of the public participating in the project brought the university's archive and its materials to life. Through their sampling decks and the repertoire they selected and performed, they enabled the archive to be heard. By sharing and displaying their stories they made its materials visible, and through these stories they showed how the lives of ageing people and things are intertwined. In the context of UK higher education, "public engagement" is typically thought of as something that follows on from research, enabling it to be disseminated beyond academia. In the case of our project, however, an exercise in public engagement spawned new research, raising questions about the relationship between music, memory and ageing, and transforming an archive that had seemed such a problem into a potential research resource.

Acknowledgments

I would like to thank all of those who participated in Music, Photographs and Stories from the Archives, including the project team at the Institute of Popular Music (Áine Mangaoang, Mike Jones, Les Roberts) and our partner organizations (the Open Eye Gallery and Liverpooljazz). Thanks must also go to the UK Arts & Humanities Research Council (Cultural Engagement scheme) and the University of Liverpool for supporting the project, and delegates at the 2016 conference of the International Association for the Study of Popular Music (UK/Ireland branch) who commented on an embryonic version of this chapter. I am indebted to the editors of this book for their insightful feedback on the later version of the chapter, and to the inspirational team of researchers involved with the international research and partnership project Ageing + Communication + Technologies (ACT). It has been a privilege to be part of this project, and I am grateful to Line Grenier, Kim Sawchuck, Constance Lafontaine and the rest of the ACT team for their encouragement and support.

Notes

1. The research was conducted between 2010 and 2013 as part of Popular Music Heritage, Cultural Memory and Cultural Identity (POPID), a project supported by the HERA Joint Research Programme (www.heranet.info), which is co-funded by AHRC, AKA, DASTI, ETF, FNR, FWF, HAZU, IRCHSS, MHEST, NWO, RANNIS, RCN, VR and the European Community FP7 2007–2013, under the Socio-economic Sciences and Humanities program.
2. Library music (also known as stock music or production music) is recorded music that can be licensed to customers for use in film, television, radio and other media.
3. As Marion Leonard (2014) explains, one authenticity can nevertheless be substituted for another. Describing a wooden stage from the church where Paul McCartney and John Lennon first met and performed, and its conservation for a museum display, Leonard notes that the conservation work "compromised the authenticity of the original object that was acquired by the museum." In another sense, however, "The conservation treatment was not about maintaining the integrity of the material as it has 'lived' over time but rather about constructing the authenticity of the object at a particular point in time so that visitors could immediately understand it as 'the real thing' and consume it as authentic" (p. 366).
4. Research like this could therefore build on work currently being undertaken for Ageing + Communication + Technologies (ACT), an

international research and partnership project established in 2014 to address the transformation of the experiences of ageing with the proliferation of new forms of mediated communications in networked societies. This chapter and book are both outputs from ACT, a project that has been creating intergenerational connections, rethinking media from the perspective of old age, and confronting ageism.

References

Antze, Paul, & Lambek, Michael (Eds.). (1996). *Tense past: Cultural essays in trauma and memory*. London: Routledge.

Appadurai, Arjun. (1986). Introduction: Commodities and the politics of value. In Arjun Appadurai (Ed.), *The social life of things: Commodities in cultural perspective* (pp. 3–63). Cambridge: Cambridge University Press.

Baker, Sarah, & Collins, Jez. (2016, March 9). Popular music heritage, community archives and the challenge of sustainability. *International Journal of Cultural Studies* [online version], 1–16.

Baker, Sarah, & Huber, Alison. (2014). Saving 'rubbish': Preserving popular music's material culture in amateur archives and museums. In Sara Cohen, Robert Knifton, Marion Leonard, & Les Roberts (Eds.), *Sites of popular music heritage: Memories, histories, places* (pp. 112–124). London: Routledge.

Barton, Laura. (2014, December 25). Guardian music critics: The songs that kept us sane in 2014. *The Guardian*. https://www.theguardian.com/music/2014/dec/25/guardian-music-writers-best-moments-2014.

Bennett, Andy. (2009). "Heritage rock": Rock music, representation and heritage discourse. *Poetics*, 37(5–6), 474–489. https://doi.org/10.1016/j.poetic.2009.09.006.

Bennett, Andy. (2013). *Music, style, and aging: Growing old disgracefully?* Philadelphia: Temple University Press.

Bennett, Andy, & Rogers, Ian. (2016). Popular music and materiality: Memorabilia and memory traces. *Popular Music and Society, 39*(1), 28–42.

Bennett, Andy, & Taylor, Jodie. (2012). Popular music and the aesthetics of ageing. *Popular Music, 31*(2), 231–243.

Blacking, John. (1973). *How musical is man?* Seattle: University of Washington Press.

Born, Georgina. (2010). Listening, mediation, event: Anthropological and sociological perspectives. *Journal of the Royal Musical Association, 135*(1), 79–89.

Bourdieu, Pierre. (1977). *Outline of a theory of practice.* Cambridge: Cambridge University Press. (Original work published 1972)

Clark, Margaret. (1967). The anthropology of aging: A new era for studies of culture and personality. *The Gerontologist, 7,* 55–64.

Cohen, Sara. (1991). *Rock culture in Liverpool: Popular music in the making.* Oxford: Oxford University Press.

Cohen, Sara. (1995). Sounding out the city: Music and the sensuous production of place. *Transactions of the Institute of British Geographers, 20*(4), 434–446.

Cohen, Sara. (2005). Country at the heart of the city: Music, heritage and regeneration in Liverpool. *Ethnomusicology, 49*(1), 25–48.

Cohen, Sara. (2007). *Decline, renewal and the city in popular music culture: Beyond the Beatles.* Aldershot, UK: Ashgate.

Cohen, Sara. (2012). Bubbles, tracks, borders and lines: Mapping music and urban landscape. *Journal of the Royal Musical Association, 137*(1), 135–171.

Cohen, Sara. (2014). 'Going to a gig': Remembering and mapping the places and journeys of live rock music in England. In Karen Burland & Stephanie Pitts (Eds.), *Coughing and clapping: Investigating audience experience* (pp. 131–147). Farnham, UK: Ashgate.

Cohen, Sara. (2016). Music as cartography: English audiences and their autobiographical memories of the musical past. In Johannes Brusila, Bruce Johnson, & John Richardson (Eds.), *Memory, space, sound* (pp. 107–123). Bristol: Intellect Books.

Cohen, Sara, Jones, Mike, & Sillitoe, Paul. (2014, May 4–December 30). *Pop, passion and politics*. Exhibition staged at the Vice-Chancellor's Lodge, University of Liverpool.

Dant, Tim. (1999). *Material culture in the social world: Values, activities, lifestyles*. Buckingham: Open University Press.

DeNora, Tia. (2000). *Music in everyday life*. Cambridge: Cambridge University Press.

Elliott, Richard. (2015). *The late voice: Age and experience in popular music*. London: Bloomsbury.

Finnegan, Ruth. (1989). *The hidden musicians: Music-making in an English town*. Cambridge: Cambridge University Press.

Forman, Murray. (2016, May 11–13), *Every day a pioneer: Aging artists and hip-hop legacies*. Paper presented at the Music, Ageing, Technology Symposium, University of Eastern Finland.

Frame, Pete. (1983). *The complete rock family trees: The development and history of rock performers including Eric Clapton, Crosby Stills Nash & Young, Led Zeppelin, . . . Genesis, Madness, T.Rex, Police*. London: Omnibus Press.

Gable, Eric, & Handler, Richard. (2011). Forget culture, remember memory? In Margaret Williamson Huber & Robert Shanafelt (Eds.), *Museums and memory* (pp. 23–44). Southern Anthropological Society Proceedings, no. 39. Knoxville, TN: Newfound Press.

Gibson, James J. (1977). The theory of affordances. In Robert Shaw & John D. Bransford (Eds.), *Perceiving, acting, and knowing: Toward an ecological psychology* (pp. 67–82). Mahwah, NJ: Lawrence Erlbaum Associates.

Graves-Brown, Paul (Ed.). (2000). *Matter, materiality and modern culture*. London: Routledge.

Grenier, Line. (2012). Ageing and/as enduring: Discussing with "Turtles [that] do not die of old age." In Guillaume Latzko-Toth & Florence Millerand (Eds.), *TEM 2012: Proceedings of the Technology and Emerging Media Track, annual conference of the Canadian Communication Association* (pp. 1–12). http://www.tem.fl.ulaval.ca/www/wp-content/PDF/Waterloo_2012/GRENIER-TEM2012.pdf.

Hogarty, Jean. (2015). Memories of the material/vestiges of the virtual: Exploring the impact of material and immaterial formats on the memory of popular music. *Rock Music Studies, 2*(2), 148–167.

Hoklas, Anne-Kathrin. (2014, June 27–28). *Generational differences regarding the role of materiality for everyday music listening practices in Germany: A qualitative case study.* Paper presented at the conference Musical Materialities in the Digital Age, University of Sussex.

Hornby, Nick. (1995). *High fidelity.* London: Victor Gollancz.

Huyssen, Andreas. (1995). *Twilight memories: Marking time in a culture of amnesia.* New York: Routledge.

Istvandity, Lauren, (2014). *Musically motivated autobiographical memories and the lifetime soundtrack.* Unpublished doctoral dissertation, Griffith University, South East Queensland, Australia.

Jennings, Ros, & Gardner, Abigail (Eds.). (2012). *'Rock on': Women, ageing and popular music.* Farnham, UK: Ashgate.

Katz, Stephen. (2005). *Cultural aging: Life course, lifestyle, and senior worlds.* Toronto: University of Toronto Press.

Katz, Stephen. (2014). Music, performance, and generation: The making of boomer rock and roll biographies. In C. Lee Harrison, Denise D. Bielby, & Anthony R. Bardo (Eds.), *Aging, media, and culture* (pp. 93–106). Lanham, MD: Lexington Books.

Kaufman, Sharon R. (1986). *The ageless self: Sources of meaning in late life.* Madison: University of Wisconsin Press.

Kopytoff, Igor. (1986). The cultural biography of things: Commoditization as process. In Arjun Appadurai (Ed.), *The social life of things: Commodities in cultural perspective* (pp. 64–92). Cambridge: Cambridge University Press.

Kotarba, Joseph A. (2013). *Baby boomer rock 'n' roll fans: The music never ends.* Lanham, MD: Scarecrow Press.

Krause, Elizabeth L. (2005). Encounters with 'the peasant': Memory work, masculinity, and low fertility in Italy. *American Ethnologist, 32*(4), 593–617.

Leonard, Marion. (2014). Staging the Beatles: Ephemerality, materiality and the production of authenticity in the museum. *International Journal of Heritage Studies, 20*(4), 357–375.

Litzinger, Ralph, A. (1998). Memory work: Reconstituting the ethnic in post-Mao China. *Cultural Anthropology, 13*(2), 224–255.

Magaudda, Paolo. (2011). When materiality 'bites back': Digital music consumption practices in the age of dematerialization. *Journal of Consumer Culture, 11*(1), 15–36.

May, Vanessa, & Muir, Stewart. (2015). Everyday belonging and ageing: Place and generational change. *Sociological Research Online, 20*(1), 1–11. http://journals.sagepub.com/doi/abs/10.5153/sro.3555.

Miller, Daniel. (2009). *Stuff*. London: Polity.

Myerhoff, Barbara. (1992). *Remembered lives: The work of ritual, storytelling, and growing older*. Ann Arbor: University of Michigan.

O'Sullivan, Caroline. (2016). *From gigging to social networking: Changing practices of indie and dance musicians in Dublin*. Unpublished doctoral dissertation, Trinity College, Dublin.

Pearson, Mike, & Shanks, Michael. (2001), *Theatre/Archaeology*. London: Routledge.

Pickering, Michael, & Keightley, Emily. (2015). *Photography, music and memory: Pieces of the past in everyday life*. London: Palgrave Macmillan.

Proust, Marcel. (2011). *À la recherche du temps perdu* [In search of lost time]. Toulon: Soleil Productions. (Original work published 1913–1927)

Reynolds, Simon. (2012). *Retromania: Pop culture's addiction to its own past* (paperback ed.). London: Faber & Faber.

Roy, Elodie A. (2015). *Media, materiality and memory: Grounding the groove*. Farnham, UK: Ashgate.

Small, Christopher. (1998). *Musicking: The meanings of performing and listening*. Middletown, CT: Wesleyan University Press.

Straw, Will. (2000). Exhausted commodities: The material culture of music. *Canadian Journal of Communication, 25*(1). http://www.cjc-online.ca/index.php/journal/article/view/1148/1067.

Straw, Will. (2003). Music and material culture. In Martin Clayton, Trevor Hebert, & Richard Middleton (Eds.), *The cultural study of music: A critical introduction* (pp. 227–236). London: Routledge.

Trouillot, Michel-Rolph. (1995). *Silencing the past: Power and the production of history.* Boston: Beacon Press.

van Dijck, José. (2007). *Mediated memories in the digital age.* Stanford, CA: Stanford University Press.

Waxer, Lise A. (2002). *The city of musical memory: Salsa, record grooves, and popular culture in Cali, Colombia.* Middletown, CT: Wesleyan University Press.

Chapter 2: Soundtrack of My Life
Ageing, Autobiography and Remembered Music

Ros Jennings

Popular music is increasingly understood as an important way for many people to construct and articulate their identities along their life course (Bennett, 2013). Intersecting with a nexus of contextual references and emotions, popular music offers a rich resource to interrogate reflections and reminiscences about ageing and identity.

José van Dijck (2004) argues that music and memory form strong links and that recorded music, in particular, "connects personal affect and emotion to collective identity and heritage" (p. 370), thus functioning as a culturally mediated memory object. The study described in this chapter explored the complex individual and collective relationships between music (mostly recorded music but not exclusively so), autobiographical memories and the formation of identities along the life course. In what follows, significance was attributed to specific pieces of music by means of a research device called the "soundtrack of my life." This involves choosing and evaluating music over the time and spaces of the life course. In the process of thinking back and forth across the life course, the music that is chosen acts as an important mechanism for people to articulate and share moments and understandings of their lives. The selected music, and the autobiographical memories used to contextualize it, are intricately entwined, mediated by affect, by emotion, and also by the cultural contexts of individual and collective engagements with it. From a memory studies perspective, what is produced is "dynamic, contagious and highly unstable" (Sturken, 2008, p. 75), an apt description in this study given the dynamics integral to creating a soundtrack of a person's life.

To ascribe importance to specific pieces of music (finding music that holds importance over the course of a lifetime), each participant must sift through memories of music along the life course and, in so doing, engage in what amounts to an interface between past and present. Identifying a lifetime soundtrack is a process that involves retrieval and reflection in the "now" (the present) while connecting with the context of or memories of the past. The soundtracks that are produced "illuminate the embodied and experienced qualities of time – as momentary, biographical, and transitional over the lifecourse" (Jarvis, Pain, & Pooley, 2011, p. 519) and, as May and Thrift (2001) explain, they occupy "neither only time or space but a multi-dimensional, partial and uneven TimeSpace" (p. 3). In the following discussion, the "soundtrack of my life" is considered to be an important way to reflect on ageing and also to articulate the TimeSpace(s) of identity through musically inflected autobiographical memories.

The "soundtrack of my life," as introduced above, which provided the methodological framing device for the study described in this chapter, is based on a feature that was published in the UK daily newspaper *The Guardian* from 2006 to 2015. The Soundtrack of My Life feature gave popular musicians and singers the opportunity to select five tracks and then explain to the journalist, who compiled the article for publication, why the musical tracks still have importance in their lives. The feature allowed the reading public to learn more about the artists and their chosen music, and to gain access to the shared intimacies of autobiographical memories. The research described in this chapter was qualitative and followed two strands of investigation. The first analyzed a sample of all the British artists, aged 50 years old or more, selected from the Soundtrack of My Life archive, which is available from the *Guardian* online (Soundtrack of My Life, 2006–15). The second strand loosely replicated the core idea of what was produced in the newspaper feature by asking two groups of people based in the United Kingdom to produce their own soundtrack. The study then brought together the findings from the archive sample and from the two groups of study participants to analyze the soundtracks, which consist of the recorded tracks or pieces of music referred to and the related autobiographical memories that accompanied them. This chapter interrogates some of the ways musically inflected autobiographical memories are mediated by age and culture to produce rich accounts of identities – identities that are enmeshed in the cultural intersections of music, age and life course in the United Kingdom in the early decades of the 21st century.

The second strand of the investigation involved a series of online email replications of the "soundtrack of my life" process undertaken by two friendship groups (one in the North of England and the other in the South West). In both friendship groups, each person chose five pieces of music and explained why the music they had chosen was important to them. As I have argued elsewhere (Jennings, 2016), in the multiple and also affective dimensions of its sharing, popular music intersects in a web of contextual references and emotions and embodied experiences. As a memory object, music notably also resonates within the body in such a way that "music that comes from outside ourselves sounds inside us as well" (Saliers & Saliers, 2006, p. 22). Consequently, music must be thought of as a technology of memory, which interacts with age in a highly complex way. In terms of the TimeSpace of the life course, the embodiment of musical cues can work to create moments when the "past is made real and present again" (p. 80). This is particularly so when memories are constructed via the mechanism of the "soundtrack of my life." As a memory object, music works together with memory to bridge past and present. In addition, according to van Dijck (2006), any analysis of reflections about music in relation to memory is based on "the assumption that the human's recovery of the past is simultaneously embodied, enabled, and embedded" (p. 358). As Lauren Istvandity (2014) contends, the nature of autobiographical memory means that it is a fallible and thus not an "effective archive" (p. 138). What is significant to her argument, and certainly to me in this study, is not the accuracy of autobiographical memory, but rather the relationship between music and memory as a function: a function that is embodied, affective, and which enables music to "act as reservoirs for memory" (p. 139) across time and space.

For me, as a musician from a musical family, music is a contextual and embodied thread that binds and loops around the experiences of my life course so far (Jennings, 2016); it influences the ways that I am in the world, including as a researcher. This concurs with Tami Spry's (2001) understanding of her own autoethnographic position in research, a position that provides "space for the living, experiencing, and researching body to be seen and felt. It is not that our bodies haven't been in our work, rather, they have been shrouded in our research by dualistic separations of Mind and Body" (p. 720). It is from this musically immersed relationship between music and autobiographical memory that I embarked on the research outlined below.

Employing the "soundtrack of my life" as self-reflexive memory work to explore music, ageing and identities across the life course

In her article titled "The Lifetime Soundtrack: Music as an Archive for Autobiographical Memory," Istvandity (2014) sets out to confirm a relationship between music, autobiographical memory and the life course. Using a qualitative study based in Queensland, Australia, she "devised the concept of the 'lifetime soundtrack' to describe the metaphorical canon of music that accompanies personal life experiences" (p. 136). Certainly in the United Kingdom, where the research set out in this chapter was conducted, the idea of the lifetime soundtrack is almost a commonplace technology of memory that operates in media as various as fanzines, music video channels, music journalism and popular radio broadcasts. It was, as I have already indicated, explicitly named feature in *The Guardian* newspaper. The coupling of music and memories in these popular media formats acts as technologies of memory, promoting, filtering, organizing and archiving interconnectivities between music and autobiographical memories and circulating them in popular culture.

One of the most conspicuous media uses of this type of "technology of memory" in the United Kingdom is on popular radio, where, as I explain below, the invitation to contextualize the music played in program playlists within autobiographical memories is used to manipulate audiences' involvements with the content of radio programs and schedules. The lifetime soundtrack functions on popular radio on multiple levels as a galvanizing concept for individual and collective connections between the meanings and memories of popular music for the listeners along their life courses. The music is cast culturally and commercially as a memory object (van Dijck, 2004) threading through the interpersonal, spatial and temporal connections of the listeners' life courses. In the United Kingdom (and from my experience also elsewhere – certainly in France, Australia and New Zealand, where I have listened to popular radio regularly), radio, on a quotidian basis, deliberately constructs links between memory and autobiographical identity for radio audiences, ranging from informal invitations to guess the year of a particular song while listening (e.g., *The Chris Evans Breakfast Show*, BBC Radio 2), to more formal practices, such as playing the musical tracks and then hearing celebrities discussing their choices as part of Tracks of My Years (*Ken Bruce*, BBC Radio 2), or perhaps most famously on *Desert Island Discs* (BBC Radio 4), where listeners hear the life course–related stories connecting to the eight pieces of music that a celebrity would take with them if they were to be stranded on a deserted island. The fact that *Desert Island Discs* in 2017 celebrated its 75th year of broadcasting is testament to the success of popular media's engagement with music and memory in the United Kingdom.

Moving away from the focus on celebrity opinions, BBC Radio 2 has recently produced a series called *The People's Songs: The Story of Modern Britain in 50 Records*, which explicitly explores post–World War II British culture and identities through subsequent decades using interviews with the British public interwoven with historical news broadcasts and popular music. The inclusion of archival news media further extends the importance afforded to cultural connectivities between music and memory, binding music and memory together commercially and deliberately mobilizing an understanding of them as being interwoven through the life course. What follows explores some of the ways that ageing and recalling music work to both give meaning to and to influence or sustain identities over time. This discussion examines the ways that thinking about music allows us to re-access a specific, though as stated earlier, fallible kind of autobiographical memory archive (Istvandity, 2014), one that hinges on music.

To explore, and also to amplify, the phenomenon of a musical hinge of autobiographical memory, the discussion that follows also considers two further elements. The first is the presence of music itself: something that, as Dave Laing (1997) has pointed out, is often rather surprisingly overlooked when academics have discussed formations of identity in relation to music. In this discussion, this tendency to disregard music is reversed. The conceit of the "soundtrack of my life" format actually privileges the remembrance of music as either a trigger to access memories or as being embedded in memories themselves. The second element acknowledges notions of performance as an element of autobiographical remembrance with regard to music, music's associated meanings, and also music's relationship to autobiographical reflections on people's identities. Performance was significant to many of the musicians who had their Soundtrack of My Life published in the *Guardian* newspaper. Their association of music with performance resonates strongly with Christopher Small's (1998) notion of "musicking," where performance is not simply "the medium through which the musical work has to pass before it reaches its goal – the listener" (p. 10), but an integral part of the way music is enjoyed. Here, in the context of this study, at least for some of the cases analyzed, performance is also of importance to the way music is remembered.

The study was framed within and influenced by self-reflexive memory work (Onyx & Small, 2001), taking the position that "the self is socially constructed through reflection – memories. The construction of self at any moment plays an important part in how the event is constructed. Memories therefore are studied in their own right; they are not judged against the 'real/true' past event" (Small, 2010, p. 2). Consequently, as Julie Stephens's (2010) work on retrospective accounts of the memories of feminists involved in the women's movement suggests, self-reflexive memory work challenges a common tendency to generate the kind of binary "before" and "after" accounts of identity that have so often been the case when reflection is not understood as relatively fluid. When exploring experiences of age and ageing, it is particularly restrictive to limit reflections involving age solely to chronologically compartmentalized stages along the life course (i.e., we are simply either young or old) rather than to recognize that our lives form or act as a continuum of our experiences (Segal, 2013). The TimeSpace relationships inherent in self-reflection tally strongly with Helene Moglen's (2008) idea of "transageing," where it is possible to feel young and old at the same time. I suggest, therefore, that when participants are asked to think back over the life course and focus on the selection of music, as in this study, autobiographical memories as articulations of age are fluid in nature. These memories enable us to, as Lynne Segal in her commentary on Moglen's (2008) work on transageing states,

> feel a multitude of identities, more or less simultaneously, or at least in quick succession. We may become aware of ourselves as both young and old, in touch with the self-centered neediness and passionate desires of the child we once were one minute, then marshalling the aloof restraints of adulthood the next. (Segal, 2008, p. 316)

The *Guardian* Soundtrack of My Life

The Guardian is a UK-based newspaper devoted to serious journalism and editorial independence ("The Scott Trust," 2015). It proclaims a commitment to liberal values and is set up financially in such a way as to deliberately preserve this ethos and approach. The paper addresses an educated and already relatively well-informed readership. Looking back through the online *Guardian* material related to life soundtracks, I found that the inspiration for the series seems to stem from a one-off interview, "Soundtrack of Her Life" (Hodgkinson, 2003). This interview was conducted with classical/pop crossover musician, composer and arranger Anne Dudley. The interview addresses a general reader and is located in the newspaper text under the banner of Music / Home Entertainment. The way the initial piece on Dudley is constructed provides the general blueprint for the ensuing newspaper feature Soundtrack of My Life, which started to appear regularly some three years later. All of the subsequent 100 occurrences were then archived by the newspaper online (Soundtrack of My Life, 2006–15; all artist quotes are drawn from this archive). Once it became a regular monthly item, the feature was placed in the newspaper's weekly specialist music section, which is published every Friday.

The change from "Soundtrack of Her life" to Soundtrack of My Life signals a significant shift in the presentation of the music-related memories that are explored. The Dudley piece differs from the regular features that were to follow in that the journalist/interviewer is present and visible in the published text. The result is a conventionally constructed journalistic interview where the journalist has a voice and the form of writing used overtly includes the interviewer's reflections. The mark of the journalist is evident in observational detail and through moments of thick description (such as Dudley's daughter interrupting the interview with a plate of biscuits as a ruse to get round parental restrictions and be able to have one herself). The interview is structured around one specific theme (musical identities positioned between classical music and pop) and uses the term "soundtrack" as a linking device between Dudley's role as an Oscar-winning film soundtrack composer and her recollections of music, musical arrangements, and artists and performers working in various genres who have influenced her in her craft of music-making and career choices along her life course so far.

The shaping voice of these published reminiscences is different from the later features, as the move to the Soundtrack of My Life modified the interviewer's role from an active presence in the text to an absence (although the journalist has organized and presented the material in a particular way, under headings that have emerged during the conversations with the artists). Rather than a flowing account, the new form now follows a formula and is organized under five specific headings that are, as far as I can tell, mutually identified by journalist and artist. The headings are journalistic devices to focus readers' attention on what has emerged in the interview process as instances of importance in the lives of each contributor: vignettes drawn from the individual reminiscences and memories that were shared in relation to the music they chose. Typical examples of headings that are designed to both capture readers' attention and to structure the articles that I analyzed are "The song that made me want to play music" (Bryan Ferry); "The track that reminds me of my parents" (Edwyn Collins) and "The song that proves I'm no rebel" (Robert Wyatt). The headings, which are externally imposed (by the journalist), nevertheless still document and communicate acts of personal remembering. Framed as they are, these musical tracks and musically inflected experiences can also be seen as being sensitive to individual and collective/cultural contexts in which they are produced (Sutton, 2008).

For the study, I established a baseline of 50 as the minimum age for inclusion for entries from the *Guardian* archive and also for participants from the friendship groups. This baseline placed participants from the *Guardian* archive sample and the second friendship group within an age grouping that corresponds with the generational tag "baby boomer" (Phillipson, 2007). This grouping is by no means homogeneous, but members share to some extent a generational habitus (Gilleard & Higgs, 2005) that has links with the sort of post-1960s ideologies Gilleard and Higgs (2007) suggest are "symbolised by the consumerist quartet of virtues – choice, autonomy, self-expression and pleasure" (p. 26). Within the *Guardian* archive, Tracey Emin was the only woman who met the age criteria to be selected. By contrast, the "soundtrack of my life" reflections produced by the two friendship groups were dominated by the musical memories of women (with only three out of a total 12 responses in the two groups coming from men). Over the two strands of analysis, therefore, a mix of gendered responses contributed to the reflections as a whole.

To maintain both the geographical and age group focus chosen for the study, I focused my analysis on the 21 entries in the *Guardian* Soundtrack of My Life online archive that were by British artists/performers aged 50 years old or older. The sample consisted of the following people:

Name	Known for (as stated in the Guardian)	Year of Birth
Jarvis Cocker	Singer best known as member of Pulp	1963
Edwyn Collins	Singer-songwriter/musician/producer/record label owner best known as member of Orange Juice	1959
Elvis Costello	Singer-songwriter/musician	1954
Ray Davies	Singer/musician/composer best known as member of The Kinks	1944
Tracey Emin	Visual artist	1963
Bryan Ferry	Singer-songwriter best known as member of Roxy Music	1945
Boy George	Singer-songwriter/deejay	1961
Bobby Gillespie	Musician/singer-songwriter best known as member of Jesus and Mary Chain/Primal Scream	1962
Terry Hall	Singer best known as member of The Specials/Fun Boy Three	1959
Roy Harper	Folk-rock singer-songwriter	1941
Peter Hook	Bass player best known as member of Joy Division/New Order	1956
Elton John	Singer-songwriter/musician	1947
Tom Jones	Singer	1940
Andrew Lloyd Webber	Musical theatre composer	1958
John Lydon	Singer-songwriter best known as member of the Sex Pistols/Public Image Ltd.	1956

Johnny Marr	Musician/singer-songwriter best known as member of The Smiths	1963
Robert Plant	Singer best known as member of Led Zeppelin	1948
Neil Tennant	Singer-songwriter best known as member of Pet Shop Boys	1954
Pete Tong	Deejay/producer/BBC Radio 1 presenter	1958
Paul Weller	Singer/musician/composer best known as member of The Jam/Style Council	1958
Robert Wyatt	Singer	1945
	Please note: An online search of the name (e.g., Edwyn Collins) and "Soundtrack of My Life" will provide the full feature.	

This sample – with one exception, Tracey Emin – features older performers who have had substantial careers in popular music. The limited information furnished about each performer assumes a knowledgeable reader, familiar with the artist and with contextual information about them. Contextual knowledge provides an additional layer to the reader's understanding of the artists' discussions (e.g., I am aware of Boy George's flamboyant queer image that has, over his life course to date, negotiated multiple and contradictory public personas as teenage heart throb, eccentric Englishman, drug addict, phenomenal vocalist and talented deejay).

In the articulation of music and memories presented in each feature, the concept of a soundtrack is overwhelmingly interpreted as a recorded musical track. This was significant in terms of the concept of "first" as a key category. The concept of "first" emerged as a catalyst concept: a record that provided a moment of autobiographical enlightenment in terms of musical identity. For instance, "This was the first time I had heard music that made me sit up and think, 'This is something else.' I was nine" (Paul Weller) or "When I first heard 'Metal Guru' it was life-changing: it was simultaneously mysterious and familiar and as such it was perfect for a teeny kid interested in the guitar and all that goes with it" (Johnny Marr).

The predominance of the recorded track solidifies the notion of technologically enabled music as being key artifacts of memory in the sample discussed, but for many of the more recent Soundtrack of My Life features, the *Guardian* online archive also provides a link to a Spotify playlist that shines a spotlight on the recorded aspect of the music that was chosen. This link extends the materials generated from the feature beyond just a memory of the music and its associated autobiographical reflections. It results in multiple strands of technology related to music and memory (e.g., online archive linked to music streaming technologies, which are in turn accessed by phones, PCs and tablets, etc., at any time and in any place). In this way the now mediatized musical memories are able to disrupt time and space in multiple ways (see van Dijck, 2011).

Since the sample selected from the *Guardian* online archive focuses on musicians and performers (including deejays), it is not surprising that their reflections focus strongly on musical creativity and performance, hence not only on music, but also on what I have explained earlier as Small's notion of "musicking." This involves recalling musical practices related to the chosen track as well as the track itself. For instance, the bass line in the track "Just My Imagination (Running Away with Me)" by The Temptations (1971), according to Peter Hook, is "a very musical bassline. I spent years trying to emulate it"; and Tom Jones explains that when he heard "Great Balls of Fire" by Jerry Lee Lewis, he knew how he wanted to sing.

The circulating metaphors of music and autobiographical reflections on identity in the 21 entries (including visual artist Tracy Emin) are largely constructed and hooked around conventional post–rock and roll concepts such as the "teenage rebel" (cited by Andrew Lloyd Webber and Edwyn Collins) or the TimeSpace of the teenage years as being musically formative (articulated by Roy Harper, Pete Tong, Terry Hall, Boy George, Tracy Emin, Andrew Lloyd Webber and Edwyn Collins). Significant here are also notions of musically driven identity transformations that speak to a particular culture at a particular time (van Dijck, 2007). When feature subjects were engaged in the process of selecting individual tracks that are still important to them, thinking back over the times and spaces of their life courses so far, it seems that it is music from their teenage years that continues to be meaningful. This is articulated not only in terms of attachment to music that was first encountered at a particular time, but also in terms of recognizing that in the process of looking back with age over their own individual life course, music was a catalyst. More specifically, music was a catalyst in their search for a performative expression – something to hook their newly emerging identities on. For instance, Terry Hall identifies the significance of David Bowie's 1975 album *Young Americans*. Hall states, "When I was 16 this album gave me a look, a sound, and a way of holding yourself." As a teenager coming to terms with his sexuality, Boy George explains:

> When you're a kid and you know you're gay, and you hear Bowie singing "a cop knelt and kissed the feet of a priest, and a queer threw up at the sight of that", and then you hear Walk on the Wild Side, you know there's hope – you know you're not the only one that has these weird thoughts.

The TimeSpace(s) of these memories work to link past and present through the process of reflecting on the life course, but in certain cases these configurations are also strongly located to a memory of place. The specificities of the contextual cultural environment located in the geography of place add a further layer to articulations of autobiographical reflections on identity. In his Soundtrack of My Life, Robert Plant reflects on hegemonic notions of masculinity linked to time, space and place. In so doing, he stresses music as a way to soothe him in his struggle to find his own masculine identity as a young man.

> Music was a panacea and a mysterious release for me. It was otherworldly, another life outside Middle England in 1960 where it was all about endeavour, learning and making sure that all your vulnerabili-

ties were not too evident so that you didn't end up looking like a sobbing klutz.

As a process of memory work, choosing tracks for the Soundtrack of My Life invites a direct interface with Tia DeNora's (2000) understanding of memory being "indexed by music." The archived online responses in each act of memory work of this study strongly suggest that in the interface between music and memory, there are many and multiple acts of continuous redefinition across the life course. For instance, Peter Hook reflects on how returning to analogue technology involves layers of mediated memory and affect: "My wife bought me new decks last Christmas, so I've started playing my old records again too. It's a great feeling to put on something you've had, and you've loved, since you were 13."

Emotional connections between music and memory that bring the past vividly into the present through the process of reflection inform many of the responses. Some of the music that was chosen invoked memories of an old boyfriend (Tracey Emin), first love (Jarvis Cocker), parents (Edwyn Collins, Elton John, Terry Hall, Pete Tong), his wife (Robert Wyatt), but apart from Ray Davies (at 72, one of the older musicians featured), who said he "wanted to come home and listen to music that is completely innocent and without hype, and that has meant going back to the records that first inspired me," there is in the subjects' musical reminiscences little sense of either simple nostalgic longing (Davis, 1979) or restorative or reflexive nostalgia (Boym, 2001). The process, nevertheless, produces strongly emotional links related to the musical choices. For Tracey Emin, the choice of the bubbly upbeat British pop song "Chirpy Chirpy Cheep Cheep" (Middle of the Road, 1971) is a surprising choice as a song that makes her feel sad until she contextualizes it.

> It doesn't necessarily have to sound sad – it's sad because the situation it reminds me of is sad. When I was a little girl and my mum left home, this song was in the charts and it was really poignant for me. The cho-

rus is: "Where's your mama gone?" When I listen to this song I go back directly into that place. I become seven again.

Some music choices were also expressed as a continuous presence along the life course rather than something conjured up by reflecting on the past. Peter Hook describes *Old Ways* (1985) by Neil Young as the record he could listen to again and again, and Boy George discusses how Joni Mitchell has been (as she has been for me) one of the emotional props he has used throughout his life: "There's been so many times in my life when I've put Joni on: there's always a song of hers for when something goes wrong in your life."

In these articulations of music and memory, time is "felt" in complex ways that disrupt traditional chronological constructs. For the musicians and deejays in the sample, their words strongly indicate an ongoing hunger to discover new music and that this is an aspect of their identities they are committed to pursuing. Robert Plant states, "My love for discovering new things is ceaseless"; Paul Weller discloses that at the time of the interview, his latest discovery was Fleet Foxes (*Fleet Foxes* [2008]); Johnny Marr declares, "I'm always hearing new music that excites me." Apart from Robert Wyatt acknowledging that he can no longer hit his high vocal register, no acknowledgment of growing old/er was explicitly expressed. In the reflections analyzed, apart from references to early and teenage experiences (particularly the period when a particular track was encountered), chronological time was barely evident. Expressions of time instead emerged as kairotic (Petruzzi, 2001) entanglements of time where connections between earlier innocence and current maturity merge.

The soundtrack of friendship groups

In contrast to the celebrity musician focus of the *Guardian* archive, the following section focuses on the "soundtrack(s) of my life" produced by two friendship groups. The participants are not in the public eye, and they are not musicians or artists. The age of participants compared to the *Guardian* cohort increased in this strand by a decade (with the oldest participants all being in their eighties), extending the participation sample beyond those associated with the post–World War II baby boomer generation to those who were born before World War II. The friendship group sample thus introduces reflections from participants who came to their age of majority before the birth of rock and roll. These people do not necessarily have the shared generational habitus that Gilleard and Higgs (2005) argue shapes those born between the end of World War II and the early 1960s, the oldest people in the friendship groups thus adding a further layer of engagement and reference in relation to autobiographical memories of popular music and popular culture.

The two friendship groups that formed the basis of the second strand of the study were recruited through personal contact. The first group consisted of members of a small informal friendship group located in a small town, situated in the North of England. They have been meeting for over 30 years (starting off as a much more formal over-fifties social group, which had a secretary, a treasurer, etc.), and members of the group are all now in their eighties. The five participants who contributed to this study were aged between 82 and 87, four women and one man. I was introduced to this group by my mother-in-law, who has been a member for over 20 years. She was the initial point of contact for me and also the conduit to the rest of the group, passing on my request to members to participate. The second friendship group, located in the South West of England, met and became friends after being referred by their GPs to a local Walking for Health Group for preventative or rehabilitation reasons. They now regularly walk their dogs together and meet socially and to pursue physical activities such as swimming. This friendship group consisted of six people (four women and two men) between 53 and 72 years of age. I made contact with the group through a doctoral student related to the Centre for Women, Ageing and Media (WAM) research group (wamuog.co.uk), where I am situated at the University of Gloucestershire, who had volunteered as a walking guide for the group.

As indicated earlier, the method adopted for this second element of the study was designed to approximate the *Guardian* Soundtrack of My Life online archive used in the first strand of the study, explored above. With the exception of two members of the North of England group (Jack and Ruth, who provided written responses, sent in the post as they did not have a working computer at the time), all the other communication with participants took place via email and Skype. Contrary to many dominant ageist assumptions, old/er age was not a barrier to the competent use of online technology by these study participants.

The memory work carried out in this strand, although replicating the Soundtrack of My Life feature, also shifted its construction slightly. In this strand, the eleven responses were constructed solely by the participants themselves (they were self-penned or typed reflections arranged under the participants' own headings), thus adding both a self-disciplining dimension to the process of remembrance (Onyx & Small, 2001) as well as providing participants with much more autonomy to shape the contents in any way they wished.

Given more freedom to shape and organize their own responses, participants constructed more detailed and vivid pictures of the musically embedded TimeSpace(s) and locations that were important to them, compared to the *Guardian* archive. This was particularly true for the responses from the octogenarians, whose reflections were generally longer than those from the second group, of younger participants. Older participants also demonstrated a greater tendency to use thick description that communicated highly evocative music-centered scenarios. For example, Jack (aged 85) and his wife Ruth (aged 82) described the feeling of joy and the magnificence of the surroundings when singing "Delilah" (Tom Jones, 1968) with friends in the Arizona desert on the way to Las Vegas. Joan (aged 83) vividly set the scene of her family's living room when she was a child, for her choice of the musical *The Desert Song* (1926). She described the room where the family used to gather round the piano, her mother playing and her sister, father and her singing "most of the songs from this light opera and so enjoyed doing so, this would be 1942." Istvandity's (2014) approach to music and memory suggests that "music can effectively store details of individual and collectivized memories" (p. 136), and this is clearly reflected in the ways that details embellish the recollections of participants from both friendship groups. From the second friendship group, Peter (aged 53) pinpointed his memory of the Talking Heads' song "Road to Nowhere" (1985) to a grimy pub in Bristol. The pub had a great jukebox that he used to "feed with his money" at the expense of being able to drink as many beers as his friends, so he could "keep hearing the music [he] liked."

As in the data from the online *Guardian* sample discussed above, the idea of tracks being integral to transformations of identity was also important to the participants of the second friendship group. For instance, Bob (aged 63) mentioned discovering "A Town Called Malice" (1982) by the Jam and changing his style of appearance to imitate the lead singer, Paul Weller. Also Sandy (aged 72) wrote of being introduced to "Constant Craving" by k.d. lang in 1992 when, after many years of struggling with identity issues, Sandy came out as a lesbian at the age of 47. This direct equation between a musical track as a marker and a shift in awareness of their identity was not evident in the responses generated by the group of participants aged 80-plus. For these participants, reflecting on music that remained important along the life course did not foreground notions of identity (or the questioning of identity) in the same way as those in the sample who were born after World War II. This is interesting in terms of supporting Margaret Cruikshank's (2009) notion that while cultural ageism works to homogenize old people, often it is the experiences gained along a long life course that can make us the most different. Additionally, it supports the view that baby boomers are at least aware of, even if they do not totally subscribe to, the surrounding cultural milieu of consumerism that Gilleard and Higgs (2005) identify.

In both groups, however, the musical tracks chosen were often recollected in relation to a youthful TimeSpace. Cathy (aged 66), for example, remembered going out with friends and dancing to "Brown Sugar" (1971) by the Rolling Stones. And Shirley (aged 84) wrote of discovering "Intermezzo" from *Cavalleria Rusticana* (Mascagni, 1890) when she was learning to play the piano in her teens. In contrast to the *Guardian* sample, participants did not articulate music as constituting an act of rebellion. Indeed, in responses from both the friendship groups, dominant popular music studies' concepts of generation gaps and generational conflict (Jennings 2015) were not articulated as drivers for musical choices. What was very clear from participants' responses was that emotional connections to songs were both nourished (van Dijck, 2006) and embedded the autobiographical memories that were shared. Shirley (84) and Rita (87) expressed the close and affective relationship between their choices of music and the sense of loss they feel at the passing of their husbands. Hearing the love duet "O soave fanciulla" from *La Bohème* (Puccini, 1896) is highly emotional for Shirley, as this was her husband's favorite piece of music. For Rita, as also noted in Istvandity's (2014) study, there was a close resonance between song lyrics and autobiography. One of her choices was "Empty Chairs at Empty Tables," from the musical *Les Misérables* (1985), which she had seen in a London stage production with her husband. "I eventually saw the film version with [. . .]'s cousin and wife sometime after [. . .] had died. There were sounds of people sniffing and crying at times – I joined in!"

In sharp contrast to the *Guardian* sample discussed above, there was a clear exploration of growing old in terms of their reflections on their identities in old age, but this was only among the octogenarians. Shirley's explanation for her choice of Paul Robeson singing the African-American spiritual "Just A-wearying for You" (traditional), especially after earlier disclosing her feelings about losing her husband, is both moving and poignant: "The words express my thoughts so vividly nowadays but, I'm afraid, always bring the tears." Joan (aged 83) has a bittersweet relationship with Aker Bilk's "Stranger on the Shore" (1962), associating it with holidays in faraway places and explaining that even though she is no longer "able to take these trips due to limitations in our health and mobility, it evokes wonderful memories." Husband and wife Bill and Ruth added a joint reflection at the end of their individual "soundtrack of my life," emphasizing the interpersonal ways that music is imbricated in their lives and their memories along their life courses so far. For them, music reinforces their sense of "how lucky [they] are that [they] can remember and appreciate all that dancing, singing and laughter." Their letter ends with the sentence "We love music!"

Conclusion

In the *Guardian* online archive sample, only two participants mentioned classical music: Suite from *The Love for Three Oranges* (Prokofiev, 1919), Andrew Lloyd Webber, and *Symphony No. 4* (Tchaikovsky, 1878), Roy Harper. For the friendship group participants who were aged over 80, classical music formed a sizable component of their choices: "O mio babbino caro" (Puccini, 1918) and Brahms's "Cradle Song" (1868), for Rita; *Cavalleria Rusticana*, Bruch's *Violin Concerto No. 1* (1866) and *La Bohème*, for Shirley; Gounod's *Ave Maria* (1853) and Johan Strauss II's "Tales from the Vienna Woods" (1868), for Margaret. These choices did not, however, preclude reflections that overlapped with a more contemporary popular music culture. Ruth cited "Simply the Best" (Tina Turner, 1991); Jack loved Abba; Margaret mentioned her love of Elvis singing "Can't Help Falling in Love" (1961) and Demis Roussos singing "Happy to Be on an Island in the Sun" (1976). Despite evidence of shared preferences for popular classical music and musicals, there was no sense of a shared musical repertoire among those aged 80 years and over, and this would be worthy of further study.

In contrast, reflections from the second friendship group and the *Guardian* online archive sample (where the age ranges were similar) were dominated by pop and rock music. Moreover, within this grouping individual reminiscences produced popular music choices that hinted at ideas of a shared music, reinforcing the notion that autobiographical memory has collective dimensions that are culturally located within a continuum of time, space and place (van Dijck,

2007) – something that was certainly the case for the post–rock and roll baby boomers in this study. Within this study, not only the musical soundtrack was articulated as being significant for many in the sample, but also certain musicians emerged whose importance to the participants rendered them iconic. The artists and tracks cited most frequently across the sample (by at least three participants) were David Bowie: "Young Americans" (1975), "Let's Dance" (1983), *The Rise and Fall of Ziggy Stardust and the Spiders from Mars* (album, 1972), *Hunky Dory* (album, 1971); Bob Dylan: "Tangled Up in Blue" (1975), "Masters of War" (1963), "Highway 61 Revisited" (1965); Marc Bolan/T. Rex: "Electric Warrior" (1971), "Ride a White Swan" (1970), "Metal Guru" (1972); Lou Reed: "I'm Waiting for the Man" (1967), *Transformer* (album, 1972), "Walk on the Wild Side" (1972). The result is a white male musical canon generated by a mostly male sample, a canon in which only one of the artists (Bob Dylan) remains alive. (David Bowie died early in 2016, after the conclusion of the Soundtrack of My Life feature.)

The most vividly depicted reflections on the music selected to form the soundtracks of their lives were produced by the study participants aged over 80. Their music-related reflections were wonderfully open and candid about the participants' current feelings, perceptions and circumstances of being old. For the baby boomer participants, music was a much stronger marker of their individual and collective identities, but articulations about growing old or old age were a significant absence in their reflections. Given that I have identified in previous work that ageing in public brings with it additional difficulties (Jennings & Gardner, 2012), then, certainly for the artists' responses shared in the publicly accessible *Guardian* online archive, it is not surprising that reflections and feelings on growing or being old are not shared. In this study, and also as a way to conduct future research on the multiple connections between music, memory and the life course, the "soundtrack of my life" process is a valuable method of exploration. The constraint of choosing only five tracks or pieces of music from a lifetime of musical possibilities puts the remembered music center stage but simultaneously elicits rich autobiographical reflections that operate within or across a fluid TimeSpace of past and present.

Radio shows cited

The Chris Evans breakfast show. BBC Radio 2. http://www.bbc.co.uk/programmes/b00p2d9w.
Desert island discs. BBC Radio 4. http://www.bbc.co.uk/programmes/b006qnmr.
The people's songs: The story of modern Britain in 50 records. BBC Radio 2. http://www.bbc.co.uk/programmes/b01l9qb8/episodes/guide.
Tracks of my years. *Ken Bruce*. BBC Radio 2. http://www.bbc.co.uk/music/playlists/zzzzf5.

References

Bennett, Andy. (2013). *Music, style and aging: Growing old disgracefully?* Philadelphia: Temple University Press.
Boym, Svetlana. (2001). *The future of nostalgia*. New York: Basic Books.
Cruikshank, Margaret. (2009). *Learning to be old: Gender, culture, and aging* (2nd ed.). Lanham, MD: Rowman & Littlefield.
Davis, Fred. (1979). *Yearning for yesterday: A sociology of nostalgia*. New York: Free Press.
DeNora, Tia. (2000). *Music in everyday life*. Cambridge: Cambridge University Press.
Gilleard, Chris, & Higgs, Paul. (2005). *Contexts of ageing: Class, cohort and community*. Cambridge, UK: Polity.
Gilleard, Chris, & Higgs, Paul. (2007). Two approaches to the social structuring of later life. *International Journal of Ageing and Later Life*, 2(2), 13–30.
Hodgkinson, Will. (2003, August 15). Soundtrack of her life. *The Guardian*. https://www.theguardian.com/music/2003/aug/15/2.

Istvandity, Lauren. (2014). The lifetime soundtrack: Music as an archive for autobiographical memory. *Popular Music History*, 9(2), 136–154. doi:10.1558/pomh.v9i2.26642.

Jarvis, Helen, Pain, Rachel, & Pooley, Colin. (2011). Multiple scales of time – Space and lifecourse. *Environment and Planning A*, 43, 519–524.

Jennings, Ros. (2015). Popular music and ageing. In Julia Twigg & Wendy Martin (Eds.), *Routledge handbook of cultural gerontology* (pp. 77–84). Abingdon, UK: Routledge.

Jennings, Ros. (2016, June 22). Ageing in and with popular culture. Public professorial lecture, University of Gloucestershire, Cheltenham (see http://wamuog.co.uk).

Jennings, Ros, & Gardner, Abigail. (2012). *'Rock on': Women, ageing and popular music*. Farnham, UK: Ashgate.

Laing, Dave. (1997). Rock anxieties and new music networks. In Angela McRobbie (Ed.), *Back to reality? Social experience and cultural studies* (pp. 116–132). Manchester: Manchester University Press.

May, Jon, & Thrift, Nigel. (2001). *Timespace: Geographies of temporality*. London: Routledge.

Moglen, Helene. (2008). Ageing and transageing: Transgenerational hauntings of the self. *Studies in Gender and Sexuality*, 9(4), 297–311.

Onyx, Jenny, & Small, Jennie. (2001). Memory-work: The method. *Qualitative Inquiry*, 7(6), 773–786.

Petruzzi, Anthony P. (2001). Kairotic rhetoric in Freire's liberatory pedagogy. *JAC: A Journal of Composition Theory*, 21(2), 349–381.

Phillipson, Chris. (2007). Understanding the baby boom generation: Comparative perspectives. *International Journal of Ageing and Later Life*, 2(2), 7–11.

Saliers, Don E., & Saliers, Emily. (2006). *A song to sing, a life to live: Reflections on music as spiritual practice*. San Francisco: Jossey-Bass.

The Scott Trust: Values and history. (2015, July 26). *The Guardian*. https://www.theguardian.com/the-scott-trust/2015/jul/26/the-scott-trust.

Segal, Lynne. (2008). All ages and none: Commentary on Helene Moglen's ageing and transageing. *Studies in Gender and Sexuality*, 9(4), 312–322.

Segal, Lynne. (2013). *Out of time: The pleasures and the perils of ageing*. London: Verso.

Small, Christopher. (1998). *Musicking: The meanings of performing and listening*. Middletown, CT: Wesleyan University Press.

Small, Jennie. (2010). *Memory-work: An introduction*. Unpublished paper, University of Technology, Sydney, Australia. https://opus.lib.uts.edu.au/bitstream/10453/19758/1/Memory-work%20-%20An%20Introduction.pdf.

Soundtrack of my life. (2006–15). *The Guardian* [Online archive]. https://www.theguardian.com/music/series/soundtrackofmylife.

Spry, Tami. (2001). Performing autoethnography: An embodied methodological praxis. *Qualitative Inquiry*, 7(6), 706–732.

Stephens, Julie. (2010). Our remembered selves: Oral history and feminist memory. *Oral History*, 38(1), 81–90.

Sturken, Marita. (2008). Memory, consumerism and media: Reflections on the emergence of the field. *Memory Studies*, 1(1), 73–78. https://doi.org/10.1177/1750698007083890.

Sutton, John. (2008). Between individual and collective memory: Coordination, interaction, distribution. *Social Research*, 75(1), 23–48.

van Dijck, José. (2004). Mediated memories: Personal cultural memory as object of cultural analysis. *Continuum*, 18(2), 261–271.

van Dijck, José. (2006). Record and hold: Popular music between personal and collective memory. *Critical Studies in Media Communication*, 23(5), 357–374.

van Dijck, José. (2007). *Mediated memories in the digital age*. Stanford, CA: Stanford University Press.

van Dijck, José. (2011). Flickr and the culture of connectivity: Sharing views, experiences, memories. *Memory Studies*, 4(4), 401–415.

Chapter 3: It's a Man's World for *The Iron Lady*
Truth, Prosthetic Memory and the Organized Forgetting of Feminism

Josephine Dolan

The Iron Lady, Phyllida Lloyd's 2012 award-winning biopic of Margaret Thatcher, Britain's first woman prime minister, opens with a street scene. The camera follows Thatcher (Meryl Streep), whose bland beige costume, halting step and stooped bearing code her as old and frail. She enters a corner shop, where the image of aged frailty is consolidated as she is pushed aside by other customers, struggles with the coins in her purse/wallet, and is forgetfully confused by the cost of the milk she purchases.[1] At this juncture, Thatcher is established as the embodiment of what Chris Gilleard and Paul Higgs (2014) would term the "fourth age," that is, the " 'cultural imaginary' of the deepest and darkest aspects of old age" (p. 241), in which dementia figures prominently. Yet, initially at least, this image of "fourth age" vulnerability is undercut by the next scene. Over breakfast, an animated and lucid Thatcher expounds on rising costs to husband Denis (Jim Broadbent) and is teased about "slipping the leash" of the security cordon that both contains and protects them. But Thatcher is then rapidly returned to "fourth age" vulnerability when the intimacy of the breakfast scene is punctured by the entry of a housekeeper/carer, and Denis, who is actually dead, is exposed as a ghostly figment of her confused imagination. In these opening scenes, then, *The Iron Lady* establishes a shifting spectatorial position that moves between an objective view of Thatcher defined in terms of bleak, confused "fourth age" decline and a subjective viewpoint aligned with her vivid, memory-saturated lived experience. Such shifts in perspective are repeated throughout the film, constantly reminding audiences that Thatcher's past is integral to her lived "fourth age" present and, at the same time, establishing the mechanism through which the film narrates its story of Margaret Thatcher's life.

In this way, *The Iron Lady* tells two intertwined stories. In one, Margaret Thatcher is in her "fourth age" and the film maps a stereotypical narrative of decline (see Wearing, 2013; Swinnen, 2015) as she gradually loses independence and cognitive function. But crucially, woven through this, and told through flashback sequences that seamlessly constitute Thatcher's memory-saturated present, the film recounts Margaret Thatcher's life story, beginning with her childhood as the middle-class daughter of a Grantham grocer who is also a local politician within the Conservative Party. In this account, Margaret Thatcher is represented as alienated from her mother and her female peer group because she identifies with her father and the masculine world of politics. A bright, industrious girl, she gains a scholarship to Oxford, and after graduation she embarks on her bid for selection to stand as an MP. Although constantly thwarted by patriarchal prejudice, Thatcher meets Denis, a supportive, forward-thinking man who becomes her husband and father to her children, and who steers her into the political career that culminates in leadership of her country and a major role on the global political stage. This chapter explores the film's narration of these interlinked stories. It is concerned with the dynamic between the film's portrayal of a confused "fourth age" woman and the life story it espouses through her memories by asking, how does the film secure the memories of a "fourth age" figure as reliable and true accounts of the past?

Before any further discussion though, an immediate issue needs to be addressed – what Jean-Louis Comolli (1978) has termed the "body too much." Comolli suggests that historical films, such as biopics, produce a surplus body in that "the historical character, filmed, has at least two bodies, that of the imagery and that of the actor who represents him [*sic*] for us" (p. 44). Comolli adds that the "body too much" does not disrupt a film's believability, since audiences are complicit in the "game" of performance. And indeed, the pleasures of viewing are enhanced by the recognition of the slippages between the believable character and the performance from which it stems. Little wonder then that biopics and other "true" stories, such as *The Queen* (Frears, 2006) or *The Iron Lady* or *Selma* (DuVernay, 2014), accrue high acclaim at award ceremonies such as the Oscars (Academy of Motion Picture Arts and Sciences) and the British Academy Film Awards, or BAFTAs (British Academy of Film and Television Arts). Moreover, *The Iron Lady* offers an especially complex surplus of bodies, in that it has different actors playing younger and older Carol Thatcher (Eloise Webb, Olivia Coleman) and Denis Thatcher (Harry Lloyd, Jim Broadbent), as well as Margaret Thatcher (Alexandra Roach, Meryl Streep). So here, just taking account of Margaret Thatcher, at least four bodies are brought into play in the combination of on-screen and off-screen embodiments. It could also be argued that the on-screen Margaret Thatcher adds to the body count by way of performances split between Roach and Streep. However, as I will later elaborate, the on-screen Margaret Thatcher should be seen as a single entity, since skillful costuming effectively stitches younger and older embodiments into a seamless continuity. But regardless of numerical definition, the film clearly mobilizes multiple embodiments of "Margaret Thatcher" and thus makes obvious that clear naming distinctions are warranted, as much for the careers of actresses whose performances deserve note as for avoiding a conflation of Margaret Thatcher the historical person, memory of whom is mediated by *The Iron Lady*, and her on-screen facsimiles. Consequently, throughout this chapter, Margaret Thatcher refers to the historical person, and Thatcher to the figure in the film variously performed by Roach and Streep.[2]

It is also worth noting that *The Iron Lady* offers yet another example of the fascination Margaret Thatcher's life and career holds for filmmakers and audiences. Setting aside regular inclusion in *Spitting Image*, the excoriating television political satire that ran for 18 series from 1984 to 1996 (Central ITV), between the time of her resignation as both prime minister and leader of the Conservative Party in November

1990 and release of *The Iron Lady* (one year before her death in 2013), Margaret Thatcher was the focus of no fewer than eight screen productions. Made for both cinema and television consumption, they include the televised single and miniseries dramas *Thatcher: The Final Days* (Sullivan, 1991); *Margaret Thatcher: The Long Walk to Finchley* (McCormack, 2004); *Margaret* (Kent, 2009), as well as documentaries from sycophants and iconoclasts alike: *Thatcher: The Downing Street Years* (Blakeway, 1993); *Tracking Down Maggie: The Unofficial Biography of Margaret Thatcher* (Broomfield, 1994); *Maggie: The First Lady* (London, 2003); *Portillo on Thatcher: The Lady's Not for Spurning* (2009); and *Margaret Thatcher: The Iron Lady* (Byron, 2012).

A forgetful present

Noting this proliferation of Thatcher texts as it crosses screen and print cultures, Louisa Hadley and Elizabeth Ho (2010) suggest that

> political texts seeking to define the "Thatcher effect" vie with biographical works trying to capture Thatcher's individual charisma as an individual, [. . .] while cultural and literary texts imaginatively reconstruct the moment of Thatcherism[,] making it available to a forgetful or nostalgic present. (p. 2)

Given the ongoing and extensive focus attracted by Margaret Thatcher, and her legacy, the idea of a "forgetful present" makes for a curious contradiction. If Thatcher and Thatcherism are so persistently remembered, how can a "forgetful present" occur, and just what is forgotten? With *The Iron Lady*, is the "forgetful present" a consequence of Thatcher's "fourth age" confusions? Or, following Hadley and Ho (2010), is the film yet another example of a Margaret Thatcher text that is symptomatic of "a symbolic and traumatic 'wound' in the contemporary imagination" (p. 4)? Developing Cathy Caruth's (1996) definition of trauma as an event "experienced too soon, too unexpectedly, to be fully known and [which] is therefore not available to consciousness until it imposes itself again, repeatedly, in the repetitive actions and nightmares of the survivor" (Hadley & Ho, 2010, p. 4), Hadley and Ho further suggest, "The persistent appearances of Thatcher in the present are certainly akin to traumatic flashback" (p. 4). Overall, Hadley and Ho argue that the multiple representations of Thatcher are symptomatic of a cultural trauma and its repressions into the unconscious, *and* the flashback memories that are indicative of rupture to such repressions. This is an attractive argument, especially with its cogent reminder that remembering and forgetting are held in a mutually supportive dynamic: that memory can only be said to exist in relation to that which is forgotten.

With that said, Hadley and Ho's argument warrants further development, since their basic premise of trauma is that memory of an event can be repressed into the unconscious and rendered unreachable, inexpressible and beyond representation – in other words, forgotten. But it needs to be added that trauma can be reached, noticed and recovered through flashback memories that are simultaneously symptomatic of repressed traumas *and* ruptures to those repressions. Given that the unconscious, the site of repressed trauma, is outside language, such ruptures mark the re-entry into language and into memory of traumatic events. Importantly, it needs to be noted that language precedes memory. It is the emergence of the repressed into language that marks the difference between forgetting and memory. Here though, following Stuart Hall (1997), I need to distinguish between Lacanian understandings of language (that is, an overarching symbolic system that underpins entry into subjectivity) and those particular and specific systems through which already constituted subjects represent experience, and which are constituted at complex intersections of technology, form and regulatory discourses. Such representational systems are embedded with the compromises of meaning making, the slippages of semiotics and the regulations of discourse (Hall, 1997). Thus memory of a trauma, via rupture to unconscious repressions, can never be a transparent or neutral process, since it is always mediated through the compromises of particular languages and specific representational systems.

All of this aligns with Myra Macdonald's (2006) argument that "all memory, however individualized in its articulation, is always a social and cultural process" (p. 329). As she says, the term " 'cultural memory' testifies to the complexities of disentangling where our memories come from: whether from direct experience, oft-repeated accounts by friends or family, or from the mediation of the popular media" (p. 329). She adds that while all memory is cultural, there is a difference between memory of events directly experienced and "prosthetic memory" that is grafted onto individual consciousness through the mediations of popular cultural forms. Macdonald stresses that prosthetic memories may well be synthetically produced, but they "nevertheless acquire the familiarity of being grafted onto our own memory bank" (p. 329). Given my point above that the representational systems of popular cultural forms are indicative of cultural trauma and ruptures to its repressions, it follows that prosthetic memory is secured through attendant forgettings, exclusions and repressions, and that forgetting is also subject to the compromises and regulation of representational systems.

Roger Bromley (1988) similarly argues, "Memory is not simply the property of individual, nor just a matter of psychological processes, but a complex cultural and historical phenomena [sic] constantly subject to revision, amplification and 'forgettings'" (p. 1). Coining the term "organized forgetting," Bromley adds that cultural memory, and thus forgetting, is always a political act predicated on acts of power that articulate and validate some stories and simultaneously repress and silence others. Such repressions and silencing are acts of symbolic violence through which "forgetting" is organized. And I would add that trauma and its rupture into cultural memory is similarly ideologically organized into that which is allowed to (re)enter language and representational systems, and that which is silenced into repression. Indeed, we need to ask, how do specific representational systems, such as *The Iron Lady*, organize cultural memory and attendant forgettings? Moreover, given my opening remarks about the tension in the film between its portrayal of a confused "fourth age" woman and its promise that her memories will offer a reliable account of Margaret Thatcher's life, we need to also consider how confidence in the reliability of the film's representation of the past is achieved alongside its regulation of prosthetic memory and organized forgetting. How does *The Iron Lady* claim that its represented memories are untainted by "fourth age" confusions, that they are reliable and true? How do these represented memories of Margaret Thatcher and Thatcherism regulate the ruptures and repressions of trauma and to what effect? How does the film play into the idea of a "forgetful present"? Indeed, how does *The Iron Lady* organize a "forgetful present"?

Cultural memory, representational systems and *The Iron Lady's* "claims to truth"

From its emergence as a technological curiosity through to its transformation into a mass industrial spectacle, cinema has been inextricably linked to the production of cultural memory. As Paul Grainge (2003) has suggested, cinema's memory production and reproduction works in two ways. First, cinema itself is a site of individual and local memory production through the materiality of its technologies, theatres and ephemera, as well as the on-screen pleasures (or dis-pleasures) of stars, particular movies, specific scenes, iconic characters, reruns, remakes and retrospectives. Second, as Grainge observed, historical memories are produced from "variations of the history film" (2003, p. 1). In other words, on-screen representational systems actively produce prosthetic memories. In some history films, the past is merely a spectacular prop in the formulation of a pleasurable and convincing fiction – think the western or a Jane Austen adaptation. This does not preclude prosthetic memories of period clothing, furnishings, transport and landscape. However, such memories are intertwined with discourses of fictionality and are effectively distanced from claims to historical accuracy and truth. In marked contrast, in a variety of ways, biopics promote themselves as dramatized history, as true stories. On this, George Custen's (1992) study of 1940s Hollywood biopics foregrounded verisimilitude, that is, the ability of film to look like life. Custen suggested that verisimilitude effectively effaces the mediations of filmmaking and establishes the biopic as historical reenactment, as a window onto past events. He added that such effacement reduces competing versions and representations of the past into a singular historical truth, which for many is "the only source of information [they] will have on a given historical subject" (p. 7), and is "de-facto, the only version of history they will ever see" (p. 17). Following Custen, it is obvious that the reductions of biopic narration not only produce cultural memories of the past, but also contribute to the processes of "organized forgetting" elaborated by Bromley.

As with all dramatized histories, the constitution of the biopic's singular truth is entwined in a pervasive belief in what Bill Nicholls (1991) has called a didactic communication circuit predicated on ideas of "an organizing agency that possesses information and knowledge, a text that conveys it, and a subject who will gain it" (p. 31), which, in turn, is shored up by the camera's "seemingly irrefutable guarantee of authenticity" (pp. 149–150). In this way, biopics such as *The Iron Lady* actively foster belief in didactic communication through claims to accurate and reliable research. For instance, prerelease publicity frequently refers to authoritative research sources – primary documents such as diaries, memoirs or respected print biographies – or even to the advice of an eyewitness. With *The Iron Lady*, its screenplay writer Abi Morgan has commented:

> There's so much source material, there's the amazing Margaret Thatcher Foundation that has a record of her entire political career and beyond, in fact, and political memoirs not only by herself but also by various cabinet ministers, journalists, so certainly when I was writing it, I was very influenced by certain memoirs and certain biographers in particular, and then when Phyllida came on, I think there was a whole

other wave of research in terms of meeting people who were more directly connected. (quoted in Douglas, 2011)

In another interview, Morgan cites the memoirs of Denis Thatcher as an influence for the personal and quirky turns of phrase depicted in scenes of Thatcher's private life and which serve to personalize the dialogue (Warburton, 2011). Additionally, I would suggest that Morgan's dialogue creates an authenticating believability in the intimacy established between Thatcher and husband Denis.

Guarantees of reliability and authenticity for the film's reenactments are also supported by the "aesthetic realism" of costume design and makeup (Gaines & Herzog, 2005, p. 19). Consolata Boyle, *The Iron Lady*'s costume designer, who had previously received critical acclaim for the lapidary detail of her work on *The Queen* (Frears, 2006), is reported to have "looked at photos and newsreels from the 1970s and 1980s, using a magnifying glass to study the clothes" ("Dressing the Iron Lady," 2011). As Justine Picardie (2011) noted, "Boyle immersed herself in research before designing Streep's costumes from scratch – examining patterns and pieces from Aquascutum and Jean Muir, and studying photographs of Thatcher's shift from Grantham grocer's daughter to the Blessed Margaret" (para. 10). But of course, as suggested by the comments on Thatcher's beige costume that opens this article, Boyle's attention to authenticating detail extends beyond the verisimilitude of period fashions to include the believable costuming of the ageing female body. In such strategies, the authentication of "fourth age" identity and period costume are fully intertwined as the film moves between Thatcher's present and her memories of earlier periods of her life.

The attention given to the detailed replications of period costume is fully supported by makeup artists and hair specialists Marese Langan, Mark Coulier and J. Roy Helland, who were deserved recipients of both Oscars and BAFTAs for the age transformations wrought upon Thatcher as she shifts between life stages, such as the vibrant, thirty-something mother and early career politician, or the embodiment of the "fourth age" imaginary. Their skill is most apparent in the contrast between scenes of Thatcher at her prime, sporting the iconic "helmet" hair, and scenes where thinning, poorly groomed hair connotes "fourth age" vulnerability and the increasing incursions of dementia. Indeed, on several occasions, the film self-consciously draws attention to hair, as in the scene of Thatcher's makeover from suburban housewife to powerful potential party leader; or in the scene where Carol Thatcher (Olivia Colman) reminds her now confused mother of the hairdresser's imminent arrival. Here, the "realist aesthetics" of the film's didactic communication circuit operate in several ways: to serve as an aide-mémoire of Prime Minister Margaret Thatcher's appearance; to authenticate the transformation of Meryl Streep into a believable facsimile of Margaret Thatcher at various stages of the life course – and hence into Thatcher; to manage Thatcher's age transformations embedded in the film's flashback structure; and to lay further claims to accuracy, and hence truth. In various ways, then, *The Iron Lady* constitutes its representational system as accurate, authentic and truthful. By extension, the "fourth age" memories of Thatcher are established as reliable and the film's grafts of prosthetic memory accrue the stamp of truth.

At the same time, it needs to be noted that "realist aesthetics" are central to the organization of narrative time. Like many biopics, *The Iron Lady* is structured through cinematic flashback, with the narrative cutting between Thatcher's present as a vulnerable "fourth ager" and her memories of childhood, early womanhood, entry into politics, falling in love, marriage and motherhood, and her political rise and decline. A further layer of complexity is added, since Thatcher's vulnerable present is established by intercuts between scenes where she "imagines" animated conversations with the now-dead Denis, and scenes where his absence signifies the increasing isolation and abjections of "fourth age" dementia. Here, intercutting is noteworthy since it establishes Thatcher's condition, while also securing a stark contrast between her subjective experience of comfort, affection and companionable warmth with Denis (whether as a contemporary figment of her dementia-induced confusions or as clear memories of their past life together) and "objective" points of view that effectively and affectively represent the cold isolation of the cared-for within the brisk efficiency of a "caring" regime. This contrast helps establish a sympathy for Thatcher that for supporters would seem well deserved, and which for others offers some mitigation to the pervasive demonization of Margaret Thatcher that all too frequently conflates neoliberal ideologies, Thatcherism and their consequences with the actions of an individual proponent.

Moreover, because of the efficacy of "realist aesthetics," we are never confused about which mind-set or which decade is being represented. Thatcher may well be confused, but the audience never is. On this, director Phyllida Lloyd has foregrounded the nuanced use of blue in Thatcher's wardrobe.

> You see a colour palette of young Margaret in beautiful blue silk, you see her at the opera with Denis, and when she goes to dine with the Dartford Conservative Association, and gradually that pale blue colour becomes a little darker when you see Margaret with Gordon Reece and Airey Neave, and then gradually when you see her become party leader you're getting more royal blue. (quoted in "Dressing the Iron Lady," 2011, para. 6)

Consider, for instance, how the dressing gown frequently worn by the older Thatcher brilliantly connotes the disorder and dishabille of dementia, just as its pale blue color signifies how her access to power has paled into insignificance. Additionally, while costume works to define Thatcher's shifts in status, as well as distinctive periods within a nonlinear narrative, it simultaneously functions to construct continuities between the performances of Roach and Streep as the younger and older Thatcher. Early in the film, the narrative cuts between dinner party scenes attended by the young and older Thatcher where each is similarly costumed in blue. The younger Thatcher wears a fitted suit, the jacket's nipped-in waist and her full skirt connoting 1950s "New

Look" fashions. The older Thatcher's lace brocade dress is less fitted, not only suggesting changing fashions and life stages, but also signifying the increased girth that accompanies loss of mobility, while making a poignant gesture to the "easy care" functionality of dresses provided for "fourth age" women placed into "care." Here, despite the film's multiple cuts between different actresses, different periods and different circumstances, blue costuming effectively stitches the young and old Thatcher into a seamless continuity. Overall, such skillful management of character, mind-set, time and place ensures there are no uneasy moments where the momentum and believability of the film is disturbed, and by extension, there is no threat to the truth claims of *The Iron Lady*'s didactic communication circuit. In turn, this suggests that the film's capacity to produce prosthetic memory, and thus organize its forgettings, is equally undisturbed by jarring ruptures to the narrative flow.

The film's capacity to mobilize prosthetic memories that are constituted as reliable and true is especially enhanced by the use of actual or simulated archival material – newsreel footage of events, television bulletins and newspaper headlines. For instance, the film's representation of her campaign and victory for Margaret Thatcher at the 1979 general election involves a highly complex series of intercuts between images of Thatcher at the podium and simulations of banner print headlines and TV news broadcasts that reference iconic signifiers of the British election process – the Conservative Party's election "battle bus," polling booths, the ballot count, predictions of success registered on the "swingometer" (the BBC's mainstay of election night coverage of emerging voting trends), and adoring post-victory crowds. Equally, the corrosive divisions of Thatcherism are represented by a combination of simulated and seemingly genuine archival footage of clashes between police and poll tax protesters;[3] clashes between police and striking miners;[4] the infamous baton charge by mounted police on the Orgreave miners' picket line;[5] and, of course, the Falklands War. The trauma of such moments, their underlying horror, is consistently figured through physically affective sounds – jeering crowds, loud angry voices, fists and boots pounding car bodywork, the piercing shrill of police whistles, the thunder of hooves, the thud of armaments. Here, the film's representational system does not simply *show* the traumas of Thatcherism. Rather it articulates Thatcherism's violent divisiveness, bringing its traumas into remembered cultural consciousness and producing visceral, prosthetic memories.

Crucially, then, the use of archival material, and/or its simulation, works as a constant reminder that this really happened, these events are real and true, and they had a lasting impact on both individuals and the nation. For audiences who lived through Thatcherism, a complex cultural memory is brought into play as their personal witness memory of the news bulletin or banner headline blends seamlessly with prosthetic memory of the stories behind them. For these audiences, such cultural memories will be highly specific and dependent upon political allegiance at an intersection with a multitude of other particular factors ranging across age, geographic location, identity politics and economic capital. For those too young to have a direct memory of Margaret Thatcher's life and Thatcherism more broadly, the film offers an encounter with grafts of prosthetic memories: grafts that are *seemingly* unmediated since they accrue from *ostensibly* immediate, eye-witness accounts. Space does not permit a full explanation for the italicized qualifications here. Suffice it to say that all film, all print culture, whether an individual output or a collaborative project, is mediated through decisions made and practices enacted in all stages of development from pre- to postproduction. Yet as I say in various contexts and various ways throughout this chapter, there remains a persistent and widespread belief that film can somehow simply "show the past." Because of this, when combined with the biopic genre's "claims to truth," even though represented through the memories of a "fourth age" figure, *The Iron Lady*'s grafts of prosthetic memories of Margaret Thatcher and Thatcherism are constituted as similarly reliable and transparent. This reliable transparency extends to the recuperation of Thatcherism's repressed traumas, such as the divisive violence noted above, which are fully imbricated into prosthetic memory of Thatcherism.

Disputed knowledge, reliable memory and organized forgetting

Notwithstanding the strategies of verisimiltude, realist aesthetics and archival material that combine to guarantee the film's "claims to truth," *The Iron Lady*'s didactic circuit of communication, its memory machine, does not go undisputed. As well illustrated by the "Historical inaccuracies" subsection of the film's Wikipedia entry ("*The Iron Lady* [Film]," 2016), the veracity of the film is frequently questioned. For instance, Wikipedia reports that the film is inaccurate in its depiction of opposition MP Michael Foot (Michael Pennington) voting against the decision to send troops to the Falklands, when in fact he voted in favor; and when it depicted Thatcher talking to her friend and ardent supporter Airey Neave (Nicholas Farrell) in the Westminster Palace car park minutes before he was killed by an IRA terrorist car bomb, when Margaret Thatcher was actually absent from Parliament that day. Equally, the most cursory Google search brings up multiple links to articles that question the film's sources, and hence accuracy and truth. As might be expected, the film's domestic scenes are a primary target. For instance, a 2012 article from Vanessa Allen of *The Mail On-line* bears the headline " 'It Bears Little Resemblance to Reality': Mrs Thatcher's Former Personal Assistant Lashes Out at Film for Portrayal of Iron Lady" and quotes personal assistant Cynthia Crawford, who began working for Margaret Thatcher in 1978, as saying, "I can assure you that all the domestic scenes in the film are just absolutely inconceivable. They're just not right and totally unrelated to the truth" (para. 11). I have little doubt of Mrs. Crawford's sincerity, nonetheless, the journalistic sanction of the elision made by Mrs. Crawford between her knowledge of part of Margaret Thatcher's life and the reliability of the entire film needs to be noted.

Similarly, other newspaper articles have questioned the accuracy and truth of *The Iron Lady*'s account of Margaret Thatcher's political career. For instance, writing in the *Telegraph*, Norman Tebbit (2011), who had been a member of her cabinet, said:

> I do not know whom the makers of the Meryl Streep film talked to. Perhaps Michael Heseltine or Geoffrey Howe, but certainly not me. To judge the film from its trailer, they confined their inquiries to the Daily Mirror and perhaps Tim Bell's public relations firm.
>
> I can speak only from personal experience, so what I saw and heard may conflict with the image the film-makers seek to establish as conventional knowledge before the serious biographies by men like Charles Moore, who did his research with care, are published following her death. (paras. 2–3)

As an example of self-aggrandizement, Tebbit's remark is second to none. Even as he acknowledges that *some* research was carried out for the film, he infers that the film's accuracy was diluted because *his* insights were neglected and forgotten, while simultaneously he trivializes other likely sources (cabinet members Michael Heseltine and Geoffrey Howe and Tim Bell's PR company) by aligning them with the tabloid rag the *Daily Mirror*, as much as through comparison with the careful gravitas of Charles Moore's then yet-to-be-published print biography.

Notably, though, the foundation of Tebbit's dispute confirms belief in a didactic communication circuit: the belief that film *can* document the truth of history in some way, provided the *right* sources are consulted. Because Tebbit privileges Moore's print biography, he also infers that the medium, or system of representation, is itself a hindrance to accuracy. Keith Beattie (2015) has observed that such claims are frequently leveled at reenactments that "meld the conventions of drama and documentary" (p. 146), and that the claim "that dramatizations are misleading carries with it the implication that a more accurate representation is available through 'traditional' documentary techniques, which supposedly refuse dramatic re-enactment" (p. 151). Beattie elaborates the term "supposedly" in a succinct account of the documentary genre's emergence in 1930s Britain that foregrounds its basic premise, what John Grierson termed "the creative treatment of actuality" (p. 37). From the outset, reenactment was always considered to be a legitimate component of the "creative treatment of actuality," and this has generated volumes of scholarly debate about the ethics and responsibilities of filmmakers in the slippages between documented facts and reenactments, as much as attempts to place boundaries around the various categories of history film – documentary, reenacted history, docudramas, drama-docs (see Paget, 1998). Curiously, biopics rarely feature in these scholarly debates (for exceptions, see Custen, 1992; Bingham, 2010; Brown & Vidal, 2014). I would suggest that in no small part this critical neglect stems from yet another founding premise of the documentary movement – that it offers a gritty and superior alternative to anything offered by popular anglophone cinemas, which in turn has resulted in a hierarchy of cultural capital for the various categories of history film: a hierarchy predicated on proximity to denigrated and devalued Hollywood productions and their ilk from other nations.

Disdain for popular dramatized history films is long-standing, as suggested by Beattie's (2015) citation of an anonymous *Guardian* review from 1980 whereby reenactments of a historical figure are deemed to be counterfeit and sham, little more than a "mish mash of fact and fiction and producer's whim" (p. 151). Such disdain is evident in Tebbit's (2011) cursory dismissal of *The Iron Lady* and his inferred suggestion that the film is inferior to Moore's print biography. In turn, Tebbit's response to *The Iron Lady* exemplifies some major concerns about dramatized history, such as the reliability of its sources, the accuracy of its facts, the truth of its story, rather than the idea of a didactic communication circuit per se. To put this another way, the concern with sources, facts, accuracy and truth registers and confirms *both* the widespread belief in a didactic communication circuit, *and* an equally widespread anxiety that the wrong facts, the wrong histories are being inserted into that circuit. So despite the elitist disdain for the biopic genre, there simultaneously exists a desire to regulate its stories, to control its sources and facts, and an ongoing anxiety about the potential failures of regulation. Given Tebbit's concern with "conventional knowledge," it is an easy leap to recognize how such anxieties and desires mark a concern with the control and regulation of prosthetic memory.

Notably, although *The Iron Lady* has been attacked for its ostensible inaccuracies and its sources trivialized, the most virulent criticisms directed at the film are concerned with its depiction of Margaret Thatcher as a "fourth age" figure manifesting the symptoms of dementia, with major public figures taking turns to condemn the film's lack of sensitivity toward a living person and her family. The scale of the furor is crystalized by Max Pemberton (2012), writing in the *Telegraph*:

> While Meryl Streep's performance is mesmerising, it is impossible not to be disturbed by her depiction of Lady Thatcher's decline into dementia. Columnists and commentators such as Charles Moore, Norman Tebbit and Douglas Hurd have opined in this newspaper and elsewhere about this distasteful approach. And David Cameron has similarly questioned the morality of making the film while she is still alive. (para. 5)

According to blogger Julie Steinberg (2011), Pemberton's verdict of "distasteful" is matched with "extremely unkind" from Charles Moore, Margaret Thatcher's official biographer. What has always struck me as odd about the negative critical reception of *The Iron Lady* is that its depiction of Margaret Thatcher's dementia was never used to attack the film's accuracy or reliability. After all, the film is frequently shot from Thatcher's point of view, with representations of the past being organized through the flashback memories of a "fourth age" figure. Repeatedly, close-ups of Thatcher's face seemingly dissolve into her deepest memories as the film moves from its present to her past. Such moves are often prefigured through framed close-ups of Thatcher gazing at an object, suggesting that these are memory prompts that rupture the seam of trauma's forgetful repressions. For instance, a framed photograph of Airey Neave prompts a memory of his murder, whilst memories of the Falklands War are prompted by a chunky bronze figurine of two soldiers raising a victory standard. Similarly, a close-up of the DVD cover for *The King and I* (Lang, 1956) dissolves into memories of courtship, and home movie footage of children Mark and Carol slides from Thatcher's memories into a delusional recovery of motherhood as the television screen animates, with Mark stepping from the confines of the set before running from room to room, while his mother seeks in some desperation to find him.[6] So not only is the film's entire representation of the past organized through the memories of a "fourth age" person suffering the confusions of dementia, there is at least one reminder of "fourth age" confusions.

Yet, as far as I have been able to ascertain, Thatcher's dementia has never been cited as a source of the film's unreliability. No doubt, for some critics, this stems from an extension to Thatcher of personal loyalties and respect held for Margaret Thatcher and/or her achievements. Seemingly, to attack the reliability of the former is tantamount to an attack on the latter. Additionally, full credit must be given to the filmmakers as they manage the depiction of Thatcher's "fourth age" dementia while simultaneously securing her memories as reliably truthful by exploiting the progressive decline of the illness. This is best illustrated by the three scenes that form *The Iron Lady*'s closing sequence: scenes that combine with the film's three-scene opening sequence to contain the film's flashback memories within discrete brackets. With Thatcher's deteriorating health already established when a routine medical checkup is brought forward, the first of the closing scenes has Denis costumed for outdoors. He walks down a hallway, away from Thatcher, toward its brilliantly lit exit. Highly distraught, she begs him to remain as the camera cuts between her tearful face and his departing back as he disappears into a pool of light that expands into a prolonged whiteout. Unmistakably, Denis has disappeared from Thatcher's memory, suggesting that she has finally declined into the later stages of blank, forgetful dementia. Confirmation of this suggestion comes in the following scene, when a confused Thatcher is wakened by daughter Carol. Symbolically, her bedroom cupboards are stripped bare of their memory prompting contents, which are now inaccessibly contained and constrained in muddled and disorganized piles of black refuse sacks. Then, the film's closing scene has Thatcher washing teacups – seemingly forgetting that she had foresworn that task when as a young woman she had embarked on her pursuit of public life. In itself, this forgetting speaks volumes about the losses of dementia, while Thatcher's blank expression offers a confirming, visceral embodiment of the pervasive discursive suturing of lost memory and lost personhood.

Setting aside the compassionate affect thus mobilized, this closing sequence maps a very clear trajectory for Thatcher's dementia, with the presence and absence of Denis suggesting the difference between retention and loss of memory. Vitally, the film's dramatization of Margaret Thatcher's public rise and fall is completed prior to Denis's disappearance: a disappearance that powerfully symbolizes and illuminates Thatcher's traumatic decline into the forgettings of dementia. Hence, the film's representational system secures its account of Margaret Thatcher's life and political career as reliable memories unclouded by the later stages of Thatcher's dementia that close the film. When combined with the biopic genre's "claims to truth," Thatcher's reliable memories are transformed into singular and uncontested prosthetic memories of Margaret Thatcher's private and public life.

The play between memory and forgetting suggested here extends beyond off-screen claims of neglected sources, and beyond Thatcher's on-screen forgetting. Notably, there is another forgetting, a traumatic repression, inscribed in Thatcher's *reliable* memories of her individual struggle to find a place in a man's world. The patriarchal framing of this forgetting is established during Thatcher's first attempt at constituency selection, when she is patronized as both a woman and the daughter of a grocer, and then after dinner, she is compelled to retire "with the ladies." This framing of a dominant patriarchal culture is reiterated in the scene of Thatcher's first day in Parliament. In this scene, shot from her viewpoint, she walks along a corridor as the camera cuts between a surrounding gauntlet of staring men and shots of her shoes that disturb a pervasive silence with their click-clacking heels. Following this, the view takes in a swirl of packed and clubbish rooms from which she is repeatedly barred; until finally, a door bearing the sign "Lady Members Room" opens to reveal a bleak unoccupied space dominated by an ironing board ("Iron Lady" playfulness duly noted!). If the symbolism of Westminster's male privilege and female exclusion were not already sufficient, the point is driven home when a floor-level shot that juxtaposes Thatcher's dainty navy and white shoes with the solidity of multiple masculine brogues is followed by an overhead shot showing a vivid, blue-suited and hatted Thatcher as a diminutive counterpoint within an engulfing mass of gray-suited men. Then later, even with a ministerial brief achieved, representations of cabinet meetings have Thatcher spatially marginalized and verbally patronized – literally and symbolically "elbowed out."

Here, the costuming that explicates Thatcher's marginalization within a patriarchal culture also prefigures her subsequent achievements and fame, since she is always distinctive. She stands out from the crowd: she stands out from a swirling mass of belligerent, shouting, gesturing men: she stands out as an isolated and solitary woman struggling to find a place in a man's world. Yet the film is equally insistent that friendship, respect, tutelage and support for Thatcher come from specific men (never women) – her father, Alfred Roberts (Iain Glen); her husband, Denis; Airey Neave and Gordon Reece (Roger Allam). Indeed, it is Neave and Reece who mastermind the makeover that transforms Thatcher into the iconic "Iron Lady." Equally, within the film's representational system, women are fully confined to that domestic space of teacups (and ironing boards) so positively rejected by Thatcher, and women are totally absent from the public sphere of politics – except, of course, for Thatcher. Validated by the film's claim to truth and accuracy, this image of a marginalized, isolated and singular woman, a lone exemplar of female political achievement in a man's world, becomes the prosthetic memory of Margaret Thatcher.

In many ways, this representation of Thatcher's isolation adds further authenticity to the film, since it encapsulates Margaret Thatcher's pronouncement "There is no such thing as society" and crystalizes the logic of neoliberal ideologies, with their fetishistic celebration of individualism and interlinked absolutions for the privileged, from any responsibility for social action in favor of the underprivileged. With that said, it must be noted that this exemplification is disturbingly gendered, since it aligns with the male/female, present/absent binary mobilized by the film's representational system. This gendered exemplification of neoliberalism illuminates a deeply troubling, structuring absence in the film: an organized forgetting. Even as *The Iron Lady* repeatedly and painstakingly makes claims to truth for the reliability of Thatcher's memories, it simultaneously neglects and forgets that Margaret Thatcher was not an isolated woman in Parliament, either historically or contemporaneously. Notably, the first woman MP was elected in 1918, 41 years before Margaret Thatcher,[7] and between 1918 and 1987, the proportion of women MPs hovered around 4 per cent of the 605 available seats. In 1959, when Margaret Thatcher was first elected, there were 24 other women MPs (Griffin, 2013). Yet any reference to these facts by way of dialogue, archival insertions, flashes of feminine color or shadowy background figures is totally excised from the film's prosthetic memories.

Vitally, this effacement of other women from *The Iron Lady*'s account of Margaret Thatcher's life should *not* be seen as a struggle over the reliability of facts and sources, nor as an abandonment of accuracy or truth. Rather, this is a recognition that a neglect, an absence, an omission, a repression, a forgetting is embedded in the film's representational system: an organized forgetting of other women who experienced the same misogynist political system as Margaret Thatcher, some of whom set enabling precedents for her achievements. This organized forgetting extends to incorporate those feminist struggles for suffrage, education, property rights, social mobility, reproductive rights, and the right to speak and be heard that enabled Margaret Thatcher, and other women politicians from earlier and later generations, and of lesser renown, to play a part in public life. This organized forgetting is fully imbricated in *The Iron Lady*'s persistent and consistent claims to truth and is fully embedded in its grafts of prosthetic memory. Thus even as the representational system of *The Iron Lady* organizes its own claims to truth, organizes its cultural memories of Thatcherism's multiple, traumatic violent conflicts, organizes prosthetic memory of Margaret Thatcher as a singular, self-determined achiever, it simultaneously organizes a forgetting of other women's achievements and the feminist politics that made them possible. Here then, with women's achievements and their feminist underpinnings organized into the grafted forgettings of *The Iron Lady*, it becomes clear that feminist politics constitute the film's traumatic repressions and that feminist politics are fully embedded in Thatcherism's forgetful present.

Conclusion

The simple conclusion to this chapter is that *The Iron Lady*'s representational system is at pains to establish its own claims to truth about Margaret Thatcher and Thatcherism, to establish that its grafts of prosthetic memory are trustworthy and reliable, *even* when told as the memories of a "fourth age" figure. But such a simple conclusion is both highly particular and reductive because it is constituted through a structuring absence, a repression, an organized forgetting of other women's achievements and the feminist activism that enabled Margaret Thatcher's political career. Indeed, such a conclusion can be seen as yet another authenticating strategy, since one of Margaret Thatcher's many declarations of self-worth was that she "owed nothing to women's lib" (Holehouse, 2013). And clearly, to launch an equally simple counter-narrative to this conclusion – a counter-narrative that mobilizes prosthetic memory articulated through an awareness of the many women of achievement and the decades of feminist politics that enabled Margaret Thatcher to assume power and influence – would be of immense value. But then, that counter-narrative already exists. How else would I know that something is repressed and forgotten by *The Iron Lady*? How else would I know that Margaret Thatcher is not the isolated example of women's achievement claimed by the film? Sadly, that knowledge, that counter-narrative circulates mostly in the rarefied circuits of academia or among the highly committed few who seek it out. For a counter-narrative to become effective, to become a widely shared prosthetic memory, rather than an organized forgetting, it needs a popular reach similar to that of *The Iron Lady*. Here I would suggest that some headway is made by the film *Suffragette* (Gavron, 2015), which, like *The Iron Lady*, was written by Abi Morgan. Where *The Iron Lady* forgets and represses memory of the struggle to obtain suffrage for British women that was the necessary and fundamental prerequisite for Margaret Thatcher's political career, *Suffragette* remembers. More importantly, its remembering is mobilized through a viscerally affective representation of an activist collectivity that sustained campaigners through the gross, reactionary physical and emotional violence enacted upon them. The film remembers the physical and emotional traumas enacted upon suffragettes: traumas repressed by the organized forgettings of *The Iron Lady* as it reiterates Margaret Thatcher's individualistic neoliberalism.

But to end here would miss the full impact of Margaret Thatcher's traumatic legacy for feminism and would miss the complexity of the (pre)postfeminist legacy now reiterated by *The Iron Lady* and those claims to truth that override the cultural imaginary of the "fourth age." In fact, *The Iron Lady* does not merely organize forgetting of other women in public life and the feminist activism that supported Margaret Thatcher's career, it also represses her failure to support other women. Many commentators suggest that one reason for Margaret Thatcher's success was that she totally distanced herself from women and women's issues. This certainly impacted on British national politics. Susan Faludi (1991) points out that during her eleven years as prime minister, Margaret Thatcher appointed only one woman, Baroness Young, to sit among the 20 or so men composing her inner cabinet of ministers.[8] Indeed, Baroness Young is one of the striking absences of the film's representational system. So too are the other 13 women who were promoted by Margaret Thatcher to hold junior ministerial positions.[9] Even as Margaret Thatcher kept able women away from the higher echelons of government, her attitude to the needs of the female electorate was, at best, contradictory. As Naomi Wolf (1994) suggests, not only did she freeze child benefit payments,[10] but despite being a working mother herself, she often criticized other women for abandoning their children to "the 'chaos' of workplace crèches – if only there were some, most mothers felt – and, by implication, to an adult life of vice and violence" (quoted in Redfern, 2001, para. 6). Consequently, the loathing directed toward Margaret Thatcher by some sections of the British electorate resulted in a widespread antipathy toward women politicians more generally. It is noteworthy that in the 1979 general election when Margaret Thatcher was voted into power, despite the fact that she had been leader of the Conservative Party since 1975, fewer women were returned as MPs than had been the case for nearly 30 years (Whelehan, 2000). Margaret Thatcher's public position did not simply turn popular opinion away from women politicians, it also served to support patriarchal assertions that there are no barriers, no institutional impediments, no glass ceilings to halt the progress of any woman with ambition. As Joan Smith (1989) explains,

> If Mrs Thatcher could do it, the argument runs, so could anyone else. The unspoken implication is that the woman making the complaint simply has not tried hard enough [. . .] Sometimes the argument is taken even further [. . .] as evidence not only that unparalleled opportunities are open to women [. . .] but that there is now a definite advantage in being a woman. (p. 112)

Here, it becomes evident that *The Iron Lady* does not merely omit and repress an already existing counter-narrative to its own "organized forgetting" of women's achievements and the feminist activism that enabled Margaret Thatcher's public life, but that simultaneously, its reiteration of Margaret Thatcher as an exceptional and singular woman achieving high success within a man's world provides the grounds for the rejection of feminism per se, effectively negating its value for all those women who follow after Thatcher. At a stroke, feminism is simultaneously forgotten and rendered redundant. Here then we can see the real power of organized forgetting: that it should never be reduced to the simple omission of facts from the past. Rather, if a full and effective counter-narrative to the organized forgettings of *The Iron Lady* is to be mobilized, the capacity of organized forgetting to rewrite the past, to shape and regulate attitudes and beliefs in the aftermath of its repressions needs to be fully embedded in the prosthetic memories of Thatcherism. As Bromley (1988) stresses,

> *Forgetting* is as important as remembering. Part of the struggle against cultural power is the challenge to forgetting posed by memory. What is "forgotten" may represent more threatening aspects of popular "memory" and have been carefully and consciously, not casually and unconsciously, omitted from the narrative economy of remembering. (p. 12, original emphasis)

Notes

1. For British audiences at least, this corner shop scene is multiply evocative. Initially, it reminds of Margaret Thatcher's early life as a grocer's daughter and how she frequently mobilized her experience of small-business economics as a rationale and justification for many of the neoliberal policies she espoused. Equally, the purchase of milk registers the nickname "Milk Snatcher," which stems from 1971, when as Education Secretary in Edward Heath's cabinet, she implemented the parliamentary bill stopping the provision of free milk to schoolchildren aged above seven. Milk provision had been introduced in 1946 by a Labour government that aimed to alleviate the underachievement associated with poverty and poor nutrition. Its suspension was

deemed by many on the left as an indication of intent to dismantle the welfare state.

2. It is a gesture of feminist concern that Margaret Thatcher is accorded the courtesy of her full name. While I totally oppose the neoliberal ideologies that underpin Thatcherism, share none of Margaret Thatcher's political views, and continue to lament the dire consequences for the working classes of policies introduced by her government, I nonetheless reject the reductive individualization of government actions that fosters the misogynist demonization of this high-achieving woman.

3. The "poll tax," officially called the Community Charge, was introduced in 1989 by Margaret Thatcher's government as an intended reform to local taxation. The aim was to replace the traditional system based on household property values with one based on a fixed rate per person. With many critics feeling that this would operate to the detriment of poorer families and to the advantage of the better off, and that the change was being forced regardless of public opinion, throughout 1989 and 1990, protest meetings rapidly escalated into full riots and wholesale street battles between police and protestors. Some commentators suggest that this highly unpopular legislation precipitated Margaret Thatcher's fall from power.

4. Considered by many to be the most bitter industrial action in British history, the miners' strike of 1984–85 aimed to stop further coal pit closures (there were over 1000 in 1920 and only 173 in 1984) in the context of falling prices for coal and increasing government subsidies for the industry. The strike triggered two sources of conflict, between striking miners and the police, and between striking miners and those who continued to work because a national vote on the issue had not been taken by the National Union of Miners (NUM), who were protected by the police as they crossed picket lines. Footage of violent clashes between striking miners and police in full riot gear became a staple of news reporting, as did the growing toll of casualties as the conflict escalated.

5. Now known as the Battle of Orgreave, this one incident that took place in a small Yorkshire pit town on June 18, 1984, has become

emblematic of the miners' strike in particular, and the toxic divisiveness of Thatcherism more generally. Then, the official version of the event was that police defended themselves against thousands of rioting miners. Contemporary footage of the event (see YouTube for multiple versions) shows mounted police wearing full riot gear swinging batons and cracking heads as they charge their horses and trample lines of defenseless men. Seventy-four miners were brought to trial for the imprisonable charge of "violent disorder," but the trials collapsed because police evidence was deemed unreliable. In June 1991, following a sustained campaign, South Yorkshire Police paid £425,000 in compensation to 39 miners for assault, wrongful arrest, unlawful detention and malicious prosecution.

6. As with the corner shop scene discussed above, the image of Thatcher seeking her son has especial resonances within British popular memory since Mark Thatcher, along with a co-driver and a mechanic, went missing for six days, January 9–15, 1982, after losing his way crossing the Sahara Desert during the Paris-Dakar motorcar rally. Attracting major news coverage, a very distressed Margaret Thatcher was seen to weep in public, and Denis Thatcher flew out to Algeria to help supervise a search that drew on the resources of four countries and involved expensive plane and helicopter searches. When the unharmed rally team were found by the Algerian military, the safe return of Mark Thatcher made him the butt of ridicule and gave license to a virulent, resentful backlash against the economic and emotional privilege displayed by the Thatchers (see Chorlton, 1982).

7. In 1918, Countess Constance Markievicz was the first elected woman MP, but as a Sinn Fein activist she never took her seat. A year later, Nancy Astor (Viscountess Astor) became the first woman to sit in the House of Commons.

8. Baroness Young, a notorious anti–gay rights campaigner, was the first woman to be appointed Leader of the House of Lords, from 1981 to 1983. The Leader of the House of Lords is the cabinet minister responsible for arranging government business in the British Parliament's second house, the House of Lords.

9. These women are Lynda Chalker, Angela Rumbold, Jean Barker (Baroness Trumpington), Peggy Fenner, Janet Young (Baroness Young), Gloria Hooper (Baroness Hooper), Marion Roe, Virginia Bottomley, Emily Blatch (Baroness Blatch), Edwina Currie, Gillian Shephard, Sally Oppenheim-Barnes (Baroness Oppenheim-Barnes), and Caroline Cox (Baroness Cox).

10. In 1945, in the context of high levels of childhood malnutrition, one of the first measures of the emergent British welfare state was a payment called "Family Allowance" that was paid directly to the mother following the birth of a second and subsequent children. This allowance was not means tested and thus ensured that all women, regardless of marital status and independent of male support, had a reliable income that could be made available to buy food for children. In 1975, this was reformed into the universal "Child Benefit" payment that included all children. These payments ran alongside a child tax allowance introduced in 1909, which largely worked to the advantage of working men, and did not necessarily benefit children and their mothers.

Films and TV productions cited

Blakeway, Deny (Director). (1993). *Thatcher: The Downing Street years* [Television series]. United Kingdom: BBC 2.

Broomfield, Nick (Director). (1994). *Tracking down Maggie: The unofficial biography of Margaret Thatcher* [Documentary].

Byron, Alan (Director). (2012). *Margaret Thatcher: The Iron Lady* [Documentary]. Revolver Entertainment. United Kingdom: Odeon Entertainment; Japan: WOWOW Cinema.

DuVernay, Ava (Director). (2014). *Selma* [Motion picture]. United States: Paramount Pictures.

Frears, Stephen (Director). (2006). *The Queen* [Motion picture]. France: Pathé Pictures.

Gavron, Sarah (Director). (2015). *Suffragette* [Motion picture]. France: Pathé Pictures.

Kent, James (Director). (2009). *Margaret*. [Television movie]. United Kingdom: BBC 2.
Lang, Walter (Director). (1956). *The king and I* [Motion picture]. United States: 20th Century Fox.
Lloyd, Phyllida (Director). (2011). *The Iron Lady* [Motion picture]. United Kingdom: 20th Century Fox; United States: The Weinstein Company; Australia: Icon Productions.
London, Nick (Director). (2003). *Maggie: The first lady* [Television series]. United Kingdom: ITV – Independent Television; United States: PBS.
McCormack, Niall (Director). (2004). *Margaret Thatcher: The long walk to Finchley* [Television series]. United Kingdom: BBC 4.
Portillo on Thatcher: The lady's not for spurning [Television documentary]. (2009). BBC 4.
Spitting image [Television series]. (1984–96). United Kingdom: Central ITV.
Sullivan, Tim (Director). (1991). *Thatcher: The final days* [Television movie]. United Kingdom: Granada ITV.

References

Allen, Vanessa. (2012). "It bears little resemblance to reality": Mrs Thatcher's former personal assistant lashes out at film for portrayal of Iron Lady. *The Mail On-line*. http://www.dailymail.co.uk/news/article-2087953/The-Iron-Lady-Margaret-Thatchers-personal-assistant-Cynthia-Crawford-criticises-film.html.
Beattie, Keith. (2015). *Documentary screens: Nonfiction film and television*. London: Palgrave Macmillan.
Bingham, Denis. (2010). *Whose lives are they anyway? The biopic as contemporary film genre*. New Brunswick, NJ: Rutgers University Press.
Bromley, Roger. (1988). *Lost narratives: Popular fictions, politics and recent history*. London: Routledge.

Brown, Tom, & Vidal, Belén (Eds.). (2014). *The biopic in contemporary film culture.* London: Routledge.

Caruth, Cathy. (1996). *Unclaimed experience: Trauma, narrative, and history.* Baltimore, MD: Johns Hopkins University Press.

Chorlton, Penny. (1982, January 14). Thatcher weeps for her missing son. *The Guardian* [Electronic version]. https://www.theguardian.com/theguardian/1982/jan/14/fromthearchive.

Comolli, Jean-Louis. (1978). Historical fiction: A body too much. Screen, 19(2), 41–54.

Custen, George. (1992). *Bio/pics: How Hollywood constructed public history.* New Brunswick, NJ: Rutgers University Press.

Douglas, Edward. (2011, December 29). Interview: Phyllida Lloyd and Abi Morgan on The Iron Lady. *ComingSoon.net.* http://www.comingsoon.net/movies/features/85409-interview-phyllida-lloyd-abi-morgan-on-the-iron-lady.

Dressing the Iron Lady. (2011). *The Stylist.* http://www.stylist.co.uk/fashion/dressing-the-iron-lady.

Faludi, Susan. (1991). *Backlash: The undeclared war against women.* London: Chatto & Windus.

Gaines, Jane, & Herzog, Charlotte. (2005). Norma Shearer as Marie Antoinette: Which body too much? In Rachel Moseley (Ed.), *Fashioning film stars: Dress, culture, identity* (pp. 11–26). London: British Film Institute.

Gilleard, Chris, & Higgs, Paul. (2014). Quality in ageing and older adults. *Quality in Ageing: Policy, Practice and Research,* 15(4), 241–243.

Grainge, Paul (Ed.). (2003). *Memory and popular film.* Manchester: Manchester University Press.

Griffin, Ben. (2013, May 7). Thatcher and the glass ceiling [Blog post]. *History of government.* https://history.blog.gov.uk/2013/05/07/thatcher-and-the-glass-ceiling.

Hadley, Louisa, & Ho, Elizabeth (Eds.). (2010). *Thatcher and after: Margaret Thatcher and her afterlife in contemporary culture.* London: Palgrave Macmillan.

Hall, Stuart. (1997). Introduction. In Stuart Hall with Paul du Gay (Eds.), *Representation: Cultural representations and signifying practices* (pp. 1–12). London: Sage Publications in association with the Open University.

Holehouse, Matthew. (2013, April 8). Margaret Thatcher: A pioneering woman with no time for feminists. *The Telegraph.* http://www.telegraph.co.uk/news/politics/margaret-thatcher/9979922/Margaret-Thatcher-a-pioneering-woman-with-no-time-for-feminists.html.

The Iron Lady (film). (2016). Wikipedia. https://en.wikipedia.org/wiki/The_Iron_Lady_(film).

Macdonald, Myra. (2006). Performing memory on television: Documentary and the 1960s. *Screen*, 4(3), 327–345.

Nichols, Bill. (1991). *Representing reality: Issues and concepts in documentary.* Bloomington: Indiana University Press.

Paget, Derek. (1998). *No other way to tell it: Dramadoc/docudrama on television.* Manchester: Manchester University Press.

Pemberton, Max. (2012, January 14). The Iron Lady and Margaret Thatcher's dementia: Why this despicable film makes voyeurs of us all. *The Telegraph.* http://www.telegraph.co.uk/news/politics/margaret-thatcher/9013910/The-Iron-Lady-and-Margaret-Thatchers-dementia-Why-this-despicable-film-makes-voyeurs-of-us-all.html.

Picardie, Justine. (2011, December 11). The making of The Iron Lady's wardrobe. *The Telegraph.* http://fashion.telegraph.co.uk/columns/justine-picardie/TMG8940986/The-Making-of-The-Iron-Ladys-Wardrobe.html.

Redfern, Catherine. (2001, August 16). Margaret Thatcher: Was she good for feminism? *The f word: Contemporary UK feminism.* https://www.thefword.org.uk/2001/08/margaret_thatcher.

Smith, Joan. (1989). *Misogynies: Reflections on myths and malice.* London: Faber & Faber.

Steinberg, Julie. (2011, December 22). 'Iron Lady' draws fire for depicting Thatcher with Alzheimer's [Blog post]. *The Wall Street Journal.*

http://blogs.wsj.com/speakeasy/2011/12/22/the-iron-lady-draws-fire-for-depicting-thatcher-with-alzheimers.

Swinnen, Aagje. (2015). Ageing in film – An overview. In Julia Twigg & Wendy Martin (Eds.), Routledge handbook for cultural gerontology (pp. 69–76). London: Routledge.

Tebbit, Norman. (2011, November 15). This is not the Margaret Thatcher I knew. *The Telegraph*. http://www.telegraph.co.uk/news/politics/margaret-thatcher/8892130/Norman-Tebbit-This-is-not-the-Margaret-Thatcher-I-knew.html.

Warburton, Heather. (2011, December 29). Screenwriter Abi Morgan: The Iron Lady interview. *Collider*. http://collider.com/abi-morgan-iron-lady-interview.

Wearing, Sadie. (2013). Dementia and the bio-politics of the biopic: From *Iris* to *The Iron Lady*. Dementia, 12(3), 315–332.

Whelehan, Imelda. (2000). *Overloaded: Popular culture and the future of feminism*. London: Women's Press.

Wolf, Naomi. (1994). *Fire with fire: The new female power and how to use it*. Toronto: Random House of Canada.

Chapter 4: Ageing with Waves
The Im/material Worlds of Two Quebec Ondists

David Madden

While youth taste cultures, male composers and male inventors continue to dominate scholarship on electronic music, popular music and technology, very few studies have been devoted to women, music and ageing. Using the early electronic musical instrument the ondes Martenot as a window to study ageing, memory and the im/material attachments between instruments and musicians, this chapter develops the beginnings of a feminist micro historiography (Steedman, 1986; Brewer, 2010) of the specialist musical interpreters of the ondes Martenot (ondes) by threading together ignored aspects of the ondes as a performing instrument. The ondes Martenot was presented publicly in 1928 at the Opéra de Paris by its inventor, Maurice Martenot, a cellist, pedagogue and former radiotelegraphic soldier in World War I. It is a monophonic electronic musical instrument that uses radio technology (two heterodyning radio waves) to produce its many sounds (cf. Laurendeau, 1990; Madden, 2013). This chapter considers the everyday musical lives, histories and practices of two ondists: Suzanne Binet-Audet and Marie Bernard, both older women living in Quebec and founding members of the Ensemble d'ondes de Montréal, with international careers in music spanning 40 to 50 years. I am interested in the ongoing lived experience of these musicians and how they have been aged *by* (Gullette, 2004) and have aged *with* Martenot's waves. Questions to be addressed include the following: How do affective relationships with musical instruments change through the passage of time? How do musical performers and instruments grow old together? The primary objective is to consider how histories of older women musicians contribute to our understandings of ageing studies and music.

The special connections between music and memory are vast, encompassing a range of practices and disciplines, from sociology, psychology and cultural studies to musicology and music therapy, among others. Typically, as Sara Cohen (2013) writes, music is understood as an autobiographic retrieval and identity formation tool and as a carrier of collective memory. As a point of departure from these established notions of music and memory, I respond to the above questions by attending to the varied entanglements between the materiality of the ondes Martenot itself, the instrument's particular sounding affordances, and the life courses and careers of these two ondists. This is the story of Binet-Audet's and Bernard's love affair with the ondes Martenot: a near-lifelong narrative of companionship and intimacy that reveals a reciprocal and transformative agency between two musicians and their instruments. This chapter critically considers the musical careers and practices of Binet-Audet and Bernard within the emerging field of ageing studies and music by using narrative and musical biographies as "ways to think *with* ageing" (Jennings & Gardner, 2012, p. 2, original emphasis). As Stephen Katz (2014) suggests, "[P]articular narratives, however intimately experienced, are also culturally grounded so that our biographical accounts are the result of intersecting conversations between self and society" (p. 93). A prominent empirical foundation for this analysis draws from my own musical experiences with Binet-Audet and Bernard, including performances and studio recording encounters, in addition to a series of semistructured interviews that I conducted with them between 2008 and 2016, sometimes with three to four years passing between each engagement. The interviews often took place over the course of full days at their homes, and we discussed their personal histories as musicians and their ongoing relationships with the ondes Martenot and with each other. I begin with a brief history of the instrument that focuses on key moments in its life course before moving on to the musical histories of Binet-Audet and

Bernard, and my experiences with them as a researcher and practicing musician.

The ondes's life course

Although this chapter shifts the focus of typical patrilineal histories of electronic music and technology (see McCartney, 2006; Rodgers, 2010, 2012) by focusing on two older women and their careers and practices as performers and composers, some contextual information on the ondes is important to set up the ways in which the life courses of Binet-Audet and Bernard are intertwined with the instrument and with each other. Additionally, in order to understand how one grows old with instruments and the material traces of our lives, one must account for the fact that instruments have their own distinct life courses, cycles and personalities; they are not merely static cultural artifacts and operate within shifting temporalities outside of our own. As Stephen Katz (2005) emphasizes in a provocative afterword from his book *Cultural Aging*, "[T]ime is governed by different and wider movements, tempos, environments, and cycles than the ones determining the span and development of our human lives" (p. 233). He continues, using the life cycle of a rose as a way to think through the multifaceted ways in which we age together with material culture:

> A rose is not just a rose, but, like other material objects, it is a living gateway to the dynamics between material culture, the contingencies of time, and the spirit of renewal that confront the new paradoxes of cultural aging and its postmodern timelessness with an eternity of other possibilities. (p. 234)

Much like Katz's ageing rose, the ondes Martenot also operates as a living material gateway and as an attachment site for thinking about history and the oscillating temporalities of life courses. As mentioned, the instrument made its public debut in 1928 in Paris, where its inventor, former radiotelegraphic soldier, pedagogue and cellist Maurice Martenot (1898–1980), demonstrated its range of sounds and sonic processing capabilities to a rather mystified, yet curious, audience at the Opéra de Paris (Laurendeau, 1990). As a result of this initial success, Martenot took the ondes on a limited world tour, making it as far as Japan in the early 1930s, and would be used by many of Western Europe's most prominent composers of the avant-garde, including Arthur Honegger and Pierre Boulez, the future founder of the Institut de Recherche et Coordination Acoustique/Musique (IRCAM). The French composer and pedagogue Olivier Messiaen (1908–1992) is perhaps the most well-known composer to feature the instrument in his compositions, most notably *Fête des belles eaux*, for six ondes, which premiered in 1937 at the Exposition Internationale des Arts et Techniques dans la Vie Moderne (EXPO) in Paris, *Trois petites liturgies de la présence divine* (1945), *Turangalîla-Symphonie* (1949) and *Saint François d'Assise* (1983).

Interestingly, the ondes has its own gendered history related to its expressive and lyrical sounding possibilities, which is accentuated by the instrument's highly sensitive and malleable interface. Martenot, the inventor, devoted his life to modifying the ondes and would make seven different models in his lifetime; the last one, transistorized, he produced in 1975.[1] The instrument has a short scale monophonic keyboard controlled (delicately) with an interpreter's right hand, which allows for subtle vibrato and microtonality, or intervals smaller than a semitone. An interpreter can also employ a ribbon, or *ruban*, which is controlled by the forefinger of the right hand, recreating many of the sonic affordances and lyricism of fretless stringed instruments, such as glissando, while moving across the entirety of the ondes's eight-octave range.[2] This very lyricism and connection to the voice/body made the ondes seem dangerous, too feminine and out of touch with the post–World War II high modernist musical sophisticates of the day, which, rather ironically, included the aforementioned Boulez, who studied with Messiaen at the Conservatoire de Paris and played the ondes. For instance, Jacques Tchamkerten (2007) writes that

Boulez's reaction to the premiere of Messiaen's *Turangalîla-Symphonie* was violent; he insisted that he would never conduct either *Turangalîla-Symphonie* or *Trois petites liturgies*, the latter of which he believed to be "brothel music" (p. 71).

This reaction directly attaches the ondes to the "discourse of 'classical music,' " which, as Tia DeNora (1997) writes, construes glissandi "as 'unclean,' that is, part of different and 'less tasteful' musical discourses" (p. 58). I have written elsewhere (Madden, 2013) about how this ideological and gendered rejection of the ondes as an instrument of composition led to a steep decline in its use by many "important" male Western European composers of the mid-20th century. However, in light of this thorough compositional silencing, a devoted group of ondists, or specialist players of the instrument, continued to study and perform with the instrument, most notably in France at the Conservatoire de Paris and in Canada at the Conservatoire de musique du Québec à Montréal (CMQM), where, after an 18-year absence from the school's curriculum from the late 1990s until 2015, it is again being taught as a performance instrument, by ondist Estelle Lemire. The most acclaimed ondist is the French musician and pedagogue Jeanne Loriod (1928–2001), who was the featured player in many of Messiaen's works and recordings of compositions; in addition, Loriod produced a three-volume work on the instrument entitled *Technique de l'onde électronique, type Martenot* (1987–99). Loriod also taught Quebec's Binet-Audet at the Conservatoire de Paris, where her relationship with the ondes began in the 1960s.

From the 1960s onwards, the ondes's sociality has been kept alive, in part, through the sustained efforts and ongoing commitment of Quebec's ondists, who range in age from 56 to 79, and who continue to perform with the instrument regularly. Even though a cadre of scholars (Laurendeau, 1990; Tchamkerten, 2007; Chapman, 2009; Madden, 2013) and museums (the Musée de la musique de la Philharmonie de Paris; the National Music Centre, Calgary) have focused on the historicity of the ondes as one of the most important electronic musical instruments of the 20th century, very little has been written about the instrument's musical practices and its specialist players, known as ondists. There are approximately 40 formally trained ondes Martenot players in the world, primarily living in France, Canada and Japan (Martel, 2013). Of those, five ondists currently reside in Quebec: Bernard, Binet-Audet, Geneviève Grenier, Jean Laurendeau and Estelle Lemire. Laurendeau is a key figure in bringing the ondes to Quebec and taught the instrument for many years at the CMQM. He wrote a book on the ondes's inventor and the instrument, entitled *Maurice Martenot, luthier de l'électronique* (1990), and is a founding member of the Ensemble d'ondes de Montréal. Lemire is also a member of the Ensemble d'ondes de Montréal and, as noted, currently teaches the ondes at the CMQM. Grenier, the youngest of the five, performs and composes with the ondes and is also a member of the Ensemble d'ondes de Montréal.

Before moving on to discuss the musical lives of Binet-Audet and Bernard and our interactions and collaborations over the past seven or eight years, I outline some of the instrument's more recent history and how certain developments might work to interrupt the ondes's life course and play with, or distort, its past. In the past 20 years, the instrument has received a resurgence of attention within popular music circuits – largely because Jonny Greenwood from the English rock group Radiohead plays one and composes with it – and from musical instrument designers, universities, and large-scale museum projects and institutions in Canada and France. In brief, this renewed interest primarily comes from the fact that the ondes is retrospectively considered one of the most important instruments bridging classical and electronic music cultures, in terms of design, sound processing, time of invention, and somewhat extensive use by certain historically established Western composers. The instrument has also taken on a technological aura – again, especially in France, where it was invented, and in Canada, where it has a developed history since the 1960s. As mentioned above, two museums in particular, the National Music Centre (Calgary, Alberta, https://nmc.ca) and the Musée de la musique de la Philharmonie de Paris, have taken lead roles in conservation projects vis-à-vis the ondes (Madden, 2013). Rather unsurprisingly, perhaps, these institutions have reinscribed normative historical narratives of music and technology by primarily directing their efforts on the instrument itself, its inventor (Maurice Martenot), and the many male composers who composed for it. For instance, the website of the Musée de la musique de la Philharmonie de Paris mainly features photographs and documentation of fragments of the ondes, such as photographs of its keyboard and *diffuseurs* (Musée de la musique, n.d.). Going further, the site notes that the Musée de la musique "contributes to the development of both musical practice and culture, and of musical knowledge and its cultural heritage" (n.d., para. 2). It is important to point out, as Sara Cohen (2013) tells us, *heritage* "is a highly political and ideological term that is used and defined in many different ways but commonly associated with a sense of ownership rather than just knowledge of the past" (p. 581).

These museums continue to focus on normative historical threads in spite of the fact that the instrument's life course was largely maintained by the ondists who studied it and performed with it following its gendered dismissal in the mid-20th century. Put more pointedly, we would most likely know very little about the instrument today, including the extent of its cultural and national relevance, if these ondists had not continued playing the instrument and thereby keeping its sounding sociality alive. It would seem that in the ondes's own life course, it has gone from discarded novelty sound maker of the early 20th century to rescued and endangered cultural artifact of national prestige in one generation. Does this, in turn, contribute to making the living ondists cultural artifacts or relics of the past? Are these ondists living in the shadow of the instrument's afterlife?

Although a detour through the cultural politics of organology – the field of studying and creating knowledge about musical instruments (see Bijsterveld & Schulp, 2004; Tresch & Dolan, 2013) – is beyond the scope of this text, it is important to emphasize that the abovementioned museum conservation projects might be oppositional to, and somewhat incommensurable with, the desires of those currently playing these instruments and those who want to continue playing them in the future. Jonathan Sterne (2007) contends that traditionally the "field of organology is largely an exercise in formal classification" (p. 5). As he emphasizes, "[L]ike the natural historians, the organologists put all the instruments in their proper place, but they do not explain their genesis, function or meaning" (p. 5). And when they do, what does it contribute to our understandings of an instrument when it is classified and approached "like a frail elderly lady" (*une vieille dame malade*), as lab manager at the Musée de la musique in Paris, Stéphane Vaiedelich, refers to an ondes Martenot that is currently being studied by a group at the museum (Philharmonia Orchestra, n.d.)?[3]

Typically, for ondists, and as many other musicians playing any "endangered" instrument might tell you, their interests lie in keeping the ondes alive as a living and sounding instrument. According to the two ondists featured in more detail below, their instruments have idiosyncratic affordances and quirks; their priority is to maintain their ongoing playability and survival. They feel this is their responsibility. Given the age of these instruments, their scarcity, and how they are designed and constructed, they often require modifications that break with Martenot's "original" specifications and blueprints. As Marie Bernard suggests, the ondes is a "complicated" and "stressful" instrument and it needs continuous care, tuning and refinement, although she has been "lucky" with her ondes and it is in very good condition (pers. comm., December 6, 2016). The abovementioned ondist Geneviève Grenier, in contrast, has stopped using the *diffuseurs* that came with her instrument and has replaced them with a more reliable powered studio monitor and a digital reverb/echo effects pedal.[4] When I recently worked with Grenier on a studio recording project, she passionately expressed that she just wants to *play* her instrument, noting that ever since Martenot's passing in 1980, certain museum projects, instrument designers and professionals working within the culture of organology have halted the life course of some instruments by meticulously preserving and displaying them (pers. comm., November 21, 2016). The irony here, of course, is that the inventor Martenot devoted his whole life to improving and modifying the ondes and would most likely be carrying out this work today if he were still alive. As Bernard stresses, "When you stop playing an instrument, it dies" (pers. comm., December 6, 2016).

At this point, I will briefly delve into my own personal musical narrative and elaborate on how my life course became entwined with the two ondists. I am a lifelong practicing musician and I play many instruments – guitar, electric bass, drums and computer, primarily – although I have never been formally trained at a music conservatory, nor have I obtained a university-level degree in music. After finishing undergraduate studies at McGill University, I embarked on a rather common career trajectory for post-graduate-educated musicians and artists living in Montreal: I took on many forms of precarious employment, from cook to construction worker, while attempting to prioritize music-making and performing in various scenes. In the mid-2000s, I enrolled in graduate school in media studies at Concordia University, hoping to bring my musical interests more into the foreground of my everyday daytime life, and began honing my interests in cultural history, practice-based scholarship (known as research-creation in Canada), popular music and gender. While nearing the completion of my first graduate degree, I was invited as a research assistant and collaborator to join a research project centered on the theremin, ondes Martenot and Hammond organ.[5] Through the collaborative and research-creation components of the project I would first meet Binet-Audet, then Bernard, and gradually begin to work with them.

The ondists' im/material worlds

Sound waves can have powerful ripples and effects as they move through space, time and objects. They simultaneously touch our bodies and travel through our ears as audible sound, wherein one form of energy (mechanical) transduces into another (electrical). Sound waves propagate at the intersection of immaterial and material worlds, and in this way, they offer expansive pathways for connecting musical and sonic experience to material and immaterial memory. It is worth mentioning that wave metaphors, minus the sound, also abound in studies of memory. As I discuss in further detail below, the two women ondists suggested during our various encounters that they are bound to the ondes Martenot because of its pure, immaterial sound and the instrument's particular materiality – the contact with the small-scale keyboard, the feel of the ring and ribbon, the touch of the instrument's wood and its sound – even if they are at times unaware of and unable to articulate these connections after so many years of playing the instrument.

Since 2008, I have participated in numerous musical collaborations and semistructured interviews with Binet-Audet and Bernard, including recording sessions at Montreal's world-famous music studio Hotel2Tango.[6] In what follows I discuss these intermittent encounters, creative bursts and key methodologies in relation to the core research questions outlined above and the musical careers of these two women with the ondes Martenot and music, more generally. This work is related to that of a growing group of scholars undertaking historical cultural studies of music (Hodkinson, 2011; Bennett, 2013; Forman, 2013; Grenier & Valois-Nadeau, 2013), of gender (Whiteley, 2003; Jennings & Gardner, 2012; Taylor, 2012), of memory (van Dijck, 2009; Hyltén-Cavallius, 2012; Cohen, 2013), and of ageing (Calasanti & Slevin, 2006; Gullette, 2011; Grenier, 2012).

The notion of the career is largely missing in music scene analysis, and more generally, anything that has to do with time and with how people's position changes in relation to the contingencies of time remains understudied. Ageing is not the same as a career, I know, but they both have to do with trajectories and with experiencing different temporalities simultaneously. This temporal mode of analysis provides a generative theoretical tool for connecting studies of cultural production and technology with studies of ageing. In addition, bringing forth and representing the musical careers of Binet-Audet and Bernard responds to the call of Rodgers (2012) and others (cf. McCartney, 2003; Bosma, 2006) to expand the scope and frameworks of existing cultural histories of electronic music by crafting feminist historiographies of technology that "emphasize the substance and diversity of work that *has* been accomplished by women" (Rodgers, 2012, p. 482, original emphasis). The intimate im/material attachments and affective engagements that these two older women musicians share with the ondes Martenot and with each other work toward creating an "elsewhere" within electronic music discourses and practices: "a space for mutual encounters between humans and technologies, between familiarity and otherness, that motivates wonder and a sense of possibility" (p. 477). It is worth noting that this elsewhere space must be built to include the diverse experiences, memories and soundings of older women and their relationships to the past, present and future.

My intention is to present two distinct portraits of ageing trajectories and diverging relationships to the past and present vis-à-vis one electronic musical instrument (the ondes Martenot). Even though Binet-Audet and Bernard share many personal bonds, markers of identity and experiences – they are both from Quebec and both have devoted their lives to the ondes Martenot, for instance – each ondist has developed a particular connection with her own instrument. By focusing on the transformations and temporalities of their everyday lives, I aim to create an intimate portrait of ageing, which in its own ways challenges and disrupts totalizing and ageist discourses that construct the ageing population as, in the words of Katz (2005), a "burdensome and cumbersome behemoth" (p. 13). My semistructured interviews and musical collaborations (including performances and studio recording projects) with Binet-Audet and Bernard took place between 2008 and 2016, often with a couple of years between each interaction and with many personal transformations in between. And yet, while I proceed in a linear fashion for the purposes of this text from one musician to the next, I must emphasize that my memory resists, as Freeman, Nienass and Daniel (2016) write, such "strict choreography" (p. 3).

Loving the ondes Martenot

I first met Binet-Audet in 2008 through the Quebec filmmaker Caroline Martel, who made a documentary on the instrument entitled *Le chant des ondes* (2012), and for whom I am forever indebted for the introduction. Binet-Audet is featured in the documentary, and during filming I was invited to participate in a recording session in Montreal at the aforementioned Hotel2Tango music studio. I played electric guitar. The recording was entirely improvised, meaning we had never played together before and did not follow any predetermined scripts, or in musical language, scores.

Binet-Audet was born in 1942 and is a world-renowned ondist who lives in Montreal. She studied organ at the Conservatoire de musique du Québec à Québec (CMQQ) and then at the Conservatoire de Paris, where she first encountered the ondes Martenot. Binet-Audet trained with the ondist Jeanne Loriod as well as with Maurice Martenot himself. She received diplomas from both the Conservatoire de Paris and the École Superieure de Musique. She has performed in many parts of the world as an ondist and has played with the Ensemble d'ondes de Montréal since its inception in the mid-1970s. Binet-Audet began playing the ondes in Paris in the 1960s after a chance encounter with ondist Jean Laurendeau that she refers to as "a stroke of luck." For Binet-Audet, listening to a performance of Messiaen's *Turangalîla-Symphonie* featuring Jeanne Loriod was "love at first sight." I interviewed Binet-Audet at her home in Montreal in the spring of 2008, and this is how she told the story of her first meeting with the instrument.

> I went to Paris in the 1960s. At the time I was very interested in Olivier Messiaen and his whole repertoire. I saw that the *Turangalîla* was playing, so I decided to go, not knowing the piece. Jeanne Loriod was playing the ondes Martenot and I did not know that either. When I heard the instrument I was staggered. Really, I fell in love, right there. It was truly love at first sight. I could relate to the sound, as if I had

found something. What was being expressed was both atavistic and very new to me.

When I left the concert I took the subway and went in the wrong direction for two stations. I got off the subway and was completely lost. I went for a walk and found myself facing the concert hall. I saw Jean Laurendeau, an ondist from Montreal. I told him about the concert and I shared my astonishing experience with this new instrument. I asked him if he happens to know this instrument. He tells me that it is the ondes Martenot and that he studies it with Jeanne Loriod. Jean then invites me to his place to play the instrument. He also played a record of Jacques Charpentier's Lalita that Jeanne Loriod had just finished. I knew right away that I really loved the instrument. (pers. comm., April 16, 2008)[7]

Some of the music that Binet-Audet and I produced together in Montreal during the one-day recording session would go toward scoring Martel's film: most prominently during the closing credits, where there is a three-minute guitar and ondes duet entitled *Vers l'or*.[8] There is tension in the piece. I would later find out from Martel that Binet-Audet was attempting to push and pull the musical time during the recording, as I held the piece's foundation with an unwavering and somewhat commanding arpeggio guitar figure. The recording session was my first encounter with the ondes as a complicated and unreliable instrument. After we had set up our instruments and done an initial sound check, one of Binet-Audet's *diffuseurs* broke down for the remainder of the day, creating an additional layer of stress to the studio environment and Binet-Audet's relationship with the instrument. This is how Binet-Audet describes her own interfacing with the instrument:

> We have many different timbres to incorporate and play with. The sound of the ondes Martenot is made up of pure sine tones and timbres are created when we add harmonics, thus changing the wave shape. It is always a play between purity and complexity; always this

relation between an electrical sound with the immaterial, the body and the soul of the player.

Sound awaits, is what happens between the musician and the sound of the instrument. The sound of ondes Martenot is something immaterial. We cannot feel anything tangible, such as the bow's stroke on the violin's string. The sound does not have the same kind of materialness as other instruments, and strangely, every instrument that has this material sound tries to purify it, to eliminate it. With the ondes, on the other hand, there's something already very pure, and the relation we have with this sound is one of complete embodiment. It is as if the sound was so pure that our body becomes this sound, to give it a human character. It is an immaterial sound touched by the body. (pers. comm., April 16, 2008)

Performing intimacies

Embodying the sound of the ondes comes by way of an ondist's physical and affective relationship to some of the instrument's most unique material features: the small-scale keyboard with its 15-centimeter white keys that players can vibrate with their right hand for vibrato effects and the ribbon, which, again, players control by placing the index finger of their right hand through a metal ring. With this particular attachment site, the intimate connection between musician and instrument is literally and metaphorically forged through a musical engagement ring. Here is how Binet-Audet describes the ondes's expressive powers. (In musical notation, *f*, or forte (loud), is a marking used to denote dynamics in musical scores.)

> Because of the way the ondes Martenot is made, and because of the highly sensitive touch, we can make perfect continuous sounds. We can also go all the way to the four *f*s, or very very loud. The continuous touch can therefore correspond very precisely with the unconscious

musical intent of the ondist. When you play music not everything is fully conscious. There is a musical form of thinking, a musical intention, and then there is what carries us, the momentum of the moment and the unconscious. Like a continuation of the nervous system, the ondes translates, just like the voice does. It is a very intimate experience. The ondes is a very malleable instrument and an ondist can totally shape the sound. (pers. comm., April 16, 2008)

Fig. 1: The ring and ribbon of the ondes Martenot, by which the ondist can create lyrical effects such as glissando.

Photo: Magdalena Olszanowski

An understanding of broader historical shifts in classical and electronic musical instrument design and development and an understanding of the pedagogical need to continue teaching the ondes shape Binet-Audet's own sense of the instrument's changing life course and its future imaginings. In this way, the ondes mediates between intimate experience and cultural memory, thereby enabling Binet-Audet and the other ondists to develop affective attachments to both the past and the future. For instance, the harpsichord remained largely out of use throughout most of the 19th century, and in the 20th century there was a renewed interest in the instrument on the part of performers, composers and instrument makers. A similar revival of the lute occurred in the second half of the 20th century, after the instrument flourished throughout most of the 16th and 17th centuries in Western Europe. Binet-Audet sees these changes as the shifting ebbs and flows of a musical instrument's life course, and like many with connections to classical music scenes, her imagination can easily stretch forwards and backwards 400 years. The ondist continues:

> I believe in a future for the ondes Martenot because I think it is an instrument that cannot be forgotten, for many reasons, including the repertoire of the French composers Messiaen and Tristan Murail. On the other hand, in one hundred years, what will remain of these pieces? Will they still be played? We must play them now so that they continue to exist. We also need to build new instruments. And most importantly, the ondes must be taught. And then eventually, yes, there will be a rebirth. I believe in this because the ondes "speaks" in such a unique way. What form will this revival take? I don't know, but the Martenot principle, the touch, the vibrato and this sound – I don't think it will ever disappear. (pers. comm., April 16, 2008)

During the past ten years, Binet-Audet's long-term relationship with the ondes has undergone several changes. The instrument's noted complicated existence and constant maintenance have affected the musician's desire to continue playing it. She rarely performs publicly with the ondes anymore, and I have had very little contact with her over the past five years. These personal anxieties with the instrument might also be exasperated by so many years of working as an interpreter and performer within a variety of classical music scenes where, as Bijsterveld and Schulp (2004) write, "professional classical music players are tied to critical-attentive audiences, watchful conductors, ever-present colleagues and well-known scores that function as the final arbiters of playing" (p. 656). The authors contend: "[A]midst these high demands, the musical instruments are both vehicles for coordination *among* the performers and, literally and metaphorically, important mainstays *for* the performers" (p. 656, original emphasis). These demands are perhaps even more heavily felt by ondists, because when they perform within the context of an orchestra they are very often working as soloists and might remain somewhat isolated from the other instrumentalists, especially when they do not have previous relationships with them. Furthermore, until the production of Martenot's model 7 in 1975, ondists would have to make tuning adjustments *throughout* an orchestral performance – usually after every movement – as model 6 could not stay in tune for extended periods of time.

Fig. 2: Marie Bernard.

Photo : Magdalena Olszanowski

Quebec and the daily pleasures of playing

Binet-Audet's hesitation to perform with the instrument led to my own chance encounter with Marie Bernard at the premiere of Martel's film on the ondes at the Montreal International Documentary Festival (RIDM) in 2012. Martel asked Binet-Audet and me to perform the abovementioned musical piece *Vers l'or* at the Cinémathèque québécoise during the reception for the film's world premiere; however, in the week leading up to the performance Binet-Audet canceled, and Bernard offered to step in. Again, I would meet an ondist through an improvisation: Bernard and I met for only a five-minute conversation to make introductions and to discuss our performance before taking the stage. We used *Vers l'or* as the foundation and point of departure for the improvisation. This time, rather than guitar, I played synthesizer and computer with audio editing software that has a variety of effects to choose from. Although my recollection of the performance remains very positive, I was unable to confirm Bernard's impressions of the night until very recently, as we did not have time to discuss the performance that night. And then time passes and questions linger.

After nearly four years of not seeing each other, I contacted Bernard in the spring of 2016 about the possibility of participating in an interview for the purposes of this text and making music together again, perhaps at a recording studio or for another performance. After six months of intermittent emails and an in-person meeting where she asked, "Why me?" we finally agreed to spend a day together at her home in Charlevoix, Quebec. Marie Bernard was born in 1951 and received first prize at the Conservatoire de musique du Québec à Montréal in the ondes Martenot competition of 1978. Throughout the 1970s, she worked on many recording sessions with the Quebec orchestrator and composer François Dompierre, which led to the production of numerous film, television and theatre scores, and also recorded the ondes with several Quebec popular music artists – perhaps most notably on Harmonium's (1975) album *Si on avait besoin d'une cinquième saison*, and with Beau Dommage (1975) on their cut

»Un incident à Bois-des-Filion«. Bernard has also composed many well-known choral works, including the *Petite suite québécoise* (1979), which is a classic among francophone choirs, and *Vaste est la vie* (2000) for 2300 choristers, in addition to collaborating with the Red Army Choir in the 1980s.

Interviewing the ondist over the course of one day at her home in Charlevoix and hearing her play the ondes left me feeling like she has done everything there is to do within Quebec's music culture. Bernard shares the property and home she helped design with her dog, a Bouvier des Flandres. The loss of her previous dog marked one of the most challenging moments in her life course: one that formed the creative foundation of her last major choral work – *8 Haikus Souffle-lumière* (2011). At the of 65 she says she has finally found what she wants to do – sing and compose original works for the ondes Martenot – after working "like a robot" for over 40 years and living what she describes as a "double life" (pers. comm., December 6, 2016). This double life entailed taking on project after project as accompanist, composer and/or orchestrator to earn a decent living while also devoting time and energy to her musical love, the ondes Martenot. Bernard owns ondes Martenot no. 295, which she keeps in near-perfect condition in an open room at her home beside a baby grand piano, ready to be played at any instant. This is how Bernard describes the beginnings of her love affair with the ondes:

> One evening in the 1970s when I was a piano student at the CMQM, practicing a sonata alone in the building, or so I thought, I heard an enchanting and mysterious sound coming from a studio down the corridor. I stopped playing, filled with wonder, hooked by the waves of sound that washed over me like a love song from the far reaches of the universe. The very next day I began to play the ondes Martenot. In 1978, I was awarded a Premier Prix du Concours as a player of this instrument. (pers. comm., December 6, 2016)

Bernard's ageing with the ondes has undergone many different moments of disruption and transformation since the 1980s, including taking intermittent breaks from the instrument in the 1990s when the musical commissions started to take up too much of her time. She keeps returning to the ondes as a musical home by finding new ways and contexts to rediscover and return to the initial love she felt for the instrument in the 1970s.

> While playing the ondes, I was also composing and arranging music for film, television, the theatre and discs, including choral works and music of all kinds. These commissions were so demanding of my time that I had to stop performing on my beloved ondes Martenot. Then, in 2000, my life changed when I met the psychoanalyst, writer and lecturer Guy Corneau (1951–2017). He asked me to participate in and provide musical accompaniment for the large seminars that he was organizing in Quebec and in Europe.
>
> Through these seminars I rediscovered the pleasure of playing and improvising with the ondes. Sliding the metal ring along its wire in front of the keyboard during moments of introspection and meditation, I let my soul sing freely, touched just like the very first time I heard the vibrations of the ondes in the 1970s. Why does sliding and dancing the ring along my instrument's wire make me feel so loving and peaceful? (pers. comm., December 6, 2016)

Throughout her over 40-year career in music, the ondist has been continually urged by colleagues, friends, partners and family members to create more of a "balanced life," one that affords time for friendships, her dog and the things she enjoys in life. Bernard has increasingly brought the ondes to the foreground of her musical life since becoming reacquainted with the pleasure of playing and improvising with the instrument in 2000, thereby reducing the amount of time she spends on commissions and living a double life. Moving to the countryside in

Charlevoix and building her dream home has eased this transition as well.

In May 2017, Bernard presented her first major public performance of original musical works using the ondes and her own voice. The catalyst for this particular musical thread emerged many years ago while she was working with the Quebec singer and artist Diane Dufresne, with whom Bernard has collaborated as a producer and songwriter on the albums *Détournement majeur* (1993), *Comme un parfum de confession* (1997) and *Effusions* (2007), among other projects. While composing a "sort of South American"–inspired song for Dufresne, Bernard decided to sing and play the music herself, accompanied by the ondes. She started weeping when she finished playing the new composition, realizing in that moment that she wanted to sing. She had dreamed of singing her whole life, and with the ondes Martenot in the 1970s, she discovered an instrument that could perform her voice as an extension of her body. Bernard now wants to bring these elements together. As she told me, "I am working on *songs*, my voice and the ondes Martenot." The spring 2017 show was in Montreal at the performance venue Agora de la danse. Bernard is using the performance as a way to garner attention from festival producers and bookers, in the hopes of securing future tours and continuing her life course with music and the ondes Martenot.

Bernard expressed to me her inner desire to vocalize and sing through the ondes's many lyrical sound-making possibilities. The noted intimacy and malleability of the instrument's interface and touch, combined with the fact that the ondes is monophonic, allows players to recreate and mimic human singing voices. Almost all of the features on Bernard's model 7 ondes from the late 1970s remain functional; only a few of the timbre adjustments are not working, and she has resisted having the instrument totally upgraded and refined with new features – cabling, keyboard modifications, etc. – for fear of making too many adjustments that might unduly "change" the instrument forever. She describes her ondes as having a "magic note," the G in its lowest register, which easily rattles the instrument's wooden *diffuseurs*. The effect of this magic note is similar to what is usually referred to as an instrument's wolf tone, wherein an amplified overtone is produced when a played note connects with the natural resonating frequency of the body of a musical instrument – most commonly in bowed instruments such as the cello. A wolf tone, or magic note, expands the sound of the played note, thereby producing a phenomenon that some liken to a wolf's howling.

In a similar way to Binet-Audet – whom Bernard refers to as her sister ondist – the ondist finds particular aspects of her musical life performing with the ondes stressful. Unlike Binet-Audet, Bernard continues to play the ondes almost daily and is still interested in performing and recording with it. In addition to the aforementioned tuning issues, which have caused Bernard many problems at performances and in the studio, certain musical works place heavy demands on players, in terms of their degree of difficulty, their particular sonic profiles, and the bodily gesturing required while playing them. Bernard finds many contemporary classical music works for the ondes "painful to play": for instance, she says that by the time she plays the final note of *Mach 2,5* (1971) for two to six ondes by the French composer Tristan Murail, her nerves feel "frayed." More specifically, the composition is very strenuous for ondists to perform as they require a high level of endurance and concentration to properly execute the continuous subtle microtonal movement throughout the piece.

While I was visiting Bernard at her home in Charlevoix, she demonstrated *Begonia Rex* (1977), a contemporary composition she loves by the Canadian composer Richard Boucher, who has created many works for the Ensemble d'ondes de Montréal. The piece requires such a range of movement with the ondes's ring that ondists sometimes break the ribbon of their instrument. As Bernard plays these works she often wishes she could be in the audience receiving them, rather than playing them, as they often leave her feeling exhausted by the time the final notes are played. However, in classical music scenes composers and conductors hold great control over players and decision-making and thereby usually decide which pieces are to be played at concerts. This intense division of labor was cemented through the romantic notion of the primacy of the musical work, which, as Georgina Born (2005) argued, "guided both conducting and performing, auguring hierarchical relations between composer and interpreters, and between conductor and players" (p. 9). Working within this particular hierarchical setting has strengthened Bernard's resolve to compose and perform her own music, while simultaneously lessening her desire to perform as an ondist within the contemporary classical music scene.

For the first time in her life, the ondist is singing on a regular basis, after spending so many years composing works for vocalists and choirs, and playing an instrument that mimics the voice. While I was at her home in December of 2016, she fittingly performed an interpretation of Joni Mitchell's (1991) late-career autobiographical reflection "Come In from the Cold," from the album *Night Ride Home*. Mitchell moves from the past to the present in the song and sings in the final verse:

> When I thought life had some meaning
> Then I thought I had some choice
> (I was running blind)
> And I made some value judgments
> In a self-important voice
> (I was outa line)
> But then absurdity came over me
> And I longed to lose control
> (Into no mind)
> Oh all I ever wanted
> Was just to come in from the cold (Mitchell, 1991)

Fig. 3: Marie Bernard at home with her ondes Martenot and dog.

Photo: Magdalena Olszanowski

Conclusion

By telling the stories of two creative interpreters of the ondes Martenot in Quebec and thereby advancing scholarship addressing the various ways that electronic musical instruments are used in social and performative contexts, this chapter works toward altering the epistemological foundations of electronic and popular music history as the soundings and contributions of women greatly increase in these settings. The approach of this study of ageing trajectories, temporalities and musical careers is to listen to these two older women artists in the places where they are making multifaceted and diverse contributions, from the recording studio, performance settings and various music scenes to music schools, orchestras and the home. Hannah Bosma (1998) argues that focusing on women as composers and performers is both an empirical-historical activity and also a symbolic one, as "it produces representations and role models of female composers" (p. 1) working, producing and playing in many different contexts, whether electronic music (including computer music, *musique concrète* and electroacoustic music), popular music or classical music scenes. As players and performers of the ondes Martenot, Suzanne Binet-Audet and Marie Bernard play crucial roles in maintaining the sociality and life course of the instrument while also making significant contributions to musical technique and style, in that they very often act as second authors in performing the works of composers and hold the responsibility of transforming sheet music into audible sound. As composers they challenge and disrupt some of the most dominant and established conceptions of Western music history, where the role of the composer is usually reserved for (mostly white) men. Their stories also inherently defy dominant narratives of youth and music.

Sverker Hyltén-Cavallius (2012) argues that "all memory requires selection and is constituted as much by forgetting and neglect as by that which is actually remembered, which means that an understanding of memory also requires us to reflect upon that which is not remembered" (p. 280). As the ondes Martenot continues to move along its conservational path in museums and other institutions of national and cultural authority, scholars must also attend to the changing life courses of the instrument itself and the ondists who play it, and how the passage of time alters their relations to each other. Musical instruments are designed to be played, modified and marked by the (daily) gestures and care afforded by musicians and those who come into contact with them. For instance, simply turning the ondes Martenot on and playing the instrument every day prevents oxidization problems and galvanic corrosion that eventually leads to the degradation of components. Any keyboard with mechanical switches faces this oxidization problem, unless one seals the switch contacts in a vacuum or with an inert gas. This kind of continuous care and playing also provides clues and messages for future generations of players and musical instrument designers, among others, both in terms of how the instrument is to be played *and* maintained, thereby potentially ensuring its survival and futher soundings. Remember, as Bernard previously stated, "When you stop playing an instrument, it dies."

The ondists' ageing narrative with the ondes Martenot reveals a continuously transforming relationship between them and their instruments, and is marked by disruption, change and renewal. My many and varied encounters with these two musicians through the years – semistructured interviews, performances and studio recording sessions – suggest that their instruments have their own changing "personalities" and life courses, and in many ways have provided them with long-term companionship, love and loss. In material terms, these attachments have been fortified through the ondes's musical engagement ring, in addition to its other idiosyncratic, delicate and malleable component parts, and through the instrument's aforementioned immaterial sound: a sound that simultaneously touches the body while also performatively acting as an extension of the body, through its connection to human voices. At the same time, these encounters suggest that the ondes Martenot is not a singular musical instrument, nor a static artifact, as Binet-Audet and Bernard have experienced their own distinct life courses with two distinct instruments. Binet-Audet's ondes Martenot has needed more modifications and maintenance through the years, and as a result, the ondist has recently stopped playing and performing with the instrument, primarily due to the increasing anxiety that she associates with it. Bernard, in contrast, is finally discovering at the age of 65, after living what she calls a "double life" for so many years, that all she wants to do is compose, perform and sing with her ondes.

Notes

1. The first six models of the instrument used heterodyning radio waves to produce its sounds. On the ondes and heterodyning signal processing, see, for instance, Laurendeau (1990) and Chapman (2009).

2. For a more thorough description of how to play the ondes Martenot, see, for instance, Laurendeau (1990) and Chapman (2009).
3. To answer that question, we can turn to the vast feminist science and technology studies (STS) literature of the past three decades that acknowledges the multifaceted ways in which the gendering of technology affects the entire trajectory of artifacts (Wajcman, 2009).
4. *Diffuseurs* (or "diffusers" in English) are the set of speakers that produce the instrument's sounds.
5. I was a research assistant for Owen Chapman (Concordia University) while he was preparing to write a Fonds de recherche du Québec – Société et culture (FRQSC) grant entitled »Radio activités: une généalogie du theremin, les ondes Martenot et l'orgue Hammond.«
6. Hotel2Tango (hotel2tango.com) has been a key site for music production in Montreal since its inception as a commercial recording studio in 2000. Situated in Montreal's Mile End neighborhood, it is a place where many well-known Montreal popular music artists have recorded, including Arcade Fire, Coeur de pirate, Godspeed You! Black Emperor, Wolf Parade, Ice Nine and Lesbians on Ecstasy.
7. This interview was conducted in French and translated by my colleague David Paquette.
8. To listen to this musical composition, refer to https://soundcloud.com/ravedm/vers-lor-extended.

Musical works cited

Beau Dommage. (1975). Un incident à Bois-des-Filion. In *Où est passée la noce?* [Vinyl]. Los Angeles: Capitol Records.

Dufresne, Diane. (1993). *Détournement majeur* [CD]. Montreal: Les Disques Amérilys.

Dufresne, Diane. (1997). *Comme un parfum de confession* [CD]. Montreal: Les Disques Amérilys.

Dufresne, Diane. (2007). *Effusions* [CD]. Montreal: Disques Présences.

Harmonium. (1975). *Si on avait besoin d'une cinquième saison* [Vinyl]. Baarn, Netherlands: PolyGram.

Mitchell, Joni. (1991). Come in from the cold. In *Night Ride Home* [CD]. New York: Geffen Records.

References

Bennett, Andy. (2013). *Music, style and aging: Growing old disgracefully?* Philadelphia: Temple University Press.

Bijsterveld, Karin, & Schulp, Marten. (2004). Breaking into a world of perfection: Innovation in today's classical musical instruments. *Social Studies of Science,* 34(5), 649–674.

Born, Georgina. (2005). On musical mediation: Ontology, technology and creativity. *Twentieth-Century Music,* 2(1), 7–30.

Bosma, Hannah. (1998). The death of the singer: Authorship and female voices in electronic music. *eContact!,* 1(3). http://econtact.ca/1_3/Bosma.html.

Bosma, Hannah. (2006). Musical washing machines, composer-performers, and other blurring boundaries: How women make a difference in electroacoustic music. *Intersections: Canadian Journal of Music,* 26(2), 97–117.

Brewer, John. (2010). Microhistory and the histories of everyday life. *Cultural and Social History: The Journal of the Social History Society,* 7(1), 87–109.

Calasanti, Toni M., & Slevin, Kathleen F. (Eds.). (2006). *Age matters: Realigning feminist thinking.* London: Routledge.

Chapman, Owen. (2009, Spring). Radio activity: Articulating the theremin, ondes Martenot and Hammond organ. *Wi: Journal of Mobile Media.* http://wi.hexagram.ca/?p=44.

Cohen, Sara. (2013). Musical memory, heritage and local identity: Remembering the popular music past in a European capital of culture. *International Journal of Cultural Policy,* 19(5), 576–594.

DeNora, Tia. (1997). Music and erotic agency: Sonic resources and sonic-sexual action. *Body and Society, 3*(2), 43–65.

Forman, Murray. (2013). Kill the static: Temporality and change in the hip-hop mainstream (and its 'Other'). In Sara Baker, Andy Bennett, & Jodie Taylor (Eds.), *Redefining mainstream popular music* (pp. 61–74). New York: Routledge.

Freeman, Lindsey A., Nienass, Benjamin, & Daniel, Rachel. (2016). Memory | Materiality | Sensuality [Editorial]. *Memory Studies, 9*(1), 3–12.

Grenier, Amanda. (2012). *Transitions and the lifecourse: Challenging the constructions of 'growing old.'* Bristol: Policy Press.

Grenier, Line, & Valois-Nadeau, Fannie. (2013). Vous êtes tous des gagnants. "Étoile des ainés" et le vieillissement réussi au Québec. *Recherches sociologiques et anthropologiques, 40*(1), 137–156.

Gullette, Margaret M. (2004). *Aged by culture.* Chicago: University of Chicago Press.

Gullette, Margaret M. (2011). *Agewise: Fighting the new ageism in America.* Chicago: University of Chicago Press.

Hodkinson, Paul. (2011). Ageing in a spectacular 'youth culture': Continuity, change and community amongst older goths. *British Journal of Sociology, 62*(2), 262–282.

Hyltén-Cavallius, Sverker. (2012). Memoryscapes and mediascapes: Musical formations of 'pensioners' in late 20th-century Sweden. *Popular Music, 31*(2), 279–295. doi :10.1017/S0261143012000050.

Jennings, Ros, & Gardner, Abigail. (2012). *'Rock on': Women, ageing and popular music.* Abingdon, UK: Ashgate.

Katz, Stephen. (2005). *Cultural aging: Life course, lifestyle, and senior worlds.* Toronto: University of Toronto Press.

Katz, Stephen. (2014). Music, performance, and generation: The making of boomer rock and roll biographies. In C. Lee Harrington, Denise D. Bielby, & Anthony R. Bardo (Eds.), *Aging, media, and culture* (pp. 93–106). Lanham, MD: Lexington Books.

Laurendeau, Jean. (1990). *Maurice Martenot, luthier de l'électronique.* Montreal: Louise Courteau.

Loriod, Jeanne. (1987–99). *Technique de l'onde électronique, type Martenot* (Vols. 1–3). Paris: Alphonse Leduc.

Madden, David. (2013, March). Advocating sonic restoration: Les ondes Martenot in practice. *Wi: Journal of Mobile Media, 7*(1). http://wi.mobilities.ca/advocating-sonic-restoration-les-ondes-martenot-in-practice.

Martel, Caroline (Director). (2012). *Le chant des ondes* [Film]. National Film Board.

Martel, Caroline. (2013). The ondes Martenot is making new waves. *Musicworks*, no. 117.

McCartney, Andra. (2003). In and out of the sound studio. *Organised Sound, 8*(1), 89–96.

McCartney, Andra. (2006). Gender, genre and electroacoustic sound-making practices. *Intersections: Canadian Journal of Music 26*(2), 20–48.

Musée de la musique de la Philharmonie de Paris. (N.d.). The establishment. https://philharmoniedeparis.fr/en/institution/presentation/establishment.

Musée de la musique de la Philharmonie de Paris. (N.d.). Musée de la musique. http://philharmoniedeparis.fr/en/museumexhibitions.

Philharmonia Orchestra (London, UK). (N.d.). *City of light: Making the ondes Martenot speak* [Video]. https://www.youtube.com/watch?v=xpj8ifQdsJA.

Rodgers, Tara. (2010). *Pink noises: Women on electronic music and sound*. Durham, NC: Duke University Press.

Rodgers, Tara. (2012). Towards a feminist historiography of electronic music. In Jonathan Sterne (Ed.), *The sound studies reader* (pp. 475–490). London: Routledge.

Steedman, Carolyn K. (1986). *Landscape for a good woman: A story of two lives*. London: Virago.

Sterne, Jonathan. (2007, September). Media or instruments? Yes. *Offscreen, 11*(8–9).

Taylor, Jodie. (2012). Performances of post-youth sexual identities in queer scenes. In Andy Bennett & Paul Hodkinson (Eds.), *Ageing and youth cultures: Music, syle and identity* (pp. 24–36). Oxford: Berg.

Tchamkerten, Jacques. (2007). From *Fête des belles eaux* to *Saint Francois d'Assise*: The evolution of the writing for ondes Martenot in the music of Olivier Messiaen. In Christopher Dingle & Nigel Simeone (Eds.), *Olivier Messiaen: Music, art and literature* (pp. 63–78). London: Ashgate.

Tresch, John, & Dolan, Emily I. (2013). Toward a new organology: Instruments of music and science. *Osiris, 28*(1), 278–298.

van Dijck, José. (2009). Remembering songs through telling stories: Pop music as a resource for memory. In Karin Bijsterveld & José van Dijck (Eds.), *Sound souvenirs: Audio technologies, memory and cultural practices* (pp. 107–122). Amsterdam: Amsterdam University Press.

Wajcman, Judy. (2009). Feminist theories of technology. *Cambridge Journal of Economics, 34*(1), 143–152.

Whiteley, Sheila. (2003). *Too much too young: Popular music, age and gender.* New York: Routledge.

Chapter 5: "Dis-placement," Ageing and Remembering
Case Study of a Transnational Family

Helmi Järviluoma

> Wonder occurs at the horizon line of what is potentially knowable, but not yet known. We learn about this horizon line when we find ourselves in a state of wonder. Surprise has guided us to something where we can invest energy and time in a profitable way.
> – Philip Fisher, *The Vehement Passions*

A few years ago I visited an intergenerational household in the Åland Islands, a region of Finland situated in the southwest, between the Finnish mainland and Sweden.[1] The ageing grandmother of the family had been born in Pakistan, and I was taken by surprise by the household's continuous internet connection with Pakistan, with a computer on a living-room table constantly connected to the Skype application. The connection seemed to play a crucial role in the life of the household, forming something which, at the time, I thought of as a firm media bridge to Asia. As a consequence, this chapter has grown out of wonder. The surprise that I experienced has guided me toward something in which I have started to invest "energy and time in a profitable way," to use the words of Philip Fisher (2002) in his book *The Vehement Passions*.

This research combines many of my earlier as well as present research interests, including my studies concerned with place, memory, music and the senses. One of these is the participatory music ethnography project Becoming Audible (BA).[2] The main goals of the project were to empower and encourage asylum seekers in Finland to create networks, to learn the language, and to keep up their spirits during the stressful period of waiting for the decision about whether they would be permitted to stay in Finland.[3] During the past decade or so, much has changed for the asylum seekers with whom we were working in the BA project. For example, the grandmother mentioned at the start of this chapter – let us call her Rubina[4] – received permission to stay in Finland. She has now reached retirement age and is drawing her pension. Rubina divides her time between Sweden (Stockholm, where her son Nabeel's family lives) and Finland (the Åland Islands, where her daughter Azizah's family lives). In other words, her mobile life repeatedly takes her between Finland and Sweden on the Baltic Sea ferries.

Fig. 1: Map showing the locations of Rubina's Nordic homes, as of 2014: Stockholm (Sweden), the Åland Islands (Finland), and (to a very minor extent) Turku (Finland)

In this chapter my aim is to focus on the intergenerational, transcultural and socio-musical remembering of Rubina's family in a digital world that has recently exploded. At the start of this chapter, I described something that I thought was a firm and constant media bridge linking the transnational family to Pakistan. After further fieldwork, the question proved to be much more complex, and my research questions developed. How do the different members of the same family – who arrived in Sweden (and Finland) at different times – remember their mediated musical past? What kind of narratives do they produce? Do they share intergenerational memories? I embarked with musical remembering in mind, but it proved to be impossible to isolate cultural mediations dealing with music from the wide range of other mediations, and different technologies used in the family.

Here, I am assuming a definition of mediation that goes beyond technical media: present moments of bodies and minds are always-already mediated, delineated and enriched by the past (e.g., see Kember & Zylinska, 2012). However, especially with reference to the ageing grandmother Rubina, it is relevant to ask whether extreme digitization impacts on the social, and socio-musical, remembering of an immigrant family. I pay careful attention throughout the analysis to the challenges and blessings connected to ageing and technology. As De Cesari and Rigney (2014) argue, it is a matter of urgency for scholars "in the field of memory studies to develop new theoretical frameworks, invent new methodological tools, and identify new sites and archival resources for studying collective remembrance beyond the nation-state" (p. 1). I hope this chapter will contribute to that emerging discussion.

Encounters in Stockholm

Over the years, Rubina and I have developed a friendship (for more about this, see Järviluoma, 2010). For the research interview, we arranged a time for me to visit the family in Stockholm in 2014, in the suburb of Loppnäs, where Rubina shares a home with her son. The upshot: this extraordinarily hospitable family hosted me for three days, refusing all my attempts to stay in a hotel. I traveled by subway to the suburb, where we had arranged to meet. Rubina arrived dressed in trousers and a long green tunic, a greenish coat and with a black scarf tied under her chin. After a hug we started walking, heading for a block of flats right next to the metro station. These high-rise buildings looked fairly badly maintained, partly because the doorways were painted in the old-fashioned colors of olive green, beige and gray, and the paint was flaked in places. The apartment itself, however, was modern and full of light. It had two bedrooms and a living room, and there was a glass door between the living room and the kitchen that let the light shine into the kitchen.

Rana, Rubina's new daughter-in-law (married to her son Nabeel), whom I had never met before, welcomed me immediately with a kiss, holding her eight-month-old baby in her arms. She was wearing *shalwar kameez* and, to my eyes, appeared unpretentious. Azizah, Rubina's daughter – she had come from the Åland Islands with the youngest of her three children, a three-year-old girl – greeted me joyfully as well. She was dressed in a mixed Swedish-Asian tunic: the cut was Swedish, while the colors and print figures struck me as Asian. In the living room we sat down on the fuchsia-colored sofas with their flowery cushions, and the youngest of the women, Rana, offered snacks and juice. Her husband was at work when I arrived: he is well educated and has a well-paying job. In the living room, I saw a large television screen, some 50 inches wide, joysticks, and an apparently new stereo system. Numerous media gadgets of different kinds could be seen beneath the television, including a Digibox (satellite receiver) and a DVD player. I also counted three computers in the living room: a desktop PC, an iPad and a laptop. We exchanged our news and talked about quite serious matters immediately: illnesses and unemployment.

During my three-day stay I conducted a group interview involving the whole family – an interesting experience. I ended up speaking to a total of four individuals – Rubina, Azizah, Nabeel and his wife, Rana – in different constellations (see more in the next section); I also spoke with the aid of Skype to Azizah's daughter in the Åland Islands.

Midway through the interview, Nabeel returned from work, and the three women repeatedly left the living room to attend to the needs of the children.

Perhaps at this point I should point out that only the grandmother, Rubina, has been a refugee, a one-time asylum seeker who, earlier in her life, belonged to the Pakistani upper-middle class. Four of her children are middle-class immigrants into Nordic countries. How has this been possible? I cannot, obviously, reveal the reason why in 2001 Rubina suddenly applied for asylum in Finland, when she was still living in Pakistan with her husband. What I can reveal is that at the age of 18 she had married a man with a flourishing international career. She moved from country to country with her family (see below for a more detailed narrative), arriving in Sweden for the first time more than 30 years ago. It is also worth mentioning that, in the end, Rubina was not granted "asylum" but received a permanent residence permit on compassionate grounds.

I next introduce the conceptual and methodological framework of the chapter, and then proceed to shed further light on the different histories or, rather, the different listening locations that Rubina and her children have in relation to their socio-musical and other social remembering, especially when it comes to media. Finally, I will attempt to draw conclusions about the different narratives that emerged from a long group interview in Stockholm in spring 2014.

Conceptual and methodological framework

> To plot only 'places of birth' and degrees of nativeness is to blind oneself to the multiplicity of attachments that people form to places through living in, remembering, and imagining them.
> – Liisa Malkki, "National Geographic"[5]

Liisa Malkki (1992) suggests that earlier refugee studies looked at refugees as human beings torn away from their roots and hence as people who have lost their culture, becoming cultureless and, in a way, naked. I will offer, in this chapter, an alternative view of one refugee and her family: Rubina is not cultureless or naked, but a transnational, ageing woman who has, during her long, utterly mobile life, formed a multiplicity of attachments to places through living in, remembering and imagining them.

During the interview in that suburban apartment in Loppnäs, Stockholm, I realized that my earlier conception of the constant media bridge linking the Åland Islands to Asia had misled me. I needed to understand the reasons for my immediate assumption that the transnational family was living as if in a Skype bubble between the Åland Islands and Pakistan. One reason was obvious. I found out later that a year before my visit to the Åland Islands, Azizah had been married: her new Pakistani spouse was present in the family via the constant Skype connection, and when he moved to Åland, the Skype connection to Pakistan became more sporadic. The bridge, and the assumed bubble, had to do with love. Azizah was pregnant and in Åland, while her husband was in Pakistan still trying to arrange his move to Finland. The second reason for my assumption was not flattering to an ethnomusicologist like me. To paraphrase the cultural anthropologist Liisa Malkki (1992), the reason may well have been that the national order of things was thinking inside me, since it is thinking inside us all.[6] Only during the Stockholm interview did I fully realize that especially for Rubina's son Nabeel, and also for her daughter Azizah, Pakistan was less of an important source of cultural heritage and memory than I had assumed, even though I knew very well from the research literature (e.g., Suutari, 2000) that the family's country of origin has less importance for so-called second-generation immigrants.

Malkki (1992) claims that our actions are surprisingly often directed or steered by a naturalized way of thinking about the world through the matrix of nations. From this perspective, it is self-evident that the world has been divided into clearly bordered national units and that a certain unit corresponds to a certain piece of land, a certain language, a certain culture, and a certain group of human beings.

We often tend to forget that refugees, or people who move for other reasons, arriving from many different societal situations and contexts, carry with them distinctively different histories (Malkki, 1992). Drawing on the works of various thinkers from various disciplines – from Arendt, via Deleuze and Guattari, to Foucault – Malkki (1992) observes: "The term 'refugees' denotes an objectified, undifferentiated mass that is meaningful primarily as an aberration of categories and an object of 'therapeutic interventions'" (p. 34).

Since Malkki started developing her arguments in the early 1990s, there has been a growth in the literature devoted to transnational ethnography (e.g., Bryceson & Vuorela, 2002; Vertovec, 2009), as well as transnational and international memory (De Cesari & Rigney, 2014; Gutman, Brown, & Sodaro, 2014). Likewise, there has been new research into the transnational experiences of older immigrants (e.g., Tiaynen, 2013; Horn & Schweppe, 2015). In the 1990s, we still had only a faint understanding of the obstacles they faced, not to mention knowing little about the ageing of specific ethnic groups and their daily life (Tanjasiri, Wallace, & Shibata, 1995; Dilworth-Anderson, Williams, & Cooper, 1999). In the 2000s and 2010s, several studies were made of certain immigrant groups reaching old age in their host countries. Of particular use on this topic was Molly George and Ruth P. Fitzgerald's study (2012) of ageing migrants in Aotearoa/New Zealand, and also studies looking at Italian, Bengali or Japanese women living in England (respectively, Ganga, 2006; Gardner, 2002; Izuhara & Shibata, 2001). In addition, Iranian immigrants in Sweden have been studied by Torres (2006), who points out that the ways in which ageing is understood are affected by a condition of immigrants' "being-in-between," where the whole idea of "home becomes a fluid construction" (p. 236). Today this sounds almost like a platitude, as well as saying that in older age the global and the local interweave in daily life (Phillipson, 2015). A theme that comes up in each and every one of these studies is the role played by the family, especially the idea that the family has a very large influence on the process through which the "host country is made familiar" (George & Fitzgerald, 2012, p. 242).

As Held and others summarized it already in 1999, "[F]ar from this being a world of 'discrete civilizations' or simply an interconnected order of states, it has become a fundamentally interconnected global order" (Held, McGrew, Goldblatt, & Perraton, 1999, p. 49). The current communication technologies have an encompassing influence on the experience of globalization and transnationalism in later life "in an adopted country," as has been convincingly shown by, among others, George and Fitzgerald (2012). They describe a moment when the person, after spending 40 to 60 years in her new country, may later in life be missing her family very much, but in present times – compared, say, to the 1960s – communication technologies have developed enormously. "In a breath-taking second, you can hear old voices on the phone easily and receive photos through email instantly" (p. 240). George and Fitzgerald's study notes many of the same aspects also noticed in my own case study. The handwritten letters have been replaced by other communication methods, although less by – expensive – phone calls than by sending emails, having Skype conversations, and sending and receiving photographs via social media.

Although grandmother Rubina came to the Nordic countries in her later life as an asylum seeker, certain features in her life story may well be connected to international retirement migration (IRM), an idea launched by Warnes, Friedrich, Kellaher and Torres (2004). Researchers have acknowledged that IRM can cause challenges that are different from those experienced by individuals migrating in early adulthood and "ageing in place." However, similarities emerge, write George and Fitzgerald (2012), "when we start to see how the two 'types of older immigrants' create continuity in their lives" (p. 241). Generally, IRM literature has focused on the experience of transnationalism, especially identity formation and constructions of home (see Huber & O'Reilly, 2004; Warnes et al., 2004; Oliver, 2008). Immigrants encountering the developmental tasks of middle and old age have also been discussed by psychoanalysts (Akhtar & Choi-Kain, 2004), who have noted that in Eastern cultures, in which collectivism is more valued than individualism, "the anticipated separation of children from the parental home is less complete" (p. 185). In the case of Rubina, it is particularly painful that she cannot turn to her spouse for support – often the immigrants cannot.

In earlier research, I have clarified and defined the overlapping concepts of social, collective and cultural memory (Järviluoma, 2009a; see also Assman, 2008), concluding that social memory is the most comprehensive, especially when it is defined basically as consisting of the memories that are shared by a group – or at least socially agreed upon: even personal remembrance often has shared frameworks (Boym, 2001; Misztal, 2003). Past is always mediated and being produced through memory work, and it is important to understand that through these acts of remembering we present ourselves both to ourselves and the others (Misztal, 2003; Järviluoma, 2009a, 2009b). I prefer to use the term "social remembering" rather than social or collective memory, perceiving the phenomenon to be dynamic, not static. Early sociological collective memory theories have been criticized because they configure societal and group memories as static (Misztal, 2003) – and the research methods have been static as well. Andreas Huyssen (2003) has already long ago argued that it is impossible by such means to grasp the dynamism and transience of our media-saturated modern culture, lived time and forgetfulness, the clashes between different social and ethnic groups, and the ever fragmenting politics of memory.

Memories acquire new elements in the active process of understanding over time (cf. Mistztal, 2003), and furthermore, considerable concrete evidence in memory studies supports the theory that the past and the ways in which it is recalled are always affected by one's current situation and state of mind (Schacter, 2001; Järviluoma, 2009b). Thus, regarding the research discussed in this chapter, I consider social and socio-musical remembering to be the most useful concepts.[7] By socio-musical remembering I quite simply mean the social remembering that deals with remembrance connected to music, and also technology related to music. In the analysis of remembering it is important to focus on the ways in which memories are being produced in the processes of telling and writing both personal and shared stories.

Researching memories of music and sound events, and inducing their remembrance, is a task that – I would modestly suggest – calls for imagination or, at least, a grounding in sophisticated concepts and methods to achieve success. Group interviewing is a method that has proven successful in "hunting down the social memory" (see Fentress, 1992). In the group interview, relationships with historical events are created through remembering, and as the interview unfolds, a comprehension is achieved about the phase within which the participants of the group are in the process of understanding the past (Järviluoma, 2009a; see also Olick & Levy, 1997; Misztal, 2003). My group interview shared numerous features with the method Hyltén-Cavallius (2012) has developed, namely collective memoryscaping, although I had not heard about it when doing my fieldwork. In his study of the musical formations of pensioners in late 20th-century Sweden, he writes, "[H]osts would point out to fellow members certain biographical or historical settings, thereby proposing a highly specific memoryscape. At other times, the work of elaborating a memoryscape out of the music in the circle would be a collaborative effort, with each member adding bits and pieces to the jigsaw of musical memory" (p. 292).

Furthermore, when discussing ageing, place and remembrance, Chaudhury and Rowles (2005) state that as the individual remembers "the event, recollection and imagination are once again at interplay in recreating the original event" (p. 11). They continue:

> This recreation of the experience is filtered through physical, psychological, and social changes that may have occurred in the person's life during the intervening time. Especially with the loss of social roles, retirement, physical frailty, and environmental changes, for many older adults the past experience of home may hold different meanings. [...] [M]emory performs not only the feat of interdependent fusion of recollection and imagination, but also allows a dynamic evolution over time based on the subjective experience and idiosyncratic life circumstance transitions that occur over the life span. The evolution of

memory over time is by nature a product of the individual's own evolution. (pp. 11–12)

I believe that I met with recently retired Rubina and her family in 2014 at a special point of her "evolution," after she had gone through serious health and family-related challenges. When interviewing Rubina and her family, I do not think I encountered many "ready-mades," key narratives that had already been frequently recounted (cf. Bönisch-Brednich, 2002, p. 70). Ready-mades typical in research on ageing immigrants include narratives on the themes of leaving, arriving, adjusting during the first year, and so on (Bönisch-Brednich, 2002). The days spent in the Stockholm apartment assumed a different form. Rubina brought up several issues from her years in the Nordic countries that she had never raised before. Without going into the detail of these matters, they were undoubtedly concerned with core issues of her family: members whom she had had to leave behind when starting her transnational life as a young adult, and difficulties concerned in trying to organize her family life according to Pakistani values while living in a completely different world, in the Nordic countries.

I knew Rubina well before this interview, having known her for ten years, and still I learned many important new things about her life. As I said, the group interview had several interviewees, and the discussions took different forms over a time span of several days: one-on-one interviews and also group conversations. Hence, I began to encounter widely differing narratives from several members of the same family who arrived in Sweden (and Finland) at different times – and occasionally also arrived several times.

Same family, different histories

Nabeel, the evening before the interview, said: "Everybody at work says I am Swedish." (FN 2014)

Rubina was born in 1952 into a Punjabi-speaking family in Lahore, Pakistan. Her father was an army officer, and her mother was a housewife. As a child, Rubina lived a very sheltered life: for example, when asked about the strongest music-related memory of her childhood, she responded not by identifying this "strongest" memory, but by saying that, in principal, listening to the radio was forbidden in her family. Her father would say, "When you have completed your education you can listen to what you like." The children nevertheless listened to the radio, although not loudly (GI 2014).

At the age of 18, Rubina married a man with an international career, and in the early 1970s she moved to Senegal, where the family lived for seven years. Following that, the family moved to India for six years, and then to Sweden for a longer period. When Rubina first came to Sweden more than 30 years ago, her children were still very small. She felt that she had been living in too many countries and so she wanted her children to be able to stay in Sweden and finish their studies (GI 2014), and this is basically what happened. Rubinstein (2005) wonders what makes us realize or feel that we have found a place "where I ought to be" (p. 124), a place of belonging. It seems that for Rubina this feeling was quite clear. She names as the main factor the education of her children, and, I would add to that, the stable Nordic model, based on equity and welfare, which lies behind the democratic education system of Sweden.

The last stage in Rubina's itinerant international life was in postwar Bosnia, where she and her husband stayed for four or five years. Then, in 2001, Rubina applied for asylum in Finland, after she had left her husband behind in Pakistan, receiving a permanent residence permit after a few years. Her husband died in Pakistan soon after that, while four out of five of her children were by then living in either Sweden or Finland. The fifth has now also moved to Sweden, a few years ago. Understandably, therefore, Rubina was very strongly drawn to the Nordic countries. Even if, technically speaking, she is a refugee, Rubina has many connections with the discussions about international retirement migration and transnational grandmothers, although those concerns were not much voiced when her case was handled in the Finnish system for asylum seekers. When she moved, she was approaching her senior years, and she has now lived 16 years of her life in two of the Nordic countries. If, then, we think about Rubina's children, they will most probably be "ageing in place" in the two Nordic countries (see section above, and Warnes et al., 2004, pp. 311–312 for the discussion on IRM). In this case, within the very same family there will be the experience of ageing in several ways in an "adopted country."

Until recently, to a large extent only Rubina attempted to maintain Pakistani ways of thinking in the family. Thus, four years ago she arranged Nabeel's second marriage, to a young Pakistani relative. Five years ago, Azizah also found a Pakistani spouse. Within the family, marriages of this kind (i.e., to Pakistani spouses) have now changed the situation. Both Nabeel and Azizah have said that over the past few years they have started to establish new contacts with Pakistan through their Pakistani spouse. Azizah says that her husband "tells about what is going on there," and as a result she has become curious about the numerous traditions she was previously ignorant of (GI 2014). Both of these adult children also say that their knowledge of what is going on in Pakistan has increased immensely in the last 10 to 15 years, primarily as a result of their mother's arrival in Finland and, later, in Sweden.

In consequence, I found it interesting to observe the ways in which the layers of social remembering emerged during the group interview. When I asked Azizah, who was about 40 years of age, about her strongest childhood memory, she replied that she had no memories of Senegal or Pakistan, whereas she still possessed a strong memory of attending school in India.

Azizah: We went by bus, and we had an assembly in the morning, where we sang the national anthem. Even after all these years I can still remember the words. The teacher stood in front of us and forced us to sing loudly. That was a very funny moment – we were almost competing to see who could sing (most) loudly. (GI 2014)

Here, cultural memory and personal memory are intermingling – and the cultural memory is of India. I wrote earlier, in the section on concepts, that I prefer to use the term "social remembering," and indeed do consider that as an umbrella term including cultural memory. However, here the latter term is relevant to remind us about a particular use of the term – in the footsteps of Pierre Nora (1996), as related to commemoration bringing and keeping together groups, and individuals, even with conflicting agendas (cf. Assman, 2008). Here a school is promoting national identity through making kids – even Azizah, who was not born in India – to sing the national anthem, and it seems that Azizah enjoyed the moment.

After her school memory Azizah jumped into a completely other world, saying that another strong music-related memory came from recently watching *Mamma Mia! The Movie* along with her own teenage daughter. I guided her back to India, asking her about the ways in which she thought India was present in her life now. She said she still listens to Indian music and watches Indian movies. Her interests are well in line with studies showing the importance of continuity for (ageing) migrants: immigrants tend to try to foster the continuity "by maintaining small, private bridges that link their identities and experiences together across time and oceans (e.g., a few household items, some holiday traditions or traditional foods, attendance at a national club a few times each year, or playing music from home on Sunday afternoons)" (George & Fitzgerald, 2012, p. 258).

Rubina likes Pakistani movies as well, and she said she feels a little sorry that it is not possible to see and hear Pakistani music on Swedish (not to mention Finnish) television. She said that she would like to listen to the Qawwali musician Rahat Fateh Ali Khan or Atif Aslam (GI 2014). Nabeel then described how his relationship to music has changed a lot over the years and through different technologies. Today he works as a computer programmer for the Swedish government, and I gained the impression that his advanced knowledge has a certain impact on the different music technologies that the family uses. In the course of the interview I asked whether the family had any CDs in the house, but it appeared that – just a few days before I arrived – they had thrown away all of Rubina's music CDs (GI 2014).

> *Rubina:* My son said, "Mama, why do you keep all these CDs?"
> [. . .]
> *Helmi:* So, do you actually have any CDs left in the house?
> *Nabeel:* No.

The son said the CDs seemed to be useless since he had a large external hard drive where all the family's music could be stored. He said that it was useless to keep CDs when he could download thousands of songs onto his external hard drive, and the family could use memory sticks to listen to their favorite music everywhere. It appeared that they no longer had even a CD player – instead, they had three computers and an iPad. We should, of course, note that technological development in the sphere of music listening is currently (2014–17) changing extremely fast. A few years ago people still tended to have a CD player in the house, or at least in their cars. Now even the last European strongholds of the car industry, such as Audi and Volkswagen, have stopped installing CD players in their new models (YLE News, 2015).

The family had kept photographs in their physical format, but there were, in fact, very few other objects from any of the countries they had been living in over the years. Mobile families like Rubina's, who – in this case, largely because of the occupation of the father – have to move constantly from one continent to the other learn to travel light. Thus, it is interesting that they have kept photos through all those years. This may have to do with the *material nucleus* of the photograph, as described by the Finnish visual culture researcher Janne Seppänen (2014) – using as a starting point the writings of Browning and Sontag: photos have, ever since their inception, been something *more* than descriptions. They are manifestations, as can be read from a text written by the British poet Elizabeth Barrett Browning only four years after the invention of photographs in 1843: "It is not merely likeness which is precious [. . .] but the association and the sense of nearness involved in the thing [. . .] the fact of the very shadow of the person lying there fixed forever!" (quoted in Sontag, 1984, p. 171; cf. the discussion on the theory of memory objects in Star, 2010).

In any case, I was astonished at the lack of CDs in the apartment – and felt even slightly guilty: I felt that the disposal of the CDs was connected to the cleaning of the house before my own arrival. In all likelihood, however, it was connected with another idea: material objects seemed to have very little significance for any member of the family. Even the new daughter-in-law, Rana, from Pakistan, who had recently married into the family, revealed that when she was moving to Sweden her husband, Nabeel, had told her not to bring any of her "odds and ends" with her from Pakistan. Rana explained that having the objects did not matter, since she had everything in her memory. The family discussed at length the differences between Pakistani culture and that of the Nordic countries, such as the fact that in Pakistan people rarely take pictures at family events: instead, they store them in their memories. As a result, many people still have fantastic memories, the ability to retain things in mind. For some reason Rana immediately continued the story, saying that it was unnecessary to send a text message or make a telephone call before visiting a household in Pakistan: you would always be welcomed. I interpreted Rana's comment as connecting photos and visits since they both have to do with different ways of mediating: if you wish to remember a family event, you imprint it on your mind without digital technology; if you wish to encounter someone you know, you do not need digital technology, but just appear in flesh and blood to the doorstep and try your luck.

Rana's mother-in-law, Rubina, also said that her most significant memory of Pakistan is the *respect* (i.e., the way in which children respect their parents and elderly people). Rubina's memory of respect takes the "place of things."[8] Her comment is not surprising. It has been widely observed that in certain Asian cultures, features such as filial piety and a sense of obligation toward older people are common (Kalavar & Van Willigen, 2005; Weng & Robinson, 2014). Kalavar and Van Willigen (2005) have studied ageing Asian Indian immigrants in the Americas and quote, for example, Mrs. K., who says that "times have changed. When she was growing up, seniors commanded respect. Today, she said, Indian seniors have to be very careful in their interactions with adult children and their spouses. While times have changed in India, she felt that the care and respect provided to seniors in India is still very strong" (p. 213). India is not the same as Pakistan, but likely there is still a degree of similarity between these neighboring countries, at least regarding intergenerational relationships. When Rubina left Pakistan, respect for one's elders was very strong. Rubina took that principle with her to Sweden, and from everything that occurred, it could be seen and heard that she was the matriarch of the family. This is obvious, for instance, from her constant efforts to arrange her children's marriages (see above), efforts that sometimes are very successful, but sometimes pave the way to serious obstacles.

Everything available, nothing fun

Rubina and Nabeel shared the stories (cf. Hyltén-Cavallius, 2012) that they could tell about Rubina's late husband, who was always keen to acquire the latest technology for listening to music in the various locations in which they lived. He ordered such items as LPs through the mail. Thus, the moments when the family listened to big black LPs of, for instance, Indian film music – those frequently became shared and treasured soundmarks or landmarks of social memory for the family.

At present, the Stockholm family store their music on memory sticks or a hard drive, but the daughter-in-law recently arrived from Pakistan has also taught them to use the "Asian YouTube" Saavn. Saavn's website (see www.saavn.com) permits its users to search for music, create playlists, make selections from existing playlists, and listen to music selected randomly from the website. It is interesting to note that, according to Leena Rao (2012) at *TechCrunch*, within four weeks of Saavn's integration with Facebook (at the start of 2012), Saavn had seen a fortyfold increase in its users.

As far as the genres and the age of the music family members listen to, either individually or together, the daughter commented, "Old is gold. We love that type of music, but there are also new singers, and sometimes we try theirs, so there's a mixture, you know" (GI 2014). In addition, their Punjabi mother tongue comes through the music, such as Qawwali (devotional) songs performed by Nusrat Fateh Ali Khan. Most members of the family emphasized that they listen to the words of the poetry itself, especially in Punjabi and Urdu.

For his part, son Nabeel also felt some kind of nostalgia for the old times. As a young boy living in Sweden, his musical taste had been strongly oriented toward Black music such as rap. He described the moments of extreme excitement that he felt when he was younger and watching the Top 40, waiting to see which title would emerge at the top of the chart. He would then go off to the music store to purchase the recordings. Now, everything is available readily and he said getting music is not as much fun as it used to be.

> *Nabeel:* My father used to have big black LPs. But I think [. . .] the technology has changed. Sometimes [it]'s good, sometimes it's bad. In those days we sat in front of the TV and waited for the MTV list and the music that we were looking for [. . .] It was very exciting [. . .] But nowadays it's too easy, it's not fun anymore, to wait for the actual release of a song, because before it's actually released on CD it's going to appear on YouTube or in the morning on the radio, when you drive to work. [. . .] It's just not the same.
> *Helmi:* It's almost too simple.
> *Nabeel:* Almost too simple. And when it's too simple, then it's boring.
> *Helmi:* (laughs) Yeah.
> *Nabeel:* (laughs) One should have to work a little bit.

The son recounted another story involving listening to music with a portable CD player, along with his Swedish girlfriend – they shared the same earphones. He considers that the technology has gone too far.

Nabeel: Before it was like this. When I was young I had a girlfriend, and we could listen to the song together and it was a lot of fun.
Helmi: You used the same earphones.
Nabeel: Yes, with each of us wearing one of them [. . .] and you could listen to a song. It would be a new song that we had bought [on] a CD, and we had a portable CD player and could listen to it, and it was a lot of fun and everything, but now it's not the same.

In his book *Mediated Memories in the Digital Age*, José van Dijck (2007) described how musical memories are enabled through the actual mechanical means of listening: the enabling apparatus frequently becomes part of the recollecting experience. This has also been observed by others – for example, by Catherine Strong (2011) in her work on the memories of grunge fans. As van Dijck (2007) succinctly put it, "Songs or albums are often interpreted as a sign of their time not only because they emerge from a socio-technological context. Remembrances are also embedded, meaning that the larger interpersonal and cultural worlds stimulate memories of the past through frames generated in the present" (p. 78). In this case, one aspect of the frames generated in the present is the accelerated development of portable technology, which for Nabeel makes everything "too easy."

Also, what is remembered and considered important by those remembering is "the setting where significant life events unfolded, where key interactions took place and where those events and interactions triggered emotions and the development of identity" (George & Fitzgerald, 2012, p. 252). For Nabeel many of the key interactions happened in Stockholm, where he listened to a CD together with a girlfriend, sharing earphones, and it is easy to hear that a long stay in this city has contributed crucially to the strong Swedish side of his identity.

In their study of the use of C-cassettes (cassette tapes) in Finland and the ways in which they have been listened to, Kilpiö, Kurkela, and Uimonen (2015) have commented that cassettes are often described in very affectionate terms. They are loved, and they are said to have been important in the construction of identity for the participants in the research. It is often said that CDs have rarely succeeded in becoming material objects with which anyone would have developed such affectionate relations.

This kind of judgment may, however, be somewhat premature at this particular moment and place in history. When I was spending time in the Stockholm apartment, which was equipped with all the latest technologies, I could not help feeling that Rubina had lost something that had been meaningful for her, not least because she had not yet learned how to use the hard drive, memory sticks and other modern technology. This meant that the particular pieces of music that were "her" music and her memorable objects were not easily available to her without assistance. In other words, her musical agency had become smaller in the household. This could be compared to the situations where ageing people stick to their old-fashioned mobile phones – they do not want to be bothered with changing their phone, and they feel that they have better uses for their time than constantly learning new technologies.

Technological change may well be a double-edged sword. What are the bridges that George and Fitzgerald (2012) talk about, if the material objects disappear completely due to digitization? When we think about CDs, we think of objects that include paratexts, pictures and perhaps lyrics. When Hyltén-Cavallius (2012) attended the music-listening circles of older adults in Sweden, he noticed that, for example, the sleeve pictures were important in provoking discussion and memories. YouTube and the Asian Saavn have pictures and videos as well, but when you are listening to the music on hard discs, frequently the only possibility is to preserve the images in memory. The necessity becomes a virtue.

Transnational communication between continents

> And as the distance becomes greater between here and home, the path becomes more important, until the path itself becomes "home". And then, when the path is guarded or gone, the signpost to the path becomes home.
> – Nora J. Rubinstein, "Psychic Homelands and the Imagination of Place"[9]

Rubina still remembers the times in Senegal and in India when the family members wrote long letters to each other, sending them great distances across the world. This then raises the question of how the family, now split between some of the Nordic countries and regions – Sweden, the Åland Islands and Finland – and the extended family in Pakistan communicate with each other, and also whether they share music in that communication. The family's network is tight, and as we know, over the years the communication technologies have changed a great deal.

Especially when dating their future spouses in Pakistan, Azizah and Nabeel used the telephone – but that has naturally proved to be highly expensive. Now, during the time I spent with the family, there were a few calls – Rana's sister called from Pakistan, and Azizah's daughter called from the Åland Islands. Most of the communication occurred via Skype and Facebook; through Facebook family members were able to share photos and also paste videos from YouTube, "and they simply click and listen to it" (GT 2014), as Rana put it. Both YouTube and the "Asian YouTube" Saavn are used a lot with smartphones and iPad, especially by Rana, who had only recently arrived from Pakistan. Desktop computers are also used to some extent for Skype and Facebook communication, but the iPad and laptop have practically taken over that role in communication: Skype has become the main means of their communication. Nabeel has mixed feelings about the increased role of technology in communication, both within the family and also more broadly, within society as a whole. "I would say that technology has brought people together very well, but at the same time it has also taken people away from each other" (GI 2014). In his work in the world of IT, one of his aims is to attempt to create programs that will help to reconnect people in a meaningful way.

In conclusion

> Without memory, we are everywhere or nowhere [. . .] Without memory, all places are equal and alien.
> [P]lace imagination is as important as place memory.
> – Nora J. Rubinstein, "Psychic Homelands and the Imagination of Place"[10]

This chapter has been only the first step in the process of wonder and reflection on dis-placement, ageing and remembering within one transnational family. Interesting questions are nevertheless already starting to appear. One such question concerns the impact that extreme digitization may have on the musical memory of an immigrant family. This in turn raises the question of why visual memories (i.e., photographs) are still retained as objects, but not the musical objects (i.e., CDs). Trust by the family in this study in the effectiveness of the internet is enormous, even though electricity is frequently available in Pakistan for only four hours a day.

In the case of the particular grandmother who has, to some extent, become familiar through this article, I observed a phenomenon of "talking family" into being similar to that noticed by Tatjana Tiaynen (2013): Rubina, as a transnational grandmother, is able to help in constructing and maintaining the "family" through digital devices in a situation where physical travel to Pakistan is almost too expensive to be paid for from a small pension.

In my group interview I also noted the construction, and thus the maintenance, of the family's musical history going on through memory work (i.e., the process of remembering). The musical memory of the family can never be labeled "completed": it is in flux (cf. DeNora, 2000). Even if the ties to, let us say, Pakistan have diminished at some point in the family history because Rubina's parents and her spouse have died, at another point the ties have grown stronger because of the new family members arriving from Pakistan, bringing with them fresh, new musical ideas and devices. At the same time, while living in the two Nordic countries the adult children and the growing number of grandchildren create ties to their host countries (cf. George & Fitzgerald, 2012) or, as in the case of young Nabeel in the 1990s, to the global rap culture via Music Television (MTV).

From Rana's and Rubina's comments about how "everything is kept in memory," it appears that remembering is always-already mediated (Kember & Zylinska, 2012), their present bodies and minds enriched by the past without technological aids, but also with them. It is clear that the transnational home has become permeable (cf. George & Fitzgerald, 2012); however, as pointed out by writers such as Caren Kaplan (1987), and Isabel Hoving (2001), much of the now fashionable poetics of nomadism and deterritorialization can ultimately be regarded as an ethnocentric denial of the importance of place. Extreme digitization may have certain controversial effects with regard to the ageing grandmother of the transnational family in question here. Namely, I have never witnessed Rubina herself starting a Skype call – and in 2014 her mobile phone was still an old-fashioned one with no "smartness." So she could only call others, receive phone calls, and send and receive text messages, and even in those cases the task was often left to one of the children. Has part of her agency been disposed of along with her CDs? On the other hand, being "modern" and also following the inevitable digitization of music and its remembering may increase her feeling of being part of her new host country, part of her family, and part of her new home. These are some of the many aspects of this research that warrant further exploration.

Notes

The epigraph for this chapter is from Philip Fisher, *The Vehement Passions* (Princeton University Press, 2002), pp. 1–2.

1. The Åland Islands, also called Åland, form a continuation of the Finnish Archipelago, but lie only 24 miles from the coast of Sweden.
2. Becoming Audible (2002–05), directed by the music researchers Taru Leppänen and Jouni Piekkari and myself, was a sub-project of a large EU-funded participatory action project titled Becoming Visible (see more in Järviluoma & Leppänen, 2012).
3. I am much indebted to the discussions within the SSHRC-funded Partnership Grant network Ageing + Communication + Technologies (ACT) and this volume's co-editors, Line Grenier and Fannie Valois-Nadeau.
4. I have changed the names of all family members, as well as the name of the suburb, to maintain participants' anonymity.
5. The epigraph for this section is from Liisa Malkki's article in *Cultural Anthropology* (1992), p. 38. For full citation, see chapter references.
6. The phenomenon has already for some time been called *methodological nationalism* (cf. De Cesari & Rigney, 2014).
7. My take on memory was developed earlier in a larger European project I led on Acoustic Environments in Change (see Järviluoma, Truax, Uimonen, Vikman & Kytö, 2009), in which I primarily focused on sonic remembering. I studied the same topic in my later project Sonic Memories and Emplaced Pasts in European Villages. At the moment I am leading a European Research Council Advanced Grant project (694893), SENSOTRA, on sensory transformations in European cities. For this project I have developed a sensobiographic methodology which, I believe, enables the study of embodied remembering and senses as active, bodily, multi-sited and multi-timed processes, combining the anthropology of the senses and the interesting developments in narrative psychology.
8. Akhtar and Choir-Kain (2004) have pointed out that disbursing of possessions can be easier for the aged since the need for material

objects has diminished: "They are less obsessed with the acquisition of status symbols and are more able to sustain a sense of self apart from material possessions" (p. 188). Chaudhury and Rowles (2005) cover the same ground when discussing self in ageing: a person's consciousness of life experiences from the perspective of growing older "enhances awareness of autobiographical aging," and they argue that "remembrance at a deeper level – evolves to a realization that becomes aware of its connection with a spiritual home" (p. 16).

9. The epigraph for this section is from Nora J. Rubinstein's essay in *Home and Identity in Late Life: International Perspectives* (2005), p. 133. For full citation, see chapter references.

10. These epigraphs are also from Rubinstein (2005), pp. 112 and 115.

Field data cited

FN 2014. Field notes.
GI 2014. Group interview in Stockholm, May 2014.

References

Akhtar, Salman, & Choi-Kain, Lois W. (2004). When evening falls: The immigrant's encounter with middle and old age. *American Journal of Psychoanalysis*, 64(2), 183–191. doi:10.1023/b:tajp.0000027272.64645.f2.

Assmann, Jan. (2008). Communicative and cultural memory. In Astrid Erll & Ansgar Nünning (Eds.), *Cultural memory studies: An international and interdisciplinary handbook* (pp. 109–118). Berlin: Walter de Gruyter.

Boym, Svetlana. (2001). *The future of nostalgia*. New York: Basic Books.

Bönisch-Brednich, Brigitte. (2002). *Keeping a low profile: An oral history of German immigration to New Zealand*. Wellington: Victoria University Press.

Bryceson, Deborah Fahy, & Vuorela, Ulla. (2002). *The transnational family: New European frontiers and global networks*. Oxford: Berg.

Chaudhury, Habib, & Rowles, Graham D. (2005). Between the shores of recollection and imagination: Self, aging, and home. In Graham D. Rowles & Habib Chaudhury (Eds.), *Home and identity in late life: International perspectives*. New York: Springer.

De Cesari, Chiara, & Rigney, Ann. (2014). Introduction. In Chiara De Cesari & Ann Rigney (Eds.), *Transnational memory: Circulation, articulation, scales* [E-book]. Berlin: Walter de Gruyter & Co.

DeNora, Tia. (2000). *Music in everyday life*. Cambridge: University of Cambridge Press.

Dilworth-Anderson, Peggye, Williams, Sharon Wallace, & Cooper, Theresa. (1999). Family caregiving to elderly African Americans: Caregiver types and structures. *Journals of Gerontology Series B: Psychological Sciences and Social Sciences, 54B*(4). doi:10.1093/geronb/54b.4.s237.

Fentress, James. (1992). *Social memory*. Oxford: Basil Blackwell.

Fisher, Philip. (2002). *The vehement passions*. Princeton: Princeton University Press.

Ganga, Deianira. (2006). From potential returnees into settlers: Nottingham's older Italians. *Journal of Ethnic and Migration Studies, 32*(8), 1395–1413. doi:1080/13691830600928789.

Gardner, Katy. (2002). *Age, narrative and migration: The life course and life histories of Bengali elders in London*. Oxford: Bloomsbury Academic.

George, Molly, & Fitzgerald, Ruth P. (2012). Forty years in Aotearoa New Zealand: White identity, home and later life in an adopted country. *Ageing and Society, 32*(2), 239–260. doi:10.1017/s0144686x11000249.

Gutman, Yifat, Brown, Adam, & Sodaro, Amy (Eds.). (2014). *Memory and the future: Transnational politics, ethics and society*. New York: Palgrave Macmillan.

Held, David, McGrew, Anthony, Goldblatt, David, & Perraton, Jonathan. (1999). *Global transformations: Politics, economics and culture*. Stanford, CA: Stanford University Press.

Horn, Vincent, & Schweppe, Cornelia. (2015). *Transnational aging: Current insights and future challenges*. New York: Routledge.

Hoving, Isabel. (2001). Tropes of women's exile: Violent journeys and the body's geography. In *In praise of new travelers: Reading Caribbean migrant women writers* (Cultural Memory in the Present Series). Stanford, CA: Stanford University Press.

Huber, A., & O'Reilly, Karen. (2004). The construction of Heimat under conditions of individualised modernity: Swiss and British elderly migrants in Spain. *Ageing and Society*, 24(3), 327–351. doi:10.1017/s0144686x03001478.

Huyssen, Andreas. (2003). *Present pasts: Urban palimpsests and the politics of memory*. Stanford, CA: Stanford University Press.

Hyltén-Cavallius, Sverker. (2012). Memoryscapes and mediascapes: Musical formations of 'pensioners' in late 20th-century Sweden. *Popular Music*, 31(2), 279–295. doi:10.1017/s0261143012000050.

Izuhara, Misa, & Shibata, Hiroshi. (2001). Migration and old age: Japanese women growing older in British society. *Journal of Comparative Family Studies*, 32(4), 571–587.

Järviluoma, Helmi. (2009a). Soundscapes and social memory in Skruv. In Helmi Järviluoma, Barry Truax, Heikki Uimonen, Noora Vikman, & Meri Kytö (Eds.), *Acoustic environments in change* (pp. 138-153). Tampere: TAMK Publications.

Järviluoma, Helmi. (2009b). Scythe-drive nostalgia and agricultural ambiences in Bissingen. In Helmi Järviluoma, Barry Truax, Heikki Uimonen, Noora Vikman, & Meri Kytö (Eds.), *Acoustic environments in change* (pp. 154–171). Tampere: TAMK Publications.

Järviluoma, Helmi. (2010). Podetko ystävyyttä? Etnografia ja biofilian haaste [The aching friendship? Ethnography and the challenge of biophilia]. In Jyrki Pöysä, Helmi Järviluoma, & Sinikka Vakimo (Eds.), *Vaeltavat metodit* [Traveling methods] (pp. 234–257). Joensuu: Finnish Folklore Society.

Järviluoma, Helmi, & Leppänen, T. (2012). Becoming Audible! Asylum seekers, participatory action research and cultural encounters. *Sit-*

uating popular musics: IASPM 16th international conference proceedings. doi:10.5429/2225-0301.2011.40.

Järviluoma, Helmi, Truax, Barry, Uimonen, Heikki, Vikman, Noora, & Kytö, Meri (Eds.). (2009). *Acoustic environments in change.* Tampere: TAMK Publications.

Kalavar, Jyotsna M., & Van Willigen, John. (2005). Older Asian Indians resettled in America: Narratives about households, culture and generation. *Journal of Cross-Cultural Gerontology,* 20(3), 213–230.

Kaplan, Caren. (1987). Deterritorializations: The rewriting of home and exile in Western feminist discourse. *Cultural Critique,* 6, 187–198.

Kember, Sarah, & Zylinska, Joanna. (2012). *Life after new media: Mediation as a vital process.* Cambridge, MA: MIT Press.

Kilpiö, Kaarina, Kurkela, Vesa, & Uimonen, Heikki. (2015). *Koko kansan kasetti: C-kasetin käyttö ja kuuntelu Suomessa* [The uses and ways of listening to C-cassette in Finland]. Helsinki: Suomalaisen Kirjallisuuden Seura Helsinki.

Malkki, Liisa. (1992). National geographic: The rooting of peoples and the territorialization of national identity among scholars and refugees. *Cultural Anthropology,* 7(1), 24–44. doi:10.1525/can.1992.7.1.02a00030.

Misztal, Barbara. (2003). *Theories of social remembering.* Maidenhead: Open University Press.

Nora, Pierre. (1996). The era of commemoration. In Pierre Nora & Lawrence D. Kritzman (Eds.), *Realms of memory: The construction of the French past: Vol. 3. Symbols.* (Arthur Goldhammer, Trans., pp. 609–637). New York: Columbia University Press.

Olick, Jeffrey K. & Levy, Daniel. (1997). Collective memory and cultural constraint: Holocaust myth and rationality in German politics. *American Sociological Review,* 62, 921–996.

Oliver, Caroline. (2008). *Retirement migration: Paradoxes of ageing.* London: Routledge.

Phillipson, Chris. (2015). Global and local ties and the reconstruction of later life. In Julia Twigg & Wendy Martin (Eds.), *Routledge handbook of cultural gerontology.* London: Routledge.

Rao, Leena. (2012, February 16). Eyeing the Indian market, Facebook partners with Saavn on global social music service. *TechCrunch*.

Rubinstein, Nora J. (2005). Psychic homelands and the imagination of place: A literary perspective. In Graham D. Rowles & Habib Chaudhury (Eds.), *Home and identity in late life: International perspectives* (pp. 111–142). New York: Springer.

Schacter, Daniel L. (2001). *Muisti. Aivot, mieli ja menneisyys.* Helsinki: Terra Cognita.

Seppänen, Janne. (2014). *Levoton valokuva* [The restless photograph]. Tampere: Vastapaino.

Sontag, Susan. (1984). *Valokuvauksesta* [On photography]. Helsinki: Lovekirjat.

Star, Susan Leigh. (2010). This is not a boundary object: Reflections on the origin of a concept. *Science, Technology, & Human Values, 35*(5), 601–617. doi:10.1177/0162243910377624.

Strong, Catherine. (2011). *Grunge: Music and memory.* London: Ashgate.

Suutari, Pekka. (2000). *Götajoen jenkka. Tanssimusiikki ruotsinsuomalaisen identiteetin rakentajana* [Dance music in constructing Finnish-Swedish identity]. Helsinki & Tukholma: Suomen Etnomusikologinen Seura & Ruotsinsuomalaisten arkisto.

Tanjasiri, Sora P., Wallace, Steven P., & Shibata, Kazue. (1995). Picture imperfect: Hidden problems among Asian Pacific Islander elderly. *Gerontologist, 35*(6), 753–760. doi:10.1093/geront/35.6.753.

Tiaynen, Tatjana. (2013). *Babushka in flux: Grandmothers and family-making between Russian Karelia and Finland.* Tampere: Acta Universitatis Tamperensis.

Torres, Sandra. (2006). Different ways of understanding the construct of successful aging: Iranian immigrants speak about what aging well means to them. *Journal of Cross-Cultural Gerontology, 21*(1-2), 1–23. https://doi.org/10.1007/s10823-006-9017-z.

van Dijck, José. (2007). *Mediated memories in the digital age.* Stanford, CA: Stanford University Press.

Vertovec, Steven. (2009). *Transnationalism.* London: Routledge.

Warnes, Anthony M., Friedrich, Klaus, Kellaher, Leonie, & Torres, Sandra. (2004). The diversity and welfare of older migrants in Europe. *Ageing and Society*, 24(3), 307–326. doi:10.1017/S0144686X04002296.

Weng, Susie S., & Robinson, Jacqueline. (2014.) Intergenerational dynamics related to aging and eldercare in Asian American families: Promoting access to services. In Halaevalu F. Ofahengaue Vakalahi, Gaynell M. Simpson, & Nancy Giunta (Eds.), *The collective spriit of aging across cultures* (pp. 157–172). New York: Springer.

YLE News. (2015, February 25). Autoista on tullut viihdekeskuksia [Cars have become entertainment centers]. http://yle.fi/uutiset/3-7822876.

Chapter 6: Resoundingly Entangled
Ageing and Memory in Étoile des aînés in Quebec

Line Grenier, Kim Sawchuk and Fannie Valois-Nadeau

Étoile des aînés is a musical talent competition for seniors that was launched in Quebec in 2009 by Chartwell Residences for Retirees, Canada's largest private-sector operator in the seniors housing market. The competition, modeled on televised music competitions such as *American Idol* and *Star Académie*, was part of Chartwell's agenda to promote a more "positive" approach to growing old (Grenier & Valois-Nadeau, 2013). Publicized as a celebration of "seniors talent," each competition attracted, on average, an audience of 200, comprised of residents as well as friends and the families of the participants.

We followed Étoile des aînés between 2012 and 2015, the year Chartwell decided to end the competition. During this three-year period, our collaborative multi-site ethnographic research involved attending events in Chartwell residences across the province. We interviewed dedicated and enthusiastic Chartwell personnel, and we spoke informally with audience members, volunteers, participants and competition judges. The latter included the official ambassador of the contest and tour judge pop singer Claudette Dion, Céline Dion's sister, later replaced by Serge Laprade, a former radio and television star. We documented contests with photos and recordings. We tracked the electronic commentaries on the websites of seniors' organizations, gathered promotional materials, and examined media coverage of competitions in local radio and newspapers. We watched and heard more than a hundred performances, some memorable and moving.

In the process, we realized that this was more than either a marketing and promotional event or an amateur singing contest for older adults.

Each and every event, each and every act comprised a complex and richly dense kaleidoscope of intense interactions between all of the protagonists involved, both on- and offstage: the audience members, the judges, the employees and volunteers, the technicians and the performers. As we came to realize, we were experiencing not simply a set of performances or a promotional event, but richly entangled "musicking" moments that exceeded the organizers' original goal: to promote positive ageing and to associate positive ageing with the Chartwell corporate name.

Why do we use the term "musicking" to describe what we heard, witnessed and felt? Musicking events, according to Christopher Small (1998), are comprised of a heterogeneous ensemble of activities, people and objects that, when brought together, "make music" (p. 9). While one of the recurrent phrases heard at Étoile des aînés referred to the vocal rendering of a song as a journey to a past, as we explain, this return through musicking is not quite so simple. During these events, we became aware of the coexistence of multiple temporalities at play. As such, these musicking moments in these seniors residences have provoked a reflection on the dynamic entanglement of music, memory and ageing.

In this chapter we analyze the affective entanglements of ageing and memory and music by unraveling one striking Étoile des aînés musicking moment: Mrs. Lucie Lafortune's stirring rendition of "Climb Ev'ry Mountain," from the 1965 American musical drama film *The Sound of Music*, in a seniors residence in Gatineau, Quebec, in 2013. After briefly introducing our twofold understanding of the concept of entanglement, we analytically describe this particular moment, which forcefully exemplifies the co-constitutive relations between memory, music and ageing that recurred during our participation as audience members at Étoile des aînés. We then explore the discursive articulation of these relations, by focusing on two salient prepositions – "aside" and "with" – through which we probe how "Climb Ev'ry Mountain" highlights the operations of multiple temporalities at play when we consider ageing and memory making as relational processes. In the final section, we turn our attention to the broader socio-cultural conjunctural trends that inform and contribute to this musicking moment and the "audible entanglements" it performs (Guilbault, 2005).

Entanglement: Two complementary understandings

We use the word "entanglement" deliberately. We borrow and adapt the concept of "entanglement" from the writings of feminist philosopher and historian of science Karen Barad (2003, 2007) as well as from ethnomusicologist and Caribbeanist Jocelyne Guilbault (2005). As Barad explicates in *Meeting the Universe Halfway*:

> To be entangled is not simply to be intertwined with another, as in the joining of separate entities, but to lack an independent self-contained existence. Existence is not an individual affair. Individuals do not pre-exist their interactions; rather individuals emerge through and as a part of their entangled intra-relating. (2007, p. ix)

Barad's notion of entanglement brings forth the relational and processual aspects of our ageing and memory making by highlighting them not only as individual, biological affairs. As we age and are involved in memory work, we inhabit complex worlds of people, material objects, animals and technologies that do not exist in isolation, but in their intra-actions. Barad uses the term "intra-action" to make the point that we are not monads, separate, indivisible "entities" that confront each other or intersect from a position of externality. Barad's concept of entanglement suggests that all of life, including music, memory and ageing, is in constant transformation and change as the result of a manifold of interactions, or what Doreen Massey (2005) calls a "meeting up of trajectories" at different registers, which are profoundly material, relational and embodied. Thinking of the entanglements of music, memory and ageing demands analytic attention to what can be disentangled in the complexities of an instance, in the collective musicking occurring at a specific event-moment. It foresounds not only what ageing and memory mean in the performance of a hit song, such as "Climb Ev'ry Mountain," but how memory and ageing are performed and dynamically enacted together in this musicking moment.

As Butler's (2016) reading of relationality underscores, "[R]elationality includes dependency on infrastructural conditions and legacies of discourse and institutional power that precede and condition our existence" (p. 11). This foregrounding of power and historical temporality is also key to a complementary understanding of the concept of entanglement developed in another field, that of ethnomusicology, by Jocelyne Guilbault. Guilbault (2005) focuses on calypso competitions in Trinidad as instantiations of "audible entanglements," arguing that "far from being 'merely' musical, audible entanglements through competitions also assemble social relations, cultural expressions and political formations" (pp. 41–42). As she so pithily articulates, competitions "performed at different historical moments, render audible and visible the specific constituencies and imaginations of longing, belonging and exclusion" (p. 62). In relation to our location in Quebec, writing about a different competition, and considered from the perspective of relational ageing and memory making, Guilbault's concept of "audible entanglements" can be deployed as a "critical analytic" to unravel the dynamics at play within Étoile des aînés.

The unfolding of a musicking moment: "Climb Ev'ry Mountain"

As we hinted at in the introduction, Étoile des aînés involves a wide range of individuals, collectives, activities, objects and technologies that come together in the performance of "Climb Ev'ry Mountain." To provide the reader with a sense of how we, as researchers and audience members, experienced the entanglements of ageing, memory and music, we return to a specific afternoon, in late June 2013, in Gatineau, Quebec's fourth most populated town.

As we enter the doorway of the residence, we encounter volunteers, residents and the personnel of Chartwell Cité-Jardin, who welcome us and other audience members to the Outaouais regional chapter of the Étoile des aînés competition. Volunteers direct people to the residence's dining room, which has been transformed for the occasion. A small stage is festooned with balloons and bears a banner that sports the title "Étoile des aînés" and Chartwell's logo. A red carpet cuts across the floor, diagonally, with the crowd assembled on each side, cordoning off the area through which special guests and members of the jury will enter the room.

At two o'clock sharp, an upbeat instrumental theme song begins to play through a powerful sound system operated by the Étoile des aînés technicians, who are situated at the back of the very full room. Everyone is clapping to the beat. A woman and a man walk to the stage. She introduces herself as Mrs. Lucie Saint-Jacques, director of Cité-Jardin. She is "very very proud to host the Étoile des aînés competition," she says,[1] and to welcome her colleague from Chartwell Domaine Notre-Dame, in the neighboring town of Aylmer, Mr. Marc Lafontaine, who will act as MC this afternoon. She mentions the presence of a few "special guests" from Chartwell's provincial office, and thanks them for sponsoring an event designed to "honor and celebrate the wonderful people that seniors like you, dear senior residents, are."

Mrs. Saint-Jacques then introduces two well-known members of the Gatineau community who will serve on the jury: Mr. Yves Marchand, musical director of the vocal group Top Passion, and Mrs. Johanne Donahue, from the music school L'Artishow. She ends by presenting the tour judge, Serge Laprade, as "someone who has lots of [female] admirers in the room." The audience welcomes him with loud cheers. The MC takes over the stage. After encouraging everyone to enjoy themselves and have fun, he reads the names of twelve men and women who, as they walk onto the red carpet, are identified as contestants. While they finish taking their seats in a reserved section near the stage, we are asked to be silent. The competition begins.

When the sixth competitor, Mrs. Lucie Lafortune, is introduced to the audience, we are told that she has participated in two prior Étoile des aînés competitions. Mrs. Lafortune walks to the stage. She uses a cane. Her hair is coiffed and she sports a colorful blouse and casual black slacks. She wears little makeup. Before she utters a word, Mrs. Lafortune places the cane on the music stand, setting it aside. The wireless microphone replaces the cane in her hand. Before singing, she tells a story that begins, "If you know *La Mélodie du bonheur*, *The Sound of Music* in English, you will know this song." As she speaks, her words provide a context for the audience to begin their own processes of remembering, of situating this present musical moment in a previous moment in time.

Mrs. Lafortune reminds the audience of who did the original performance in the movie, where the song is sung and when it is sung in the diegesis. "This is the song sung by the Mother Abbess at the convent in Salzburg." She continues, comparing herself to the actress onscreen who so memorably performs the song about to be sung. "I do not have the stature of Peggy Wood," she says, a comment that draws laughter from the audience, for Mrs. Lafortune is a tiny woman. "I do not have her voice either," she adds. Yet, she states, it is important for her to "keep" this song, "because the words of the song have helped me." She still has not revealed the precise name of the tune, relying instead on the audience to imaginatively participate by guessing its name.

Mrs. Lafortune's recollection of this song at a particular moment in her life is precise and so, in the next instance of engaging in this memory making practice, she brings us back to her biographical past. As she does so, she not only tells the audience about herself, but also invites them to recall a particular historical period in Quebec. Her intro gives the words that follow a resonance especially for those who may have shared or likewise lived through this same moment or learned about it at home, in school or in public discourse.

She continues: "In 1965, in this epoch, I was a nun – I had been for ten years – and I had doubts." Many people in the audience nod their head: they recognize the era she is alluding to, a period of intense change known as the Quiet Revolution (Révolution tranquille), a politically and culturally charged moment that shook the power of the Roman Catholic Church in Quebec. After having been strongly anchored in all aspects of Quebec life for over a century, during this era the values, ideas and institutions of the Church were being questioned and in some instances rejected and replaced. Confidently articulating each word, Mrs. Lafortune explains that "listening to Peggy Wood's voice talking about the plains, the mountains, and all of that, as the Mother Abbess said, I had to look clearly at myself." Her personal past, at that moment, is understood to be part of a much broader collective objective.

Mrs. Lafortune ends her prologue to the unnamed song that is about to be sung with a punch line: "Four years later, in 1969, I left the convent, and my life has been a fairy tale ever since." Applause bursts forth from the crowd, who share in her recounting of her story. They yell "Bravo!," fully understanding how difficult a decision that must have been. They too would know, or know of, the courage that such a decision would have taken at this moment in time, a time when there were so few options available to women, whose social roles were circumscribed to that of mother, nurse, teacher or nun, because the Church controlled the French educational and health institutions in the province. But Mrs. Lafortune's narration is not finished. "I am singing this to remind us that we all need to follow our dreams," she concludes. In other words, this not only a song about her past. It is not only a song dredged up from the past for this audience. "Climb Ev'ry Mountain" *will* be a song that she sings to the audience in this present moment, for this present moment is a reminder that "we should follow our dreams." It is a song she will sing to remind us all that there is a future. Mrs. Lafortune then points to the technician, indicating it is now time to push the button on the playback machine. We hear an opening set of harped chords and grace notes, which could, in fact, be the introduction to many different tunes. After a few bars Mrs. Lafortune starts singing "De plaines en montagnes" and, as do many in the audience, we recognize the beginning of the French version of "Climb Ev'ry Mountain."

Like most of the musicking moments at Étoile des aînés, Mrs. Lafortune's choice of musical accompaniment is a prerecorded version. In this case, a soundtrack with just one instrument, the piano, opens up the aural space that allows Mrs. Lafortune to occupy it fully with her voice. The story she has shared with the audience defers the moment of performance. By creating a prologue, she cleverly invokes a past moment and at the same time creates a moment of suspense, or temporal deferment, because she does not name the tune at all.

Mrs. Lafortune's opening narrative mixes her past with the past of the audience. Her decision to speak in the present about following their future dreams is a reminder that at any age, there is the possibility of a future. There is, in other words, a complex entanglement of temporalities at play. These temporal entanglements are shared, albeit not necessarily the same way, by everyone in attendance: volunteers, audience members, the MC, the technicians, the judges who partake in this musicking moment. At the same time, this recollection and return to the past for their future creates an affective charge, through her act of deferment, that sets the stage for the performance to come.

Mrs. Lafortune begins the song in French, and as she sings, it is evident that she has rehearsed this tune over and over again. There is no evidence of stage fright in her voice or in her comportment. Her gestures indicate that she knows, intimately, each cue on the soundtrack. She has a mezzo-soprano voice that bespeaks her newfound confidence and underscores the long-term implications of her initial decision to leave the convent. Her voice convinces us, who listen, that her past decision is still the right one, that it has brought her to this moment in the present. Mrs. Lafortune's diction is precise and she has vocal technique. Her breathing throughout the song is practiced. Her enunciation and pronunciation are embodiments of her past education in the convent and her social class. She makes the song sound easy.

The jury is captivated, and so is the audience: she holds them in the palm of her hand from the moment she delivers her story throughout the duration of the song.

As Mrs. Lafortune moves into the last verse, she switches to the English version. She ends the song with a crescendo. The musical soundtrack slows down, providing dramatic emphasis. Mrs. Lafortune underscores the final words by raising her index finger. She sings and points toward the audience, her finger moving in rhythm to the punch line of both the song and her introductory remarks: "Till you find your dream." She sustains each note. Her voice amplifies, her arms rise and she makes a sweeping gesture toward the entire audience, drawing them into the past evoked by the music into this present moment of the finale. Her finger in the air, she transforms the final line of the song into "Yes, your own dream." Her finger circles, pointing to the ceiling, indicating to one and all that she is wrapping up.

The audience's thunderous applause expresses their enthusiasm at Lucie Lafortune's moving performance. As the applause wanes, Mrs. Lafortune's posture changes. The contrast is remarkable. While she is performing, as her amplified voice reaches out to her audience, Mrs. Lafortune occupies the entire space of the stage. Her comportment, while singing, has given the impression that she is growing taller with every phrase. When she finishes, Mrs. Lafortune's shoulders drop and she hunches them together. She lowers her arms, leans over the microphone stand. She sets aside the microphone and picks up the cane, which she had temporarily set aside. Mrs. Lafortune will later voluntarily hide her cane from view when the event's official photographer takes her picture as one of the winners.

When the MC comes back onto the stage, Mrs. Lafortune awaits the comments of the judges. They praise her determination, the force of her character and the theatricality of her delivery. "Your performance provides a portrait of an epoch," says one judge. "You sang a song which is meaningful to you today, a song which describes you," adds the main judge, Serge Laprade. Still moved, another judge further remarks: "You know what your biggest strength is? Your performance brings us elsewhere."

"Your performance brings us elsewhere" or "Your performance made us travel." Expressions of traveling though time to another era, to another space, to another moment were among the most recurrent comments made by the judges to all competitors throughout Étoile des aînés competitions. The togetherness intimated and enunciated by traveling though time and space together on the wings of a hit song from a musical past pertains not only to the individuals and groups in attendance. This constitution of an instance of being together *through* musicking foregrounds, as well, the participation of the seniors, the contestants' families, the community and various other publics (Grenier & Valois-Nadeau, 2013) in attendance, whose presence and participation create an ephemeral collectivity.

This "traveling together" trope evokes the twofold spatio-temporal process that repeatedly happens to and with "us," the audience, during Étoile des aînés. Through these acts of musicking we are invited to experience a going back in time that is a movement to a specific place. We experience as well a being *between* places: we are still in a dining room in Gatineau in the co-presence of a group of older residents, humming along to the tune we are hearing, or clapping together at the end of the song. Musicking moments, like the one under analysis here, provide conditions for experiencing the complexity of ageing in time as a being *now* and *then* in the same place, as well as being *here* and *there* at the same time (Vásquez, 2013). We are at once sitting in a dining room, the same place (the here), as we experience the song in the present, a song that invites us to each return to a moment in our past (the then). We are, as a result, both here and there, together at this time.

Entangled relationalities: Aside and with

To probe the specificity of this entanglement of ageing and memory through music that suggests the multiple coexistence of temporalities at Étoile des aînés, we now turn our attention, for a moment, to the ways these relationalities are expressed through the prepositions *aside* and *with*. In discourse, prepositions are words that act as connectors and/or as orientational markers that, according to *Merriam-Webster's Learner's Dictionary*, "show direction, location, or time." As we have noted above, Mrs. Lafortune returns to a hit song that she had put *aside*; she keeps "Climb Ev'ry Mountain" with her to bring out when it is needed. This is, as well, a song that she performs *for* others, but in this musicking moment, it was performed *with* others. These two propositions, aside and with, stand out as we narrativize, recall, describe and analyze the musicking moment and the temporal unfoldings articulated in the song and its performance.

Aside: The workings of return

The vocal rendering of "Climb Ev'ry Mountain," as a musicking moment, is framed by the story Mrs. Lafortune tells, at the beginning, when she recounts her moment of decision and connects it to a specific scene in the film *The Sound of Music*. Performing "Climb Ev'ry Mountain" is a return to a specific moment in her life as well as to a song that was key throughout the three- to four-year period that preceded her making a decision that would be potentially life changing, that is, leaving the convent. "Climb Ev'ry Mountain" returns both Mrs. Lafortune and the listeners to key junctures in the scenario of the film, when Maria's future as a postulant and a member of the convent are questioned. However, the "journey" that is undertaken collectively through the performance of this song is another kind of journey. For some people in attendance, it is also a return to a period in Quebec's history and in women's history therein – one during which becoming a nun, a nurse, a teacher or a housewife was a woman's sole legitimate destiny. For others in attendance, born in another moment in time, "Climb Ev'ry Mountain" is a return to the eve of the Second World War, for the romantic story of Maria the nun-turned-governess and Captain von Trapp is set during the rise of Nazism in Austria.

This return to the historical past through the evocation of a song that has been set aside is, however, not performed as an episode of nostalgia, of a "bittersweet longing for former times and spaces," even though it does involve the sort of "interlinking imagination of the future" (Niemeyer, 2014, p. 1) that sometimes accompanies this type of return. It relates not so much to a lost past but points to the continuing relevancy *of this moment for others in the present* as well as to the future it might inspire and orient. To return does not mean going back to something that is finished, but it can involve, as Ahmed (2016) argues, "working over things that are not over" (p. 200), be it, we would add, one's existential questions over matters of faith, pleasures of singing, dreams or life itself. And here we invoke a moment in the performance that captures what returning to something that has been put aside does. As Mrs. Lafortune's substitution of the microphone for the cane at the end of the song suggests, she not only brings back the song for her audience: she brings back something that she has temporarily set aside as she begins her song. Her cane.

The gesture of setting this cane aside, then bringing it back, is significant. The cane is set aside by the contestant/singer when the song begins and is brought back by the senior/older woman when the song ends. In this gesture, the ageing body's vulnerabilities and mobility limitations, as well as the embodied gendered expectations of politeness and respectability, are rendered visible. Of course, the older Mrs. Lafortune – whose age is not revealed like it is for almost all of the other contestants – was never really "gone." Yet this identity, in this moment, was somehow overshadowed by the intimation and return to a Mrs. Lafortune almost 50 years younger, almost 50 years ago. This particular gesture folded into this musicking moment offers a glimpse into what Anca Cristofovici describes as the "permanently fluctuating relationship between younger and older selves," whose appearances and disappearances are "better seen as continuities and discontinuities over a lifetime" (quoted in Segal, 2013, p. 34). As Lynne Segal (2013) claims in her analysis of ageing and temporality, the occurrence of these fluctuations between younger and older selves "can help to subvert the most familiar typecasting of ageing" (p. 32).

But there is another kind of *aside* that is at work in the return that is created through the performance of "Climb Ev'ry Mountain." Mrs. Lafortune talks about the importance of "keeping" the song "Climb Ev'ry Mountain" and the practice of bringing it out at particular moments. This act of keeping something to the side, then bringing it out again, is commensurate with the practices of listening to *La Mélodie du bonheur* in Quebec. This film is "kept" present within Quebec's popular cinematic culture by being screened every year as a part of the special holiday film programming on local television. Watching it is a ritualistic activity for many of us. Indeed, for one of us, watching it constitutes a moment of memory making given that it has been an important ritual activity she did over the last ten years of her mother's life, while for the other, it brings back a visceral memory of a first movie theatre experience.

There is a significance not only in the film but in this particular song, which became a "hit." In contrast to other songs from the musical that may be sung at different moments during the year (e.g., "Do-Re-Mi," which is often learned by children in school), "Climb Ev'ry Mountain" has a specific affective charge that is associated with its location in the movie: it occurs at a point of dramatic decision. In the film it acts as a bifurcating moment for the main character, Maria, whose decisional moment acts as a kind of allegory for the experiences of other women, which again is specific to the history of women in Quebec. In *The Sound of Music*, "Climb Ev'ry Mountain" is sung for Maria, who is being advised by the Mother Abbess. It is a message from one doubting nun to another, and is a demand, in lyrics, for self-honesty without guilt and regret. In this musicking moment, it is brought to us by Mrs. Lafortune, who associates it with her own bifurcating, decisional moment, a moment of private significance at a crossroads in her life that she chooses to render public. We are not given details of the specific outcome of this turning point in Mrs. Lafortune's life. We do not know exactly what she chose. We only know that she chose to leave the convent and that this choosing continues to resonate for her, in her present. It is the recounting of this decisional moment and the repeated enactment that matter.

This musicking moment, in other words, brings to the fore the vagaries of temporal experience of ageing and memory. Growing old as well as memory making are far from linear; growing old and memory making are not just about the continual return to the past, as if the present and the future have no meaning. As we age, as we grow old, as we remember, reminisce, recollect and make memories, various sounds, people, objects and discrete episodes in the life span are temporarily set aside to be brought up again later, in a different moment, in a different space. As we hear and we witness in this musicking moment, ageing and memory are entangled through acts of returning, which, as Sarah Ahmed (2016) writes, "brings up subjects as well as objects that are in the present but exceed the present: returning evokes a time that is not quite now, a place that is not quite here" (p. 199). The musicking moment which unfolds in Gatineau on that June afternoon of 2013 brings forth a constellation of what it means to age and to make memory with others, including to age and to make memory with a song as it ages and is remembered, recollected, memorialized.

With: Multiple registers of co-presence

"Climb Ev'ry Mountain" is a hit song that itself has aged, along with those who sing it. A hit song has a particular power of recollection. Its every occurrence creates an echo of the past in the present and the promise of an anticipated future of different repetitions. Hits are like haunting melodies, or earworms: "As a musical tune or fragment which can insidiously and obsessively impose itself, like a foreign body, into the listener, the 'earworm' acts as a virus clinging to the memories of its host" (Guesdon & Le Guern, 2014, p. 71). Hit songs have their own temporalities. As Guesdon and Le Guern (2014) argue, "[T]he hit is always 'already known' and yet produces something new by mixing triviality and singularity; an original *déjà vu* (or *déjà entendu*, already heard) entity" (p. 72).

Through their life course, hit songs such as "Climb Ev'ry Mountain" move in and out of different states – commodity, sound souvenir (Bijsterveld & van Dijck, 2009), karaoke selection, YouTube video, cultural heritage, and so on. While they may be slow or fast, reversible or permanent, and more or less noticeable, these movements not only mark what, following Kopytoff (1986), we call the social biography of the hit, but also shape *how* they age and are involved in memory making practices. Given that pop music's relation to its own past is increasingly experienced through quotes, parodies, homages, remakes and remixes, a feature many analysts consider to be the trademark of today's retro culture (Hogarty, 2016), retromania (Reynolds, 2011) or retropia (Bauman, 2017), hits are among the cultural things that seem to age without getting old. In other words, in thinking through the entanglements of music, memory and ageing, we ask how we age, not only how we age together, but also how we age together with other entities in our world, including the songs we carry with us, may set aside, and to which we return. This is also a reminder that it is not only people who age. Songs, too, age.

In the afterword to his collection of essays on cultural ageing, Stephen Katz (2009) suggests that "our ideas, metaphors, and meanings of aging are materially inscribed," and yet, he adds, it is notable "how little account we take of the material life of ageing around and outside of our particular human experience of it" (p. 233). Katz embarks on a reflexive exercise in his immediate home surroundings "to see what kinds of aging, outside of myself exist" (p. 233). His attention is drawn to an African drum, cast-iron frying pans and the compost in the yard. Each of these objects, he notes, has different qualities, and they are ageing at different rates. His comments indicate a recognition that ageing processes are not just human. Everything around us, from the tables we eat off to the clothes we wear, does indeed age. What we think is important to add is that these objects do not simply age outside and around us. They also age alongside us, beside us, with us.

"Climb Ev'ry Mountain" is a song that is ageing and has both endured and persisted through time. As philosopher Levi R. Bryant (2012) suggests, "Persistence is not a *static* feature of objects, but is rather an *activity* on the part of objects" (para. 6, emphasis original). He adds that in thinking about persistence, we must also ask how things endure. Endurance, he writes, "is something that objects must *do*, not something that objects *have* as a default mode until perturbed from the outside in such a way as to be destroyed" (para. 6, emphasis original). Endurance can therefore be defined "as the multiplicity and succession of durations, which relies on the ongoing accomplishment of continuity in/through diversity" (Grenier, 2012, p. 10). This understanding of endurance resonates with that of Isabelle Stengers, for whom it is "the achievement of that which, through its adventures, 'goes on mattering,' " thereby "succeed[ing] in maintaining some thread of conformity between past and present" (quoted in Grenier, 2012, p. 10). "Climb Ev'ry Mountain" is a hit song that is a part of the dynamic ageing trajectories expressed in this musical moment that have persisted and endured.

Resounding trajectories

What is experienced in this musicking moment is the complexity of memory making and ageing in time, as a meeting up of "coexisting trajectories," or what the late Doreen Massey calls "stories-so-far" (Massey, 2005). According to Massey (1993), any experience of a place is the coming together of a collection of previously unrelated "stories-so-far" that makes a place unique, and produces its uniqueness out of interactions. She wrote that "stories-so-far" emerge

> out of particular interactions and mutual articulations of social relations, social processes, experiences and understandings, in a situation

of co-presence, but where a large proportion of those relations, experiences and understandings are actually constructed on a far larger scale than what we happen to define for that moment as the place itself. (p. 68)

In spatio-temporal terms, the musicking moment invoked by performances such as Mrs. Lafortune's rendition of "Climb Ev'ry Mountain" cannot be reduced to either a dot on the map of the province of Quebec that would represent the city of Gatineau where it took place, or the bounded area of the dining room of the Cité-Jardin residence where the competition was staged. Although it took place in 2013, it is made up of a much broader range of temporalities, periods and rhythms than those suggested by the calendar, as our descriptive analysis in the previous sections draws out. We are not only privy to Madame Lafortune's past; we share in the *present* Madame Lafortune's invocation for us to imagine a future. However, the journey being articulated is not only one related to the lives of individuals, it is also one connected to broader socio-cultural trends that more or less silently inform and contribute to this musicking moment. Drawing from Guilbault's (2005) analysis of calypso competitions in Trinidad, we can understand these intersecting musicking events and moments, these "stories-so far," as "instantiations" of "audible entanglements" that are connected to broader socio-historical trends. These trends include transformations of the articulation of music and youth, demographic changes and ageing policies, and residences that crisscross this 2013 rendition of "Climb Ev'ry Mountain," sung at Étoile des aînés.

In the first instance, it is important to consider "Climb Ev'ry Mountain" as a part of the soundscape of popular music that is tied to the cultural industries. *The Sound of Music*, for example, is simultaneously a Broadway hit, a musical, a film and a recording. As Andy Bennett (2013) remarked, "[A]lmost every living generation in the Westernized world today has grown up in an age when popular music has been a pivotal element of the global media and cultural industries" (p. 1). *The Sound of Music* and "Climb Ev'ry Mountain" may not be a part of the musical history associated with the boomer generation of the sixties, such as the rock and roll of the Woodstock generation. Yet it is a part of the musical memory of a cohort of individuals born between the mid-'40s and the mid-'60s, who matured in postwar conditions (prosperity, new media and communication networks, and affluent consumerism, among others). The boomers have not only invested "youth" with new meanings (Chambers, 1986), this group has also made music "their way of representing itself to itself as a collective" (Katz, 2014, p. 94). This articulation has oriented the artist-development and marketing strategies of the music industries (Frith, 1990) and, more broadly, shaped popular music, including the songs from musicals, as a key mediation of social life and public culture (Grossberg, 1992; Street, 2013). While this is a part of a global trend, there are local valences.

In Quebec, youth-oriented popular music discourses, repertoires and practices have been at the forefront of mediated public culture, especially since the advent of *yéyé* and other local appropriations of pop/rock musics, as well as the burgeoning of the singer-songwriter-based movement, in the '60s to '70s. In light of the experiences of older fans, the practices of post-youth subculture audiences (Bennett, 2006, 2018; Taylor, 2010; Hodkinson, 2011; Bennett & Taylor, 2012), and the critical and commercial success of older performers, including post-menopausal women (Gardner, 2012; Jennings, 2012), the connection of popular music to youth appears, however, to be unsettled. In fact, recent studies have, as their starting point, the recognition that popular music has ceased to be the "preserve of youthful artists and consumers" (Jennings & Gardner, 2012, p. 3) and that its cultural significance "is no longer tied exclusively to youth" (Bennett, 2013, p. 2).

This brings us back to Chartwell, which at the time that Étoile des aînés was launched, conceived of this contest as part of its marketing strategy to break into the Quebec market for seniors residences. Indeed, one cynical reading of the contest is as a marketing ploy to boost the name recognition of this international company within Quebec. While ageing has been (and still is) framed as a social "problem," it has also been considered a business opportunity by the media and cultural industries. In the music sector, strategies were designed to reconnect "older" people, notably baby boomers, to their musical pasts (Katz, 2014). This has meant an intensified commodification of nostalgia (Bull, 2009; Hodson, 2012) and "retro" (Reynolds, 2011), combined with increased visibility of official and nonofficial music heritage (Bennett, 2009; Cohen, 2012; Cohen & Roberts, 2013); an increased reliance on catalogs and archives to reissue hits from the past or material never released before, and to develop new acts to recycle and reinterpret these hits; numerous comeback tours or concerts of generational icons (Tinker, 2012); and the explosion of tribute bands (Homan, 2006) and intergenerational entertainment projects. These various developments attest to the presence of a thriving "grey" market (Sawchuk, 1995), which Chartwell tapped into by relying on the highly popular format of contemporary televised music shows, and transforming it into a live music event by and for seniors.

These broader, often global trends or trajectories reverberate at local levels. Étoile des aînés happened in specific places, at a very precise moment in time. On the one hand, each competition occupied a particular place in daily life at the residence. It occurred during the afternoon, between a menu of activities offered at each residence, from bingo and swimming lessons to beanbag games and Mass, and right before dinner. As Murray Forman and Jan Fairley (2012) observe, integrated into the institutional recreation activities of senior residences, music has been "recast as an element of professional instrumentalism that is structured within the logic of commercial elder care" (p. 196). Music performances by and for seniors like the ones organized by Chartwell serve not only marketing and promotion purposes; they also provide entertainment for "ostensibly idle and potentially bored residents" (p. 196).

On the other hand, each competition foresounded the discourses of "active ageing," which, inspired by the guidelines developed by international agencies such as the World Health Organization (2002), is the driving force behind the ageing policy that was introduced by the Government of Quebec in 2013. At every musicking event we witnessed, we heard local organizers, judges or MCs reiterate that while the competition was designed to celebrate the talent of seniors, it was also meant to encourage residents – participants as well as other senior audience members – to actively engage in creative leisure activities such as singing or playing music. Numerous references were made to the rich potential of music to support well-being, hence to help maintain a healthy and active life, and to fully participating in the community as key to "successful ageing" (Grenier & Valois-Nadeau, 2013). These references included those made by participants who sung the praises of singing, for themselves and for others, as a means to forget the aches and pains of their ageing bodies, and also to relate differently with their children and grandchildren or have fun with their peers.

In conclusion

The moment of musicking we have analyzed foresounds multiple expressions of temporality and experiences of time passing not only for Mrs. Lafortune, but in all of the senses discussed above, as well as at an experiential level. Simultaneously, those who are partaking in the event are traveling back to a moment in time, associating disparate events, sounds and people located in different periods. They are sensing at one and the same time being here and there, now and then. They are reminded, in this act of listening along, of lessons learned from previous experiences. Together, we, audience members are invited to imagine coming back to an affective place that one might not have even been to yet. It is not simply a return to a past moment, a journey along one single trajectory to a shared past. This entangled moment of musicking is a reminder, as Craig Jennex (2016) puts it, that music is primarily a temporal medium: "[I]t unfolds in time, is organized through time, and seems to offer listeners unique relations to feelings of time (of time passing, of living in the moment, of remembering or feeling nostalgic, of losing a sense of time, among others)" (p. 89). It is in this complex interplay of temporalities and relationality that ageing and memory can be said to be entangled through any musicking moment, including this particular performance of "Climb Ev'ry Mountain."

Through this musicking moment particular musical repertoires, objects, performances, discourses and practices work to link the specific "present-pasts" and "becoming" of individual and collective experiences to particular local resources and public trajectories. How are they linked? What kind of connections are created? Answering these questions means going back to "relationality" as entanglement, not just in conceptual terms, but in analytical terms. Working through the entanglements of this moment requires a nuanced way of thinking about not only what is connected, but also how it is brought together. As different trajectories come together, collide and sometimes crash, we are reminded that these relationalities resonate and influence who we are, what we do, how we remember and make memory, and how we age.

Note

1. This and the following excerpts from the event were recorded and then translated from French. We want to thank Chartwell Residences for Retirees and Étoile des aînés' local organizers for their warm welcome of our research project, and for generously letting us record competitions, take photographs at various events, talk with participants and judges, and access promotional material.

References

Ahmed, Sarah. (2016). Return as moodiness. *TOPIA: Canadian Journal of Cultural Studies, 35*, 199–202.

Barad, Karen. (2003). Posthumanist performativity: Toward an understanding of how matter comes to matter. *Signs, 28*(3), 801–831.

Barad, Karen. (2007). *Meeting the universe halfway: Quantum physics and the entanglement of matter and meaning*. Durham, NC: Duke University Press.

Bauman, Zygmunt. (2017). *Retrotopia*. Cambridge, UK: Polity.

Bennett, Andy. (2006). Punk's not dead: The continuing significance of punk tock for an older generation of fans. *Sociology, 40*(2), 219–235. https://doi.org/10.1177/0038038506062030.

Bennett, Andy. (2009). "Heritage rock": Rock music, representation and heritage discourse. *Poetics, 37*(5–6), 474–489. https://doi.org/10.1016/j.poetic.2009.09.006.

Bennett, Andy. (2013). *Music, style, and aging: Growing old disgracefully?* Philadelphia: Temple University Press.

Bennett, Andy. (2018). Popular music scenes and aging bodies. *Journal of Aging Studies, 45*, 49–53. https://doi.org/10.1016/j.jaging.2018.01.007.

Bennett, Andy, & Taylor, Jodie. (2012). Popular music and the aesthetics of ageing. *Popular Music, 31*(2), 231–243. https://doi.org/10.1017/S0261143012000013.

Bijsterveld, Karin, & van Dijck, José (Eds.). (2009). *Sound souvenirs: Audio technologies, memory and cultural practices*. Amsterdam: Amsterdam University Press.

Bryant, Levi R. (2012, January 12). The dynamic life of objects [Blog post]. *Larval subjects*. https://larvalsubjects.wordpress.com/2012/01/12/the-dynamic-life-of-objects.

Bull, Michael. (2009). The auditory nostalgia of iPod culture. In Karin Bijsterveld & José van Dijck (Eds.), *Sound souvenirs: Audio technologies, memory and cultural practices* (pp. 83–93). Amsterdam: Amsterdam University Press.

Butler, Judith. (2016). Rethinking vulnerability and resistance. In Judith Butler, Zeynep Gambetti, & Leticia Sabsay (Eds.), *Vulnerability in resistance* (pp. 12-27). Durham, NC: Duke University Press.

Chambers, Ian. (1986). *Urban rhythms: Pop music and popular culture* (Reprint ed.). New York: Palgrave Macmillan.

Cohen, Sara. (2012). Musical memory, heritage and local identity: Remembering the popular music past in a European Capital of Culture. *International Journal of Cultural Policy, 19*(5), 576–594. https://doi.org/10.1080/10286632.2012.676641.

Cohen, Sara, & Roberts, Les. (2013). Unauthorising popular music heritage: Outline of a critical framework. *International Journal of Heritage Studies, 20*(3), 241–261. https://doi.org/10.1080/13527258.2012.750619.

Forman, Murray, & Fairley, Jan. (2012). Introduction: As time goes by. *Popular Music, 31*(2), 193–197. https://doi.org/10.1017/S0261143012000049.

Frith, Simon. (1990). Video pop: Picking up the pieces. In Simon Frith (Ed.), *Facing the music: Essays on pop, rock, and culture* (pp. 88–130). London: Mandarin Books.

Gardner, Abigail. (2012). Framing grace: Shock and awe at the ageless black body. In Ros Jennings & Abigail Gardner (Eds.), *'Rock on': Women, ageing and popular music* (pp. 65–86). Farnham, UK: Ashgate.

Grenier, Line. (2012). "Ageing and/as enduring: Discussing with "Turtles [that] do not die of old age." In Guillaume Latzko-Toth & Florence Millerand (Eds.), *TEM 2012: Proceedings of Technology and Emerging Media track, annual conference of the Canadian Communication Association* (pp. 1–12). http://www.tem.fl.ulaval.ca/www/wp-content/PDF/Waterloo_2012/GRENIER-TEM2012.pdf.

Grenier, Line, & Valois-Nadeau, Fannie. (2013). »Vous êtes tous des gagnants«. Étoile des aînés et le vieillissement actif au Québec. *Recherches Sociologiques et Anthropologiques, 44*(1), 137–156.

Grossberg, Lawrence. (1992). *We gotta get out of this place: Popular conservatism and postmodern culture.* New York: Routledge.

Guesdon, Maël, & Le Guern, Philippe. (2014). Retromania: Crisis of the progressive ideal and pop music spectrality. In Katharina Niemeyer (Ed.), *Media and nostalgia: Yearning for the past, present and future* (pp. 70–80). New York: Palgrave Macmillan.

Guilbault, Jocelyne. (2005). Audible entanglements: Nation and diasporas in Trinidad's calypso music scene. *Small Axe*, 9(1), 40–63. https://doi.org/10.1353/smx.2005.0006.

Hodkinson, Paul. (2011). Ageing in a spectacular 'youth culture': Continuity, change and community amongst older goths. *British Journal of Sociology*, 62(2), 262–282. https://doi.org/10.1111/j.1468-4446.2011.01364.x.

Hodson, Jaigris. (2012). When I'm sixty-four: Beatles rock band and the commodification of nostalgia. *Loading... Journal of the Canadian Game Studies Association*, 6(10), 71–90.

Hogarty, Jean. (2016). *Popular music and retro culture in the digital era* (Routledge Advances in Sociology). New York: Routledge.

Homan, Shane (Ed.). (2006). *Access all eras: Tribute bands and global pop culture*. Milton Keynes, UK: Open University Press.

Jennex, Craig. (2016). Resoundingly queer: Cover song as collective return. *TOPIA: Canadian Journal of Cultural Studies*, 35, 87–106.

Jennings, Ros. (2012). It's all just a little bit of history repeating: Pop stars, audiences, performance and ageing – Exploring the performance strategies of Shirley Bassey and Petula Clark. In Ros Jennings & Abigail Gardner (Eds.), *'Rock on': Women, ageing and popular music* (pp. 35–51). Farnham, UK: Ashgate.

Jennings, Ros, & Gardner, Abigail. (2012). Introduction: Women, ageing and popular music. In Ros Jennings & Abigail Gardner (Eds.), *'Rock on': Women, ageing and popular music* (pp. 1–15). Farnham, UK: Ashgate.

Katz, Stephen. (2009). *Cultural aging: Life course, lifestyle, and senior worlds* (2nd ed.). Toronto: University of Toronto Press.

Katz, Stephen. (2014). Music, performance, generation: The making of boomer rock and roll biographies. In C. Lee Harrington, Denise D. Bielby, & Anthony R. Bardo(Eds.), *Ageing, media, and culture* (pp. 93–106). Lanham, MD: Lexington Books.

Kopytoff, Igor. (1986). The cultural biography of things: Commoditization as a process. In Arjun Appadurai (Ed.), *The social life of things:*

Commodities in cultural perspective (pp. 64–91). New York: Cambridge University Press.

Massey, Doreen B. (1993). Power-geometry and a progressive sense of place. In Jon Bird, Barry Curtis, Tim Putnam, & Lisa Tickner (Eds.), *Mapping the futures: Local culture, global change* (Futures: New Perspectives for Cultural Analysis, pp. 59–69). New York: Routledge.

Massey, Doreen B. (2005). *For space*. Thousand Oaks, CA: Sage.

Niemeyer, Katharina (Ed.). (2014). *Media and nostalgia: Yearning for the past, present and future*. New York: Palgrave Macmillan.

Reynolds, Simon. (2011). *Retromania: Pop culture's addiction to its own past*. New York: Faber & Faber.

Sawchuk, Kimberly A. (1995). From gloom to boom: Aging, identity and target markets. In Mike Featherstone & Andrew Wernick (Eds.), *Images of aging: Cultural representations of later life* (pp. 116–134). London: Routledge.

Segal, Lynne. (2013). *Out of time: The pleasures and perils of ageing*. New York: Verso.

Small, Christopher G. (1998). *Musicking: The meanings of performing and listening*. Hanover: Wesleyan.

Street, John. (2013). *Music and politics*. Hoboken, NJ: John Wiley & Sons.

Taylor, Jodie. (2010). Queer temporalities and the significance of 'music scene' participation in the social identities of middle-aged queers. *Sociology, 44*(5), 893–907. https://doi.org/10.1177/0038038510375735.

Tinker, Chris. (2012). *Âge tendre et têtes de bois*: Nostalgia, television and popular music in contemporary France. *French Cultural Studies, 23*(3), 239–255. https://doi.org/10.1177/0957155812443203.

Vásquez, Consuelo. (2013). Spacing organizations: Or how to be here and there at the same time. In Daniel Robichaud & Francois Cooren (Eds.), *Organization and organizing: Materiality, agency, and discourse* (pp. 127–149). New York: Routledge.

World Health Organization (Ed.). (2002). *Reducing risks, promoting healthy life*. Geneva: World Health Organization.

Acknowledgements

The editors would like to acknowledge the Social Sciences and Humanities Research, Canada (SSHRC) for financial contribution to Ageing + Communication + Technologies: Experiencing Digital World in Later Life (ACT), an international research and partnership project in which all contributors are involved. Our thanks to Kim Sawchuk and Constance Lafontaine of Concordia University, respectively Director and Associate Director of ACT, for their ongoing support. We are also indebted to Roberta Maierhofer and Ülla Kriebernegg of Graz University, who wholeheartedly welcomed our edited collection project to the Ageing studies series. The carte blanche they gave us was key to our explorations of uncharted territories in ageing and memory studies.

Samuel Thulin made a significant contribution by taking up the challenge of mediating between two linguistic worlds and helping us find the right words and formulations in English for our introductory chapter. We would like to give special thanks to Naomi Pauls for her invaluable assistance. Her outstanding editing work, praised by all contributors, extended well beyond correcting typos and spelling mistakes. She was meticulous in her revisions and provided tremendous input with regards to the book.

To the authors who generously embarked on this adventure, we extend our sincere gratitude. We thank you for the confidence you showed in us, the time and energy you invested in the project, and your willingness to jump into the study of cultural mediations of ageing and memory with both feet. Your analyses contribute to opening up a critical space for reflection about the hidden complexity behind "senior moments."

Contributors

Sara Cohen is a professor at the University of Liverpool, where she holds the James and Constance Alsop Chair of Music and is director of the Institute of Popular Music. She has a DPhil in social anthropology from Oxford University and is author of *Rock Culture in Liverpool: Popular Music in the Making* (Oxford University Press, 1991) and *Decline, Renewal and the City in Popular Music Culture: Beyond the Beatles* (Ashgate, 2007). She is a co-applicant on the Ageing + Communication + Technologies project: Experiencing a Digital World in Later Life (ACT) supported by the Social Sciences and Humanities Research Council of Canada (SSHRC).

Josephine Dolan is an independent age scholar and a Visiting Reader with the UK's Centre for Women, Ageing and Media (WAM). She is the author of the 2017 book *Contemporary Cinema and 'Old Age': Gender and the Silvering of Stardom* (Palgrave Macmillan) and numerous articles. She is closely linked to Canada's SSHRC-funded Ageing + Communication + Technologies project, as well as to the European Network in Aging Studies, the North American Network in Aging Studies and Spain's Grup Dedal-Lit. She was guest editor (with Julia Hallam) of "Screening 'Old Age'," a 2017 special issue of the *Journal of British Cinema and Television*, and in 2012 co-edited (with Estella Tincknell) *Aging Femininities: Troubling Representations* (Cambridge Scholars).

Line Grenier is a full professor in the Department of Communication at the Université de Montréal and a popular music studies scholar. For the past few years, she has been conducting research on music and ageing within the framework of the international research partnership ACT (Ageing + Communication + Technologies), for which she is coordinating the Critical Mediations stream. Her current work is devoted to the deaf cultures of ageing and, more specifically, to the musical experiences of deaf adult signers in Montreal.

Helmi Järviluoma is a professor of cultural studies at the University of Eastern Finland and principal investigator of the European Research Council's project Sensory Transformations and Transgenerational Environmental Relationships in Europe, 1950–2020. Her areas of expertise include sensory remembering, sensory history and ethnography, qualitative methodology (especially regarding gender), music and social movements. Her publications include the results of a large interdisciplinary follow-up project, *Acoustic Environments in Change* (co-editor, Tampere University of Applied Sciences, 2009), and *Gender and Qualitative Methods* (co-author, Sage, 2003/2010). During the past decade she has also made several radio features, combining art and research, for the Finnish Broadcasting Company's Radio Atelier.

Ros Jennings is co-director of the Research Centre for Women, Ageing and Media (WAM) and head of postgraduate research at the University of Gloucestershire, UK. She is author of "The WAM Manifesto" (2012) and has recently published several articles on older women in relation to popular music, popular television and late style performances. She is co-editor with Abigail Gardner of *'Rock On': Women, Ageing and Popular Music* (Ashgate, 2012); co-author with Abigail Gardner of *Aging and Popular Music in Europe* (Routledge, forthcoming); and co-author with Hannah Grist of *Carers, Care Homes and the British Media: Caring for Older People* (Palgrave Macmillan, forthcoming).

David Madden is an assistant professor of screen arts at Pepperdine University. His research considers the cultural politics of electronic music from the intersections of history, technology, ageing and gender. Currently he is undertaking a micro-historiography of the performers of the ondes Martenot and writing a historical book on electronic music (McGill-Queen's University Press, forthcoming). He is also a musician, community arts organizer and artist, whose work crosses screens, dance floors and media.

Kim Sawchuk is a professor in the Department of Communication Studies at Concordia University. She holds a Concordia University Research Chair in Mobile Media Studies and she is the director of the multi-methodological research project Ageing + Communication + Technologies: Experiencing a Digital World in Later Life (ACT).

Fannie Valois-Nadeau is a postdoctoral fellow at the Centre de recherches cultures-arts-sociétés (CÉLAT). She is also a lecturer in sociology at Université du Québec en Outaouais (UQO) and a professional researcher who specializes in cultural studies. She holds a PhD in communication, and her research interests intersect popular culture, memory studies, cultural events, sport studies and philanthropy. During the past years, she has conducted research on material and media cultures of memory and temporalities. She is a member of the Culture populaire, connaissance et critique (CPCC) laboratory and a visiting researcher at the Groupe Interdisciplinaire de Recherche sur les Cultures et les Arts en Mouvement (GIRCAM).

Cultural Studies

Elisa Ganivet
Border Wall Aesthetics
Artworks in Border Spaces

2019, 250 p., hardcover, ill.
79,99 € (DE), 978-3-8376-4777-8
E-Book: 79,99 € (DE), ISBN 978-3-8394-4777-2

Jocelyne Porcher, Jean Estebanez (eds.)
Animal Labor
A New Perspective on Human-Animal Relations

2019, 182 p., hardcover
99,99 € (DE), 978-3-8376-4364-0
E-Book: 99,99 € (DE), ISBN 978-3-8394-4364-4

Andreas Sudmann (ed.)
The Democratization of Artificial Intelligence
Net Politics in the Era of Learning Algorithms

2019, 334 p., pb., col. ill.
49,99 € (DE), 978-3-8376-4719-8
E-Book: 49,99 € (DE), ISBN 978-3-8394-4719-2

All print, e-book and open access versions of the titles in our list
are available in our online shop www.transcript-verlag.de/en!

Cultural Studies

Burcu Dogramaci, Kerstin Pinther (eds.)
Design Dispersed
Forms of Migration and Flight

2019, 274 p., pb., col. ill.
34,99 € (DE), 978-3-8376-4705-1
E-Book: 34,99 € (DE), ISBN 978-3-8394-4705-5

Pál Kelemen, Nicolas Pethes (eds.)
Philology in the Making
Analog/Digital Cultures of Scholarly Writing and Reading

2019, 316 p., pb., ill.
34,99 € (DE), 978-3-8376-4770-9
E-Book: 34,99 € (DE), ISBN 978-3-8394-4770-3

Chris Goldie, Darcy White (eds.)
Northern Light
Landscape, Photography and Evocations of the North

2018, 174 p., hardcover, ill.
79,99 € (DE), 978-3-8376-3975-9
E-Book: 79,99 € (DE), ISBN 978-3-8394-3975-3

**All print, e-book and open access versions of the titles in our list
are available in our online shop www.transcript-verlag.de/en!**

GPSR Authorized Representative: Easy Access System Europe, Mustamäe tee 50, 10621 Tallinn, Estonia, gpsr.requests@easproject.com

www.ingramcontent.com/pod-product-compliance
Lightning Source LLC
Chambersburg PA
CBHW051540020426
42333CB00016B/2026